STATE AND FINANCIAL SYSTEMS
IN EUROPE AND THE USA

State and Financial Systems in Europe and the USA

Historical Perspectives on Regulation and Supervision in the Nineteenth and Twentieth Centuries

Edited by

STEFANO BATTILOSSI and JAIME REIS

ASHGATE

Published by
Ashgate Publishing Limited
Wey Court East
Union Road
Farnham
Surrey, GU9 7PT
England

Ashgate Publishing Company
Suite 420
101 Cherry Street
Burlington
VT 05401-4405
USA

www.ashgate.com

British Library Cataloguing in Publication Data
   State and financial systems in Europe and the USA : historical perspectives on regulation and supervision in the nineteenth and twentieth centuries. — (Studies in banking and financial history)
   1. Banks and banking—State supervision—Europe—History—19th century. 2. Banks and banking—State supervision—Europe—History—20th century. 3. Banks and banking—State supervision—United States—History—19th century. 4. Banks and banking—State supervision—United States—History—20th century. 5. Money market—Europe—History—19th century. 6. Money market—Europe—History—20th century. 7. Money market—United States—History—19th century. 8. Money market—United States—History—20th century.
   I. Series II. Battilossi, Stefano, 1961– III. Reis, Jaime.
   332.1'094'09034—dc22

Library of Congress Cataloging-in-Publication Data
Battilossi, Stefano, 1961–
   State and financial systems in Europe and the USA : historical perspectives on regulation and supervision in the nineteenth and twentieth centuries / Stefano Battilossi and Jaime Reis.
      p. cm. — (Studies in banking and financial history)
   Includes bibliographical references and index.
   ISBN 978-0-7546-6594-6 (hardcover : alk. paper) 1. Finance—Government policy—Europe—History. 2. Finance—Government policy—United States—History. I. Reis, Jaime. II. Title.
   HG186.A2B38 2009
   332.1094—dc22

                                                                                    2009034596

ISBN 9780754665946 (hbk)
ISBN 9780754699583 (ebk)

Mixed Sources
Product group from well-managed forests and other controlled sources
www.fsc.org Cert no. SA-COC-1565
© 1996 Forest Stewardship Council

Printed and bound in Great Britain by
MPG Books Group, UK

Contents

List of Tables

List of Figures

Notes on Contributors

Stefano Battilossi is Associate Professor of Economic History at Universidad Carlos III Madrid. He holds a PhD in History from the University of Turin, and carried out his post-doc research at the LSE and the European University Institute. His research interests include international banking in the 19th and 20th centuries, the regulation of financial systems in historical perspective, and business cycles and economic policy in Europe after 1945. He has published in the *Financial History Review*, *European Review of Economic History* and *Economic History Review*. He is an author and co-author of books on Italy's banking and financial history, and a co-editor of *European Banks and the American Challenge. Competition and Cooperation in International Banking under Bretton Woods* (with Y. Cassis, Oxford University Press, 2002). Since 2009 he has been an Editor of the *Financial History Review*.

Piet Clement obtained a PhD in History at the Katholieke Universiteit Leuven, Belgium. Since 1995, he has been working as historian and Head of the Archives at the Bank for International Settlements in Basel, Switzerland. His publications include: H. Van der Wee and P. Clement, '1945–1995. L'economia tra crescita e transizione', in P. Bairoch and E. Hobsbawm, *Storia d'Europa* (Einaudi, 1996); 'Nazi Germany and the Service of the Dawes and Young Loans', *Financial History Review*, 11, 1 (2004); G. Toniolo with the assistance of P. Clement, *Central Bank Cooperation at the Bank for International Settlements. 1930–1973* (Cambridge University Press, 2005); C. Borio, G. Toniolo and P. Clement (eds), *Past and Future of Central Bank Cooperation* (Cambridge University Press, 2008).

Philip L. Cottrell is professor of economic and social history at Leicester University. He has published widely in the areas of international financial, business, economic and social history.

Paolo Di Martino (PhD, University of Pisa, Italy), is currently lecturer in British economic history at the University of Manchester (UK). Previously, he has worked at the Universities of Bristol (UK), and Birmingham (UK), and has been Junior Visiting Fellow at the Department of Economic History at the London School of Economics. His research focuses on the relation between legal institutions and economic performance in comparative perspective. On this topic, he has published various chapters in edited books and articles in international journals, including *Business History* (2005) and the *Economic History Review* (with M. Vasta, forthcoming).

Peter Englund is a professor of banking at the Stockholm School of Economics and a professor of real estate finance at the University of Amsterdam. He holds a PhD from Stockholm School of Economics and has previously been a professor of economics at Uppsala University. He has been a scientific advisor to the Sveriges Riksbank and is the secretary of the Prize Committee of the Prize in Economic Sciences in Memory of Alfred Nobel. He has published in academic journals in the fields of banking, public economics and housing and real estate.

Richard S. Grossman is Professor of Economics, Wesleyan University and a Scholar at the Institute for Quantitative Social Science, Harvard University. He is the author of *Unsettled Account. The Evolution of Banking in the Industrialized World since 1800* (Princeton University Press, 2010). He has held visiting faculty appointments at Harvard, Yale and the Hebrew University of Jerusalem, and received research support from the National Science Foundation and the German Marshall Fund of the United States. His work has appeared in the *American Economic Review*, *Journal of Economic History*, *Journal of Money, Credit, and Banking*, and other scholarly journals and newspapers.

Pablo Martín-Aceña is Professor of Economics and Economic History at the University of Alcalá (Madrid), President of the Spanish Economic History Association, former editor of the *Revista de Historia Económica*, and visiting scholar at the Karl Marx University of Economics (Budapest), Harvard University (Boston, Mass), Leuven University (Leuven, Belgium), El Colegio de Mexico (Mexico DF), Paris X-Nanterre and Science Politiques in Paris. Two relevant publications are *The Economic Development in Spain since 1870* (with J. Simpson, Edward Elgar, London, 1995) and *Monetary Standards in the Periphery* (with Jaime Reis, Macmillan Press, 2000). He has also published articles in the *Journal of European Economic History* and the *Financial History Review* as well as in various Spanish academic journals.

Ranald C. Michie is Professor of History at the University of Durham, England. Over a career spanning almost 40 years he has built up a reputation in two areas of financial history. The first is the history of stock exchanges within the context of securities markets. This culminated in the publication of *The Global Securities Market. A History* (Oxford University Press, 2006). The second is the history of the City of London as a financial centre, where his most recent publication has been *Guilty Money. The City of London in Victorian and Edwardian Culture* (Pickering and Chatto, 2009).

Laure Quennouëlle-Corre is a researcher at the CNRS (Centre national de la recherche scientifique) in Paris. Her main research areas are: history of capital markets; Paris as a financial centre; history of the French ministry of Finance. Her publications include *L'Etat-banquier et la croissance. La direction du Trésor 1947–1967* (Paris, CHEFF, 2000); 'The State, the Banks and Financing of Investments in France from

World War II to the 1970s', *Financial History Review*, 12, 1 (2005), pp. 63–86; with Y. Cassis (eds), *Institutions, Markets and Capital Flows. 19th–20th Centuries: Why are Financial Centres Attractive?* (Oxford University Press, forthcoming).

Jaime Reis is a senior research fellow at the Instituto de Ciências Sociais of the University of Lisbon. He holds a PhD in History from the University of Oxford and has taught at the Universities of Vanderbilt, Leicester, Glasgow, Nova de Lisboa and the European University Institute. He is a former president of the European Historical Economics Society and an editor since 2008 of the *European Review of Economic History*. He belongs to the Lisbon Academy of Sciences. He has published on the history of money and banking, labour markets, human capital and agriculture, in Europe and Latin America.

Catherine Schenk, FRHS AcSS is Professor of International Economic History at the University of Glasgow. She has published widely on international banking and monetary history with particular emphasis on East Asia and on Britain's international monetary relations. She has been visiting research fellow at the Hong Kong Monetary Authority and the International Monetary Fund. Her latest books are *Hong Kong SAR's Monetary and Exchange Rate Challenges. Historical Perspectives* (Palgrave Macmillan, 2009) and *Decline of Sterling. Managing the Retreat of an International Currency 1945–1992* (Cambridge University Press, 2010).

André Straus is researcher at the CNRS (Centre national de la recherche scientifique). His research covers finance and the modern French economy, with a focus on manufacturing, the emergence of new technologies, the growth of financial institutions, in particular insurance companies, and the centrality of the state. His publications include, with P. Fridenson (eds), *Le capitalisme français, blocages et dynamismes d'une croissance* (Fayard, 2007); 'Le financement de l'industrie française', in *Histoire de la France industrielle* (Larousse, 1996); *The Financing of the French Economy 1880–2000* (Peter Lang International, forthcoming).

Teresa Tortella has been Head of the Archives and Numismatic Service of the Bank of Spain from 1978 to March 2009. She graduated in History from the Universidad Complutense of Madrid in 1962. Having worked for the National Archives in Madrid from 1974 to 1977, she joined the Banco de España as Head of the Historical Archives in 1978 and was appointed Head of the Numismatic Service in 1990. Tortella became a member of the ICA Business Archives Committee in 1983 and of ICA/SBL Steering Committee in 1990. She was also a member of the EABH Academic Advisory Council from 1989 to 2007 (Vice Chair 1993 to 1998). Her publications include *Los primeros billetes españoles. Las 'Cédulas' del Banco de San Carlos 1782–1829* (1997); *A Guide to Sources of Information on Foreign Investment in Spain 1780–1914* (2000); *Spanish Banknotes 1940–2001* (2004); *Spanish Banknotes 1874–1939* (2005). She is currently working on her next book: *El Banco de España desde dentro*, a domestic history of the Bank of Spain.

Vesa Vihriälä is, since February 2004, State Under-Secretary in the Finnish Prime Minister's Office and Head of the Secretariat of the Economic Council. Dr Vihriälä received his Master, Licentiate and Doctoral degrees from the University of Helsinki, where he also worked as a researcher in 1981–84. In addition, he has studied at the Massachusetts Institute of Technology. Before being appointed to his current position, Dr Vihriälä had a long career at the Bank of Finland. He worked on monetary policy and financial market regulation in the 1980s and had a central position in the crisis-management activities of the central bank during Finland's banking crisis of the early 1990s. Vihriälä has also worked as an economist at the OECD (1989–91) and as the Managing Director of Pellervo Economic Research Institute (1997–2004).

Eugene N. White is Professor of Economics at Rutgers University and a Research Associate of the NBER. His most recent book is *Conflicts of Interest in the Financial Services Industry. What Should We Do About Them?* (ICMB/CEPR, 2003) with Andrew Crockett, Trevor Harris and Frederic Mishkin. He has written extensively on stock market booms and crashes, deposit insurance, banking regulation, and war finance. He is currently at work on studies of the evolution of the microstructure of the New York and Paris stock exchanges, war economies, and real-estate and stock-market bubbles.

Acknowledgements

The chapters published in this volume were originally prepared for the annual conference of the European Association for Banking and Financial History (EABH) held in Lisbon on 26–27 May 2006. The editors gratefully acknowledge the generosity of the Caixa Geral de Depósitos, which sponsored the event, and in particular the support of Carlos Santos Ferreira, Chairman of the Caixa.

We also want to thank Manfred Pohl (EABH), Luis de Abreu de Nunes (Banco de Portugal) and Nuno Valério (Universidad Técnica de Lisboa), who sat with us on the Academic Committee of the conference and shared the responsibility for selecting the papers. The conference would not have been possible without the brilliant assistance of Gabriella Massaglia, Emer Magee and Marnie Giuranna (EABH), Margarida Santos Ferraz, Lídia Pita Barros and Zacarias Dias (Caixa Geral de Depositos), who most efficiently managed the organization of the event.

This volume also greatly benefited from the lively discussion that took place at the conference. We are grateful to all those who so actively contributed to making it a success. Francesca Carnevali (University of Birmingham), Luigi Zingales (University of Chicago), Sigitas Skuodas and Dalia Lasaite (Stockolm School of Economics in Riga) presented papers which are not included in the volume. International experts engaged in passionate panel debates: João Salgueiro (Portuguese Bankers Association), Manuel Jacinto Nunes (School of Economics and Management Lisbon – ISEG), Hugo Bänziger (Deutsche Bank), Vitor Constâncio (Banco de Portugal), Malcolm Knight (Bank for International Settlements), Gertrude Tumpell-Gugerer (European Central Bank), David Marsh (Marsh & Co.), Antonio Borges (Goldman Sachs International), Harold James (Princeton University), David T. Llewellyn (Loughborough University), Liliana Rojas-Suarez (Centre for Global Development). The Chairman of EABH, Jean-Claude Trichet, also Chairman of the European Central Bank, and Fernando Teixeira dos Santos, the Portuguese Minister of Finance, addressed the conference too.

We are deeply indebted to our friends and colleagues who, after the conference, acted as anonymous referees of the papers, contributing so timely and effectively to improving the volume. We owe also a debt of gratitude to Monika Pohle Fraser and Iain L. Fraser for carrying out an excellent job of copy-editing the volume, as well as for being patient with our delays.

We finally want to pay a warm tribute to the memory and legacy of Gerald Feldman, a great scholar, a wise and witty man and a good friend, who chaired a session at the conference and was, as ever, generous in advice and guidance.

Introduction
The Making of Financial Regulation and Deregulation:
A Long View

Stefano Battilossi and Jaime Reis

The global financial crisis triggered in 2007–08 by the collapse of the US subprime mortgage market has dramatically revived the discussion on financial regulation in industrialized economies. Generalized regulatory failure and forbearance have been blamed by Dominique Strauss-Kahn, Managing Director of the IMF, as a major factor of the excess risk taken up by banks.[1] Confidence in market-based self-regulation has been shaken as internal systems of risk control failed to prevent the accumulation of enormous losses in international banks of the highest reputation. As Lawrence Summers, a former Secretary of Treasury under the Clinton Administration, has admitted, 'it should be recognized that to a substantial extent self-regulation is deregulation. Allowing institutions to determine capital levels based on risk models of their own design is tantamount to letting them set their own capital levels. We have seen institutions hurt again and again by events to which their models implied probabilities of less than one in a million'.[2] The effectiveness of prudential regulation to discipline bank managers has been severely questioned, namely on grounds of their motivation. 'Those of us who have looked to the self-interest of lending institutions to protect shareholders' equity, myself included, are in a state of shocked disbelief,' former chairman of the FED, Alan Greenspan, told a Congressional hearing.[3]

The limits of financial supervision have been revealed by the SEC's failure to detect giant pyramidal frauds like Bernard Madoff's in time. Yet only few months earlier, the Bush Administration's Treasury Secretary and former chairman of Goldman Sachs, Henry Paulson, blamed the Sarbanes-Oxley Act, enacted after the wave of corporate and accounting scandals of 2001, for 'excessive regulation', calling for a lighter regulatory touch.[4] But many of those who, back in the long boom of the 1990s, staunchly opposed tougher regulation on derivatives have now confessed that the business of spreading risk through financial engineering has got out of control. The extraordinary characteristics of the present crisis have required extraordinary interventions by the authorities. In the USA, the Federal

---

[1]   *Financial Times*, 25 September 2008.
[2]   *Financial Times*, 1 June 2008.
[3]   *New York Times*, 23 October 2008.
[4]   *New York Times*, 27 July 2008.

Reserve's safety net has for the first time been extended to investment banks. Both in the USA and in Europe, governments have rushed to arrange emergency plans with massive injections of taxpayer money to recapitalize ailing institutions and preserve the public's confidence in the banking system. Whatever its gravity and duration, the crisis has put into a radically new perspective the long wave of financial deregulation that started in industrial and emerging economies at the end of the 1970s. There can be no doubt that the regulatory regime of financial services on both shores of the Atlantic will emerge profoundly reshaped by the global crisis.

How did we get here? What factors have driven the ebb and flow of financial regulation over the last two centuries? What lessons can we draw from the past regarding the impact of financial crises on the regulatory attitude of governments? And what has history to say about the making of financial regulation and deregulation?

Two theoretical approaches compete to explain the historic cycles of financial regulation, one based on a public-interest motivation and another one emphasizing the role of private interests. In the public-interest view, governments are conceived of as benevolent social planners which intervene to regulate and oversee financial systems when informal rules of practice and self-regulation (i.e. market rules collectively administered by market actors) prove incapable of preventing market inefficiencies. The special features of banking intermediation make financial institutions particularly vulnerable to crises. They act as delegated monitors of borrowers on behalf of depositors and confront problems of adverse selection (*ex ante* screening) and moral hazard (*ex post* monitoring). The bank-depositor relationship also entails a moral hazard problem, as banks have incentives to increase leverage (thus operating on low capital-deposit ratios) in order to increase returns on equity. Leverage, 'transformation' (turning liquid deposits into illiquid assets) and asset opaqueness expose them to runs and panics with potentially systemic externalities.[5] Therefore, policymakers are called upon to intervene in order to ensure the safety and soundness of the management of risky assets by the banking system, and to prevent contagion effects that may disrupt the working of the payment and credit systems, thus leading to systemic crises and social welfare losses.

This economic rationale underlies the concept of banking as a matter of public interest and has justified traditional means of prudential regulation, such as capital requirements to create a buffer against losses, as well as to act as a disciplinary device for banks' risk-taking. Motivations of this sort are also advanced for structural regulations such as controls on bank chartering and restrictions on entry aimed at preventing disruptive competition. By increasing the franchise value of licensed or incumbent intermediaries, these are assumed to limit bankers' incentives to take

---

[5]   D.W. Diamond, 'Financial Intermediation and Delegated Monitoring', *Review of Economic Studies*, 51 (1984), pp. 393–414; D.W. Diamond and P.H. Dybvig, 'Bank Runs, Deposit Insurance and Liquidity', *Journal of Political Economy*, 91, 3 (1983), pp. 401–19.

risks and encourage a cautious conduct of business.[6] Likewise, the introduction of deposit insurance serves to promote financial stability, by protecting uninformed depositors and preventing panics. However, deposit insurance carries high costs in terms of weakened market discipline, given that depositors and debt-holders have less incentive to monitor banks, up to the point where they become indifferent between solvent and insolvent institutions. In addition, they magnify moral hazard since managers may increase leverage and asset risk to maximize shareholder value, thus in fact maximizing the value of the insured subsidy.[7] A deposit insurance scheme therefore requires a prudential regulation of banks' risk-taking complemented by some supervision of the banking system by public authorities (mainly but not exclusively performed by central banks) in the form of regular disclosure of balance sheets and on-site inspections.

In the same vein, imperfections and failures in markets for financial assets provide an economic rationale for regulating capital markets. Risk-taking by individual firms can generate negative externalities for other firms and individuals that are not their counterparties. Market discipline is insufficient to deal with the social costs of disrupted financial market activities and the ensuing loss of wealth and output. Likewise, private firms have incentives that limit the amount and the quality of information they provide to the public, as the social benefit of information is greater than the private benefit to those who produce it. This justifies government intervention in its multiple forms – from public licensing of market intermediaries to disclosure requirements and prohibition of insider trading – in order to discipline risk taking, assure transparency and deter frauds, manipulations and other forms of misconduct.[8] Historically, the regulatory and supervisory reforms promoted by the Roosevelt Administration during the Great Depression – from the Glass-Steagall Act of 1933 to the Securities Act and the Securities Exchange Act of 1933–34 – are often regarded as paramount examples of public intervention aiming at limiting the social losses of financial instability.

The competing view of financial regulation to this one has been developed by a recent tradition of theoretical and empirical research based on a political-economy approach. In this approach, financial regulation can be interpreted as the outcome of a policy-making   process in which special interests with different objective functions and political influences compete to use the coercive power of the state in order to appropriate rents. This literature considers politics and political institutions as the main drivers of the laws, regulations and controls which affect the financial system. It investigates how the preferences of politicians and interest groups may enhance – or hinder – financial development and influence the financial

---

[6]   M.C. Keeley, 'Deposit Insurance, Risk, and Market Power in Banking', *American Economic Review*, 80, 5 (1990), pp. 1183–2000.

[7]   M. Klausner, 'Bank Regulatory Reform and Bank Structure', in M. Klausner, L.J. White (eds), *Structural Change in Banking* (Homewood IL, 1993).

[8]   R. Dodd, The Economic Rationale for Financial Market Regulation, Financial Policy Forum, Special Policy Report no. 12, 2002.

decisions of corporations, the working of the banking sector and the operation of financial markets.[9] Legal and political reforms can be modelled as an outcome of the interplay of governments and policymakers with incumbent interests within a set of institutional mechanisms which may range from corruption to lobbying, up to the capture of the policy-making process by economically entrenched groups.

Recent studies explore how political institutions throughout the 19th and 20th centuries managed the conflict of interest which is endemic in the relationship between the state and the financial system. On the one hand, this involves the role of the government in strengthening the rights of private financial claimholders through the enforcement of financial contracts. On the other, it focuses on the capture of financial markets and intermediaries as a source of government revenue.[10] In this perspective, the rise of interstate branching prohibition and entry barriers – a manifestation of an 'abiding fear of bigness'[11] so distinctive of the US banking system – can be explained as a consequence of the large dependence of states' finances on bank chartering and other bank-related revenues, and successful rent-seeking by local bankers.[12] Likewise, the introduction of Federal Deposit Insurance in 1933, far from being an emergency measure principally aimed at protecting small depositors in the turmoil of the Great Depression, represented a political victory of small, unstable unit banks which had vainly advocated federal legislation on banks' liability insurance for half a century.[13]

The political-economy approach also puts the regulation of financial markets in a different perspective. Some contend, for instance, that the 'Blue Sky Laws'

---

[9]   M. Pagano, P. Volpin, 'The Political Economy of Finance', *Oxford Review of Economic Policy*, 17, 4 (2001), pp. 502–19; S. Haber, R. Perotti, The Political Economy of Financial Systems, Timbergen Institution Discussion Paper, no. 045/2, 2008.

[10]   H. Bodenhorn, *State Banking in Early America. A New Economic History* (Oxford, 2003) and id., 'Bank Chartering and Political Corruption in Antebellum New York. Free Banking as Reform', in E. Glaeser and C. Goldin (eds), *Corruption and Reform. Lessons from America's Economic History* (Chicago, 2006), pp. 231–57. See also S. Haber, A. Razo and N. Maurer, *The Politics of Property Rights. Political Instability, Credible Commitments, and Economic Growth in Mexico 1876–1929* (Cambridge, 2003), and the papers collected in S. Haber, D.C. North and B. Weingast (eds), *Political Institutions and Financial Development* (Stanford, 2007).

[11]   J.H. Kareken, 'Federal Bank Regulatory Policy. A Description and Some Observations', *The Journal of Business*, 59, 1 (1986), pp. 3–48, p. 6.

[12]   The seminal contributions on this issue are E.N. White, 'The Political Economy of Banking Regulation, 1864–1933', *Journal of Economic History*, 42, 1 (1982), pp. 33–40; and id., *The Regulation and Reform of the American Banking System, 1900–1929* (Princeton, 1983). See also N. Economides, R.G. Hubbard and D. Palia, 'The Political Economy of Branch Restrictions and Deposit Insurance', *Journal of Law and Economics*, 29 (1996), pp. 667–704.

[13]   C.A. Calomiris and E.N. White, 'The Origins of Federal Deposit Insurance', in C. Goldin and G. Libecap (eds), *The Regulated Economy. A Historical Approach to Political Economy* (Chicago, 1994), pp. 145–88.

enacted by several American states between 1911 and 1933 to regulate the offer and sale of securities to the public were not so much a device to address widespread frauds as rather the result of bankers' political pressure to limit the threat of disintermediation brought home by the development of securities markets. Likewise, some features of the Securities Act of 1933, typically regarded as a 'full disclosure' statute, can be properly understood as a means to protect separate wholesale and retail investment banks from the competition of integrated firms.[14]

Finally, the political-economy approach also pays attention to how limited government and democratization were positively, although not monotonically, related to financial development in the nineteenth century – eroding entry barriers and broadening the access to finance – in both the USA[15] and Europe.[16] From this point of view, the degree of political participation is considered a critical element that influences political decisions over finance. Research suggests that the narrower the social basis of political regimes – such as those under suffrage restrictions or autocracies – the more exclusionary is likely to be the ensuing regulatory regime. Democratic, information-rich and transparent environments may allow the voice of advocates of public interest to be heard, whereas in weak democratic institutions, incumbent interests are better positioned to capture the process of regulation and policy-making.[17] This would explain why autocratic regimes tend to increase regulatory restrictions on financial markets and intermediaries, as well as to establish state control over finance in order to maximize their borrowing powers and constrain the emergence of competing power centres. Monopoly rights, barriers to entry or regulations can thus be used to grant rents to connected elites and incumbent interests in return of political support, thus favouring the emergence of an oligopolistic structure of financial systems. Within autocratic regimes, lobbying and regulation capture can be enhanced by the absence of political rights, the opaqueness of the law-making process and the concentration

---

[14] P.G. Mahoney, 'The Origins of the Blue-Sky Laws. A Test of Competing Hypotheses', *Journal of Law and Economics*, 46, 1 (2003), pp. 229–51; and idem, 'The Political Economy of the Securities Act of 1933', *Journal of Legal Studies*, 30, 1 (2001), pp. 1–31.

[15] J. Wallis, R. Sylla and J. Legler, 'The Interaction of Taxation and Regulation in 19th Century US Banking', in C. Goldin and G. Libecap (eds), *The Regulated Economy. A Historical Approach to Political Economy* (Chicago, 1994), pp. 122–44; E. Benmelech and T. Moskowitz, The Political Economy of Financial Regulation. Evidence from US State Usury Laws in the 18th and 19th centuries, NBER Working Paper no. 12851, 2007.

[16] K. Ng, 'Free Banking Laws and Barriers to Entry in Banking, 1838–1860', *Journal of Economic History*, 48, 4 (1998), pp. 877–89; J.L. Brosz and R.S. Grossman, 'Paying for Privilege. The Political Economy of Bank of England Charters, 1694–1844', *Explorations in Economic History*, 41, 1 (2004), pp. 48–72; N. Lamoreaux and J.-L. Rosenthal, Corporate Governance and the Plight of Minority Shareholders in the US before the Great Depression, NBER Working Paper no. 10900, 2004.

[17] E.H. Feijen and E. Perotti, The Political Economy of Financial Fragility, CEPR Discussion Papers no. 5317, 2005.

of political powers, as recent studies of financial regulation in Tsarist Russia, Porfirian Mexico and Franco's Spain seem to suggest.[18]

Some of the essays collected in this volume suggest that the two approaches should not be considered as mutually exclusive. Indeed, financial regulation can, over the long run, be thought of as a dynamic process driven by a continuous tension between public and private interests. Historically, financial and banking crises were often interpreted as signals of market failures and provided critical focal points for public debates and policy makers' interventions. However, the outcome in terms of legislation and regulation was shaped by historically-determined and country-specific institutions (the legal framework, the nature of the state, the articulation of the political system) within which the interplay of private interests took place.

In the first chapter, Phil Cottrell ('*Conservative abroad, liberal at home':* *British Banking Regulation during the Nineteenth Century*) analyses the interaction of different constituencies in the evolving regulation of banks in the first half of the nineteenth century in response to recurrent commercial crises. In a system dominated by private banking houses, the rise of joint-stock banks, permitted after 1826, was perceived by many as a risky innovation since, as in Samuel Gurney's words, 'business was best conducted personally by those whose entire fortunes were at risk'. The preservation of unlimited liability, the introduction of minimum capital requirements and the existence of large controlling shareholders answerable to depositors were debated as regulatory instruments to safeguard the holders of banks' liabilities against possible abuses. At the same time, restrictions on the geographical expansion of joint-stock banks were discussed to preserve the Bank of England's privileges in the London metropolitan area and to limit competition between old and new banks. Cottrell describes how the political clash between incumbents and new entrants led in 1833 to the rejection by the House of Commons of the compromise proposed by Chancellor of the Exchequer Althorp for chartered note-issuing joint-stock banks. The chapter also describes how regulations and restrictions designed for chartered colonial banks helped set a new regulatory framework for domestic banks in the aftermath of the joint-stock banking 'mania' of the late 1830s. This led to the so-called 'onerous regulation' included in the Joint Stock Banking Act of 1844 in spite of the active and critical involvement of the banking community in the design of the new legislation.

The influence of private interests in determining cross-country differences in bankruptcy procedures is the subject of Paolo Di Martino's contribution in

---

[18]   B. Anan'ich, 'State Power and Finance in Russia, 1802–1917', in R. Sylla et al. (eds), *The State, the Financial System and Economic Modernization* (Cambridge, 1999), pp. 210–23; N. Maurer and A. Gomberg, 'When the State is Untrustworthy. Public Finance and Private Banking in Porfirian Mexico', *Journal of Economic History*, 64, 4 (2004), pp. 1087–1107; N. Maurer and S. Haber, 'Related Lending and Economic Performance. Evidence from Mexico', *Journal of Economic History*, 67, 3 (2007), pp. 551–81; S.A. Perez, *Banking on Privilege. The Politics of Spanish Financial Reform* (Ithaca, 1997).

chapter 2 (*Lobbying, Institutional Inertia, and the Efficiency Issue in State Regulation: Evidence from the Evolution of Bankruptcy Laws and Procedures in Italy, England, and the US (c.1870–1939)*). Historically, bankruptcy laws have had to find a difficult balance. On the one hand, they are concerned with the protection of creditors' rights, which guarantees ex ante the availability of cheaper and more abundant credit to firms, but can generate *ex post* inefficiencies and social costs due to frequent firm liquidations. On the other, strong protection of debtors may enhance ex ante moral hazard but generates ex post efficiency gains by preventing or reducing debt overhang, unnecessary liquidation of collateral and negative externalities to third parties (such as customers and employees). Di Martino argues that in the interwar period experts both in the United States and Italy perceived the British regulation of bankruptcy as 'optimal', thanks to soundly regulated debt discharge, efficient use of friendly settlement and the public nature of procedures. In both countries, however, bankruptcy laws deviated substantially from the British pattern as a consequence of considerations of political economy. In the USA the political influence of the pro-debtor lobby led to a Bankruptcy Law which gave more emphasis to debt discharge than to protecting creditors' rights. In turn, in Italy the strong pro-creditor legal tradition of the Napoleonic code proved critical in shaping the attitude of lawyers and lawmakers, thus failing to enact efficient alternatives to firm liquidation.

In chapter 3, Eugene White (*Regulation and Governance: A Secular Perspective on the Development of the American Financial System*) suggests that major turning points in the history of US financial regulation can be better explained as adjustments to productivity shocks in the real economy than as responses to crises. Technological changes related to the 'New Economy' of the 1920s challenged the existing institutions and financial techniques. These were based on a 'pyramided structure of reserves and correspondent balances link[ing] thousands of small banks with incompletely diversified loan portfolios [that] left the financial system particularly subject to shocks'. Uncertainty about the expected return on capital-intensive investment carried out by vertically-integrated big business magnified information asymmetries in the financial sector, making it harder for traditional banks to screen and monitor borrowers. The rise of specialized investment banks, such as JP Morgan, and rating agencies provided market information that mitigated the problem of monitoring by investors. At the same time, existing regulation constrained the ability of commercial banks to cope with the ongoing transformations. This led them to develop separate security affiliates to overcome geographic restrictions and carry out their investment banking business, with the result that they evolved towards a universal-banking pattern. In the turmoil of the Great Depression, these universal banks were blamed for abuses and manipulations – an accusation vindicated by recent research. Indeed the market considered universal banks more trustworthy than independent investment banks, and much of the criticism raised during Congressional hearings proved ill founded.[19] The Glass-Steagall Act was less a response to market failure than a victory of the powerful lobby of investment bankers. Likewise, the 'loosely organized cartel with barriers to entry and price controls' that resulted from the Banking Acts of 1933–35 protected the rents of small unit banks by preventing the consolidation and geographical diversification of large banks. As White explains, '[the crisis] made it difficult to identify the real problems of the financial system and (…) left the door open to adroit political entrepreneurs with their pet schemes'.

Since the interwar period and until the 1970s, financial regulation in industrialized economies has gone far beyond traditional prudential rules. With few exceptions (West Germany most notably), European governments extensively made use of policy instruments such as compulsory and non-remunerated reserve requirements, cash and liquidity ratios, interest-rate controls, credit ceilings and directives on credit allocation. Such regulations were implemented either by suasion, as in the case of the UK,[20] or more often by command-and-control administrative instructions. In some cases, such as Italy and France, this escalation was reinforced by government ownership of major banks, which gave the State an unprecedented pervasive role in intermediating and allocating capital. Domestic regulation was often complemented by external controls on foreign exchange and capital markets embedded in the regulatory design of the Bretton Woods system. They became a permanent feature of many European financial systems, with West Germany providing the only counter-example of precocious liberalization – although briefly reversed in the early 1970s.[21]

Usually, the bulk of the regulatory framework (both domestic and external) was inherited from the interwar period. New constraints were, however, introduced in the 1960s and 1970s as a way to enhance monetary management. Central banks in this period in Europe diverged as to targeting options (money, domestic credit, exchange rate) and often chose combined approaches.[22] In any case, reserve requirements, qualitative and quantitative controls, and indirect controls were

---

[19]   E.N. White, 'Before the Glass-Steagall Act. An Analysis of the Investment Banking Activities of National Banks', *Explorations in Economic History*, 23, 1 (1986), pp. 33–55; R.S. Kroszner and R.G. Rajan, 'Is the Glass-Steagall Act Justified? A Study of the US Experience with Universal Banking before 1933', *American Economic Review*, 84, 4 (1994), pp. 810–32.

[20]   J.E. Wadsworth (ed.), *The Banks and the Monetary System in the UK 1959–1971* (London, 1973), pp. 99–130.

[21]   H.-J. Voth, 'Convertibility, Currency Controls and the Cost of Capital in Western Europe, 1950–1999', *International Journal of Finance and Economics*, 8, 3 (2003), pp. 255–76; C. Wyplosz, 'Exchange Rate Regimes. Some Lessons from Post-war Europe', in G. Caprio et al. (eds), *Financial Liberalization. How Far, How Fast?* (Cambridge, 2001), pp. 125–58.

[22]   A.C.F. Houben, *The Evolution of Monetary Policy Strategies in Europe* (Dordrecht, Boston and London, 2000), pp. 141–81.

deployed allegedly in order to enhance the effectiveness of monetary policy in controlling domestic liquidity and bank lending. The process peaked in the 1970s and its intensification led in many countries to a comprehensive regime of financial repression. This was 'a set of policies, laws, regulation, taxes, distortions, qualitative and quantitative restrictions, which do not allow financial intermediaries to operate at their full technological potential'.[23] It was soon acknowledged, however, that such compacts of 'conduct' constraints, while preventing banking systems from operating efficiently, rarely achieved their alleged objective of improving efficiency in monetary management. Another general consequence was the underdevelopment of capital markets and the uncontested dominance of the government as a borrower. Yet, many European governments were generally slow in reforming their banking and financial systems. Why were regimes of financial restriction so pervasive and resilient in Europe?

Political economy interpretations of domestic and external financial constraints emphasize their role as a potential source of revenue for governments. Arguably they provide access to artificially cheap domestic funding from the banking system or capital markets, usually in combination with seigniorage and inflationary finance. This may prove especially appealing to governments with low revenues from income taxes as a consequence of widespread corruption, technical or political constraints on the verification of income across social groups, or large underground economies.[24] Institutional and political characteristics, such as political instability or dependent central banks, may increase the government's incentive to resort systematically to implicit revenues, as a weak incumbent government does not fully internalize the future costs of debt servicing and may deliberately resort to over-borrowing.[25] Empirical evidence for capital controls in a sample of 20 OECD countries between the 1960s and the 1980s has been found to be consistent with an inflation-tax explanation. In addition, capital controls have also shown a close association with higher inflation, higher reliance on seigniorage and lower real interest rates in a different sample of 19 industrialized and 42 developing countries in the period 1966–89.[26]

---

[23]   N. Roubini, X. Sala-i-Martin, 'A Growth Model of Inflation, Tax Evasion and Financial Repression', *Journal of Monetary Economics*, 35, 2 (1995), pp. 275–301.

[24]   A. Giovannini and M. De Melo, 'Government Revenues from Financial Repression', *American Economic Review*, 83, 4 (1993), pp. 953–63; J.P. Nicolini, 'Tax Evasion and the Optimal Inflation Tax', *Journal of Development Economics*, 55, 1 (1998), pp. 215–32.

[25]   A. Alesina and G. Tabellini, 'External Debt, Capital Flight and Political Risk', *Journal of International Economics*, 27, 3–4 (1989), pp. 199–220.

[26]   A. Alesina, V. Grilli and G. M. Milesi-Ferretti, 'The Political Economy of Capital Controls', in L. Leiderman and A. Razin (eds), *Capital Mobility. The Impact on Consumption, Investment and Growth* (Cambridge, 1994), pp. 289–321; V. Grilli, G.M. Milesi Ferretti, Economic Effects and Structural Determinants of Capital Controls, *IMF Staff Papers*, 42, 1995, pp. 517–51.

Adopting a different approach, Rajan and Zingales offer a comprehensive interpretation of the interwar and postwar reversal of financial markets' development based on an interest group theory.[27] In the increasingly closed economies of the 1930s, incumbents (including dominant banks and industrial firms) opposed the development of capital markets, since the latter tended to erode the value of incumbency and to enhance competition, thus undermining their own dominant positions. Such a reversal was strongest in Civil Law countries since it proved easier there for interest groups to influence the policy-making process and capture the legal system. Indeed, it was overturned only in the late 20th century, when international trade and financial openness rendered it unprofitable for incumbents to keep capital markets underdeveloped. Until then, however, Continental systems exhibited a long-lasting pattern of 'relationship finance' – a facet of a more general 'relationship capitalism' under which governments could satisfy the rapidly increasing demand for social insurance stemming from uninsured masses. An alternative explanation is provided by Perotti and von Thadden, who propose a democratic voting model. This suggests that in Continental countries affected by a huge inflationary shock in the post-WW1 period the impoverished middle class was hit by the devaluation of their long-term nominal assets and called for higher social insurance. This shifted their electoral support towards a corporatist system of financial allocation and ultimately weakened financial markets and increased politicized control over finance. The new societal consensus in favour of corporatist governance and labour protection was further strengthened by the political changes set in motion by the Great Depression.[28]

These interpretations are particularly interesting since they adopt a long-run perspective. The secular dimension of state intervention in the financial systems of Britain and France is explored in chapters 4 and 5 by Ranald Michie and Laure Quennouëlle-Corre with André Straus, respectively. In the aftermath of WW2, the two countries exhibited an apparent convergence towards highly regulated banking systems and financial markets, with nationalized central banks strongly dependent on the government, which implemented binding exchange and capital controls. The underlying political economy of the two financial systems, however, remained substantially different. As Michie (*The London Stock Exchange and the British Government in the Twentieth Century*) argues, over the twentieth century the British Treasury interfered significantly in the operations of the London Stock Exchange (LSE) only in emergency periods, such as the two world wars (in order to fund the escalating national debt) and the abandonment of Gold Standard in 1931. Most binding regulations, such as increased controls on dealers and brokers, the prohibition of forward transactions or the imposition of minimum prices, were intended as extraordinary measures and reflected policy coordination

[27]   R. Rajan and L. Zingales, 'The Great Reversals. The Politics of Financial Development in the 20th Century', *Journal of Financial Economics*, 69, 1 (2003), pp. 5–50.

[28]   E. Perotti and E.-L. von Thadden, 'The Political Economy of Corporate Control and Labor Rents', *Journal of Political Economy*, 114, 1 (2006), pp. 145–75.

achieved between the Treasury, the Bank of England and the members of the Stock Exchange. In normal periods, on the contrary, public authorities resorted to moral suasion and the LSE remained 'a privately owned financial institution exercising some control over securities and investment on behalf of the government'. This supervisory 'semi-official position' reflected an implicit bargain under which the government recognized the LSE as the only authorized securities market in return for its policing of the market and supporting national policies. The monopolistic rents generated by this agreement were undermined by the abolition of exchange and capital controls in 1979 and quickly disappeared with the full deregulation and internationalization of the market after the 'Big Bang' in 1986.

In the case of France, the presence of the state in the financial system was much more pervasive, multifaceted and influential than in most countries. It also went a longer way back. Quennouëlle-Corre and Straus (*The State in the French Financial System during the Twentieth Century: A Specific Case?*) interpret this outcome as a consequence of the nature of the French legal system and some critical economic and political events. On the capital-market side, stockbrokers ('agents de change') were public officials appointed by the Ministry of Finance, with their number established by law, while bankers and merchants were excluded from operating in the Bourse (which favoured the thriving of the unofficial, unregulated 'Coulisse' market). The government also supervised the activity of the market and could deny authorization for listing and issuing foreign securities. The banking system, in turn, was characterized by the early prominence of a number of 'public' channels of financial intermediation, such as saving banks (which received strong political support), postal savings and the 'Caisse de Depots et Consignations', all of which played a critical role in financial deepening. Slow growth and uncertainty in the 1930s paved the way for a dramatic increase in the direct financing of the government by the banking system. This shift was officially sanctioned by the heavy 'dirigiste' regulation enacted under the Vichy regime in 1941, which separated commercial from investment banking, introduced a regime of official authorization for bank entry and branching, and brought all public financial intermediaries and cooperative banks under the supervision of the Ministry of Finance. A peculiarly French institution, the 'Circuit du Tresor', aimed at channelling credit from the banking system towards the Treasury, also emerged then. This structure served very well the purposes of postwar 'indicative' planning, and was perfected thanks to the postwar nationalization and later cartelization of the largest deposit banks. The administered financial system, characterized by the pervasive regulation of interest rates, ensured the allocation of bank credit to 'priority' sectors and gave the government, state-owned institutions and local authorities priority in tapping domestic capital markets.

Ever since the nineteenth century, the issue of prudent regulation and financial stability has been intimately related to the pursuit of monetary stability and the emergence of central banking. In Britain, the Joint-Stock Banking Act of 1844 can be considered a parallel outcome of the debate that led in the same year to the Bank Charter Act, which gave the Bank of England a monopoly on note issue.

In the USA, the National Banking Acts of 1863–64 combined the introduction of binding rules for bank chartering under a unified federal regulatory authority (the Comptroller of the Currency) with the introduction of a national currency. Bagehot's rule, according to which central banks should lend freely and quickly at a penalty rate to illiquid but solvent banks, gradually became conventional wisdom in central banking[29] – although the rule too often proves hard to follow in practice, and many criticize its moral hazard effects, especially when emergency liquidity is provided systematically and unconditionally.[30] The Bank of England's credible pre-commitment is often quoted as a key determinant of the absence of major financial crises in Britain after the 1860s, although some argue that the Lender of last Resort function (LOLR) made its headway in British official policy only after WW1.[31] The reluctant and insufficient provision of last-resort credit by the Federal Reserve on the outset of the Great Depression is generally blamed for the wave of nationwide banking panics that shook the US economy in the early 1930s.[32] The evolution of central banks, from special commercial institutions with private shareholders and special privileges, to government banks, pooling gold reserves and providing rediscounting facilities, was lengthy and far from seamless.[33] In chapter 6, Richard Grossman (*The Emergence of Central Banks and Banking Supervision in Comparative Perspective*) reminds us that, in the nineteenth century, the key motivations behind the establishment of national banks (later to become central banks) certainly did not include any LOLR function. Nor was the latter performed necessarily by central banks, as the history of the USA before 1913, Canada and other countries demonstrates.[34] The emergence of LOLR activities between the late nineteenth century and the outbreak of WW1 raised interesting moral-hazard problems and had a significant impact on public confidence in gold-based monetary regimes.[35] It also provided a new economic rationale for the introduction

---

[29]   G. Caprio and P. Honohan, Banking Crises, Institute for International Integration Studies Trinity College Dublin, Discussion Paper no. 242, 2008.

[30]   An excellent introduction to this subject is X. Freixas, C. Giannini, G. Hoggarth and F. Soussa, 'Lender of Last Resort. A Review of the Literature', in C. Goodhart and G. Illing (eds), *Financial Crises, Contagion, and the Lender of Last Resort. A Reader* (Oxford, 2002), pp. 39–44.

[31]   J.H. Wood, 'Bagehot's Lender of Last Resort. A Hollow Hallowed Tradition', *The Independent Review*, 7, 3 (2003), pp. 343–51.

[32]   M. Friedman and A. Schwartz, *A Monetary History of the United States 1867–1960* (Princeton, 1963), pp. 301–59.

[33]   C. Goodhart, F. Capie and N. Schnadt, 'The Development of Central Banking', in F. Capie et al., *The Future of Central Banking. The Tercentenary Symposium of the Bank of England* (Cambridge, 1994), pp. 1–91.

[34]   M. Bordo, 'The Lender of Last Resort. Alternative Views and Historical Experience', in C. Goodhart and G. Illing (eds), *Financial Crises, Contagion, and the Lender of Last Resort. A Reader* (Oxford, 2002), pp. 108–25.

[35]   B. Eichengreen, *Globalizing Capital* (Princeton, 1996), pp. 35–8.

of some form of public supervision on banks with access to central bank's high-powered money. In a similar vein, the central position held by central banks in the financial system and their network of correspondent balances with commercial banks made them the natural candidates to perform this new function. This pattern was not generalized, however (the Nordic countries, Switzerland and other small European countries followed a different path), and gained momentum only after WW1. But, as Grossman shows, to establish when exactly central banks assumed supervisory responsibilities or when informal supervision turned into formal powers proves as elusive and controversial as to determine when their transition to modern central banking was completed. His empirical evidence also suggests that younger central banks created around the turn of the century were more likely to be invested with supervisory duties than their older counterparts, possibly because their organizational structure, ownership and management were more flexible and better able to adjust to new public tasks.

by-product of the public duties gradually assumed by central banks in the early twentieth century was their role as monitors of the national economy, providers of statistical information and advisers of economic policy-makers. In chapter 7, Pablo Martín Aceña and Teresa Tortella (*Regulation and Supervision: The Rise of Central Banks' Research Departments*) provide a timeline of the establishment of in-house Research Departments at European central banks and trace a parallel history of two of them in the interwar years, the 'Servizio studi econonomici e statistici', at the Bank of Italy, and the 'Servicio de Estudios', at the Bank of Spain.

The last quarter of the twentieth century has witnessed a major shift away from the long-established pattern of restricted financial systems towards financial globalization. By the early 1980s liberalization of capital flows and deregulation had risen to the top of the agenda of policy-makers in all industrialized countries. Explaining why this happened is not straightforward from a political-economy perspective. A popular idea among economists points to the impact of exogenous forces on the size of the rents generated by regulation to their initial beneficiaries. Technological progress, especially the dramatic reduction in the real cost of processing and transmitting information, and associated financial innovations are usually mentioned as the most powerful agents of change in the financial sector. Kroszner and Strahan suggest that new technologies in both deposit-taking and lending shifted the political balance of power from small banks towards growth-oriented large banks.[36] This is confirmed by the fact that deregulation occurred earlier in states with fewer small banks, in states where small banks were financially weak, and in states with more smaller and more bank-dependent firms.

In fact, regulation itself was in some cases a driver of change. Government-imposed constraints, by reducing financial firms' utility, provided incentives for them

---

[36]   R.S. Kroszner and P.E. Strahan, 'What Drives Deregulation? Economics and Politics of the Relaxation of Bank Branching Restrictions', *Quarterly Journal of Economics*, 114, 4 (1999), pp. 1437–67.

to circumvent regulation and for their unregulated competitors to disintermediate them through product and process innovations. Innovations, in turn, either led to re-regulation, which may have entailed attempts to bring unregulated products or firms under the existing regulatory regime, or to a relaxation of constraints on regulated incumbents. The latter was especially likely when change was too fast for regulators to keep pace with it and tended to bring the regulated equilibrium close to the unregulated one. This gave more influence to pro-deregulation interest groups and raised demand for deregulation by incumbents as well.

This 'regulatory dialectic' was most evident in the USA.[37] Here, mutual savings banks, which were prevented by regulation from adjusting interest on deposits to unusually high and volatile interest rates, suffered from serious disintermediation in the 1960s and 70s in favour of unregulated institutions such as money market funds. The ensuing disruption of the mortgage market and the building industry created the conditions for the deregulation of thrifts and savings banks in 1980. Likewise, regulated commercial banks were increasingly disintermediated in their wholesale business by non-depository institutions and alternative markets (such as Treasury bonds and commercial paper). A first circumventing reaction was a product innovation, the Certificate of Deposit (CDs), which US regulatory authorities then re-regulated. A second circumventing response was regulatory arbitrage. US banks 'invaded' the City of London and used their foreign branches to intermediate dollar-denominated deposits and CDs – the so called Eurodollars. This became an unregulated international money market towards which British authorities maintained a hands-off attitude insofar as its activities remained confined to external intermediation (cross-currency and cross-country), with no impact on the external situation of the British pound, and regulation succeeded in keeping British banks largely out of the business. Again, US regulators responded to strategic foreign branching by introducing penalty reserve requirements on funds borrowed in London.[38]

The rise of pressure for deregulation gained momentum as from the 1980s. In the USA, time-honoured pillars of the old regulatory regime were eroded and finally brought down. Under the Depository Institutions Deregulation and Monetary Control Act of 1980 and the Garn-St. Germain Depository Institutions Act of 1982, ceilings on deposit interest rates were removed and the traditional

---

[37]   E. Kane, 'Accelerating Inflation, Technological Innovation, and the Decreasing Effectiveness of Banking Regulation', *Journal of Finance*, 36, 2 (1981), pp. 355–67; and idem, 'Technological and Regulatory Forces in the Developing Fusion of Financial-Services Competition', *Journal of Finance*, 39, 3 (1984), pp. 759–72.

[38]   On the impact of regulation on the emergence of the Eurodollar market, see S. Battilossi and Y. Cassis (eds), *European Banks and the American Challenge. Competition and Cooperation in International Banking under Bretton Woods* (Oxford, 2002); and especially R. Sylla, 'US Banks and Europe. Strategy and Attitudes', pp. 53–73. On the discussion among central bankers, G. Toniolo, *Central Bank Cooperation at the Bank for International Settlements, 1930–1973* (Cambridge, 2005), pp. 452–71.

banking system deregulated in order to promote competition. The Neal-Riegle Interstate Banking Act of 1994, which had for twenty years codified at national level the effect of state-level deregulation, lifted geographic restrictions on branching. Finally, the firewalls erected by the Glass-Steagall Act of 1933 and the Bank Holding Company Act of 1956 between commercial and investment banking and insurance companies were demolished (Gramm-Leah-Bliley Act of 1999). Again, federal legislation sanctioned what many state legislatures and banking authorities had been increasingly allowing, by expanding banks' powers and paving the way for a return to universal banking and the creation of giant financial conglomerates.[39]

In Western Europe, equally profound changes took places both at national and regional levels. Competition was promoted and scope and scale in banking enhanced by removing 'conduct' regulations on interest rates and bank portfolios, as well as by gradually lifting restrictions on entry, branching, mergers and acquisitions (M&A), ownership and activities in securities and insurance.[40] Capital controls were lifted earlier and more comprehensively in countries, such as the USA and West Germany, which had resorted to capital controls only as emergency devices in the turmoil of the mid-1970s. Long-standing exchange and capital controls were also swiftly removed in the UK by 1979.[41] On the Continent, liberalization was slowed down by macroeconomic adjustment and disinflation in the first half of the 1980s and controls were, therefore, phased out more gradually and controversially. Countries such as Italy, Spain and Portugal only reluctantly accomplished full financial liberalization in the early 1990s under the political pressure generated by the EU Single Market programme.[42] National capital markets entered a phase of rapid expansion and deep institutional transformation. In the UK, the 'Big Bang' of 1986 precipitated a sudden change in the microstructure of the London Stock Exchange against the interests and the restrictive practices of traditional incumbents ('Old Boys') and in favour of foreign competitors.[43] This turned the City into the world leading financial centre, while on the Continent,

---

[39]   Federal Deposit Insurance Corporation (FDIC), *History of the 1980s. Lessons for the Future*, vol. 1, *An Examination of the Banking Crises of the 1980s and early 1990s* (Washington, 1997), pp. 87–135. See also K. Spong, *Banking Regulation. Its Purposes, Implementation and Effects* (Kansas City, 2000).

[40]   For a survey, see E.P.M. Gardener and P. Molyneux, *Changes in Western European Banking* (London, 1994).

[41]   R.C. Marston, *International Financial Integration. A Study of Interest Differentials between the Major Industrial Countries* (Cambridge, 1995), pp. 43–69.

[42]   A.F.P. Bakker, *The Liberalization of Capital Movements in Europe. The Monetary Committee and Financial Integration, 1958–1994* (Dordrecht, Boston and London, 1996), pp. 147–212.

[43]   R. Michie, *The London Stock Exchange. A History* (Oxford, 2001), pp. 543–95.

Paris, Frankfurt and Amsterdam also acquired a new international status and set in motion a competitive dynamic.[44]

The end of financial restriction has brought prudential regulation to the forefront of policy-making again. But financial globalization has also raised the challenging issues of regulatory convergence and competing regulatory jurisdictions, especially in Europe. Safety nets remain the result of policy rules formulated and implemented mainly at national level. In the process of creating a Single Market for financial services, the second EU Banking Directive of 1989 allowed the harmonization of minimum standard prudential requirements. Since 1992 most European countries have adopted the so-called 'Basel I' agreement, a prudential regulatory framework based on minimum capital requirement approved in 1988 by the Basel Committee on Banking Supervision at the Bank for International Settlements. Within the EU, the principle of mutual recognition has removed all regulatory barriers to the emergence of a single banking market and created a level playing field for universal banking.[45] At the same time, banking supervision has remained decentralized in the hands of national regulators with very different approaches. Some central banks, in Italy, Spain, Portugal, Greece, and the Netherlands, have retained it, while other EU countries have opted for integrated financial sector regulators. Since the early 20th century, Sweden has had a single regulatory authority, the Royal Inspectorate of Banks and Securities, exercising supervision of commercial banking, securities trading and stock-exchange operations and since 1991 also incorporating supervision of insurance. This model was adopted by the UK in 2000, when the Financial Service Authority, an independent and non-governmental body, took over banking supervision from the Bank of England, and financial-market regulation and supervision from the London Stock Exchange. Later, a similar pattern was adopted by Germany, with the merger, in 2002, of the Federal Banking Supervisory Office and the Federal Securities Supervisory Office into the newly created Federal Financial Services Authority.

A more fragmented situation has emerged in the regulation of financial markets. All European countries have adopted new prudential regulation on disclosure, listing, Initial Public Offerings (IPOs), M&A, and insider trading. The EU, through the Investment Service Directive of 1993, has allowed national governments to keep their own legal and regulatory frameworks, hoping that mutual recognition would suffice to deepen financial-market integration. However, scope for regulatory arbitrage and competition has remained large, and

---

[44]   W. Seifert et al., *European Capital Markets* (Basingstoke, 2000), pp. 87–107.

[45]   J.-P. Danthine, F. Giavazzi, X. Vives, E.L. von Thadden, *Monitoring European Integration*, vol. 9 (London, 1999); E.P.M. Gardener, P. Molyneux and J. Williams, 'Competitive Banking in the EU and Euroland', in A.W. Mullineux and V. Murinde (eds), *Handbook of International Banking* (Cheltenham, 2003), pp. 130–55.

the transposition of EU directives into national laws has been extremely slow.[46] The Lamfalussy Report of 2001 identified about 40 public authorities dealing with securities-market regulation and supervision, with mixed competences and different responsibilities. It also emphasized that the development of integrated European securities markets and the implementation of the mutual recognition system was being held up by the absence of clear Europe-wide regulation on critical issues such as prospectuses, cross-border collateral, market abuse and investment service provision. It pointed to the lack of an agreed interpretation of European rules and to differences in bankruptcy and judicial procedures, taxation, corporate governance and competition policies, listing and disclosure requirements, and takeover rules.[47]

As a matter of fact, the widened geographic, functional and organizational scope of suppliers of financial services has led to the emergence of what Edward Kane has called 'an international market for financial service regulation'.[48] On the one hand, rivalry between private and public suppliers of financial regulation across countries may have protected borrowers, depositors and investors from the over-regulation produced by a monopolistic supplier or a regulatory cartel. On the other, this fragmentation has also magnified the uncertainty about the size of implicit or explicit insurance subsidies guaranteed by national parent authorities to increasingly internationalized risk-bearing institutions. Any failure to meet these implicit guarantees could dangerously shake confidence in the global financial architecture, lead to shrinking foreign trade in financial services and push governments back to old and new policies of financial restriction. For this reason, all players (both regulated and regulators) have a partial community of interest in order to avoid financial instability.

Playing this kind of cooperative game has not proved an easy task, however. Indeed, in chapter 8, Catherine Schenk (*The Regulation of International Financial Markets from the 1950s to the 1990s*) shows, through the lenses of US and British records, how difficult and controversial it was for monetary and financial authorities of industrialized countries to find a common ground for a cooperative solution to the regulation and supervision of international banks. Early attempts were dominated in the 1960s and early 1970s by the discussion on how to bring under control the unregulated Eurodollar market based in London, but operated mainly

---

[46] See the papers collected in J.M. Kremers, D. Schoenmaker and P. Wierts (eds), *Financial Supervision in Europe* (Cheltenham, 2003); and in particular C. Goodhart, 'The Political Economy of Financial Harmonization in Europe', pp. 129–38.

[47] *Lamfalussy Report* (Final Report of the Committee of Wise Men on the Regulation of European Securities Markets), 15 February 2001, pp. 10–12.

[48] E. Kane, 'Competitive Financial Reregulation. An International Perspective', in R. Portes and A. Swoboda (eds), *Threats to International Financial Stability* (Cambridge, 1987), pp. 111–45; and idem, 'Tension between Competition and Coordination in International Financial Regulation', in C. England (ed.), *Governing Banking's Future. Markets vs Regulation* (Boston, 1991), pp. 33–47.

by US and other foreign banks. The debate generated much heat but virtually no practical result. Both the US and British authorities reached the conclusion that the benefits (providing relief to US banks and corporations in times of domestic credit stringency and enhancing London's status as an international financial centre) largely outweighed its inflationary potential and the destabilizing consequences of short-term capital flows. Subsequent debate among central bank officials at the Bank for International Settlements on cooperative regulation and supervision of the Eurodollar market and the provision of lender-of-last-resort facilities to international banks proved equally inconclusive. Only later, with the 'Concordats' of 1975 and 1983, did an agreement emerge regarding the division of supervisory responsibility on multinational banks between parent and host authorities. The adoption of the Capital Adequacy Requirements issued by the Basel Committee in 1987 (the so-called 'Basel I') represented the only cooperative success in almost thirty years of attempts. But, as Piet Clement gloomily argues in chapter 9 (*The Missing Link: International Banking Supervision in the Archives of the BIS*), historians interested in investigating the making of such agreements are likely to be denied access to most of the BIS records for a long time ahead on grounds of confidentiality and sensitivity. They will just have to content themselves with the background material released by the Basel Committee.

A general consensus exists that from the mid 1970s, and in the wake of thirty years of unusual financial stability, the frequency of systemic or near-systemic banking crises has increased as a consequence of the process of deregulation and liberalization. This was often accompanied by serious currency crises and is not only true of developing countries, but also of industrialized ones.[49] Three of the 'Big Five' systemic banking crises suffered by industrial economies took place in Europe and were preceded by financial liberalization: Norway in 1987 and Finland and Sweden in 1991.[50] The US Savings and Loans crises of the 1980s – an episode of comparable magnitude – also affected a recently deregulated sector of the banking system. In all these cases, competition induced deregulation and unsound practices and excess risk taking ensued, compounded by long expansionary cycles in asset prices. Their reversal eventually led to widespread losses and failures, with governments obliged to intervene in order to bail out distressed financial institutions. Indeed, financial liberalization seems to have brought about the re-emergence of boom and bust cycles, with longer expansions in credit and asset prices, followed by sudden, disruptive contractions. Consumption and investment decisions by no longer credit-constrained households and firms seems to have

---

[49]   M. Bordo and B. Eichengreen, 'Is our Current International Economic Environment Unusually Crisis Prone?', in D. Gruen and L. Gower (eds), *Capital Flows and the International Financial System* (Sydney, 1999), pp. 18–74. See also the papers included in G. Caprio, J.A. Hanson and R. Litan (eds), *Financial Crises. Lessons from the Past, Preparation for the Future* (Washington DC, 2005).

[50]   C. Reinhart and K. Rogoff, Banking Crises. An Equal Opportunity Menace, NBER Working Paper no. 14587, 2008.

responded, to an unprecedented extent, to highly pro-cyclical perceptions of wealth and risk, leading to a build-up of financial imbalances – that is, overextensions of private balance sheets – which eventually unwound under the pressure of confidence crises or of monetary intervention of an anti-inflationary nature.[51]

In the last chapter of the volume, Peter Englund and Vesa Vihriälä (*Banking Crises in the North: A Comparative Analysis of Finland and Sweden*) dissect the dynamics of the Swedish and Finnish banking crises of the early 1990s. Both banking systems emerged in the 1980s from a long period of tight regulation just to enter a lending boom driven by increased bank competition, improved access to foreign funds, increased demand for credit by once credit-constrained households and small firms, and asset-price escalation. When in 1990–91 the cycle was reversed, asset prices began to fall and the boom turned into a bust, bringing down finance companies and banks heavily exposed to the housing market. However, Englund and Vihriälä argue that the roots of the crises cannot be traced back exclusively to liberalization, weak supervision and excess risk-taking during the credit boom. In fact, the reversal was exacerbated by a combination of exogenous shocks (such as the collapse of the Soviet Union market for Finnish exporters) and policy mistakes. In the case of Sweden, the mistake was the decision to defend the fixed exchange rate of the Krona during the turmoil of the EMS crisis of 1992. In the Finnish case, the decision to devalue (instead of floating) the Markka in 1991 forced monetary authorities to keep interest rates high in order to defend the exchange rate from new speculative attacks. The floating of the Markka was only delayed, but the devaluation hit hard the foreign-currency debt of the corporate sector, inflicting further losses on the banking sector.

At the present time, the world appears to be on the verge of a vast movement towards encompassing financial regulation, which will probably configure something akin to the Great Reversal which swept most countries during the 1920s and 1930s. A general need is naturally felt for a crystal ball in which to read the signs regarding the nature and direction that matters in this respect are likely to take. Whether a policy-maker, a practitioner or just a member of the public, the attraction of a volume on the history of financial regulation and de-regulation will thus lie for many in the hope that the lessons of the past may be helpful in trying to understand what this second Great Reversal is likely to contain.

Can the knowledge gleaned from these chapters place one in a better position for predicting the shape of the financial world and of the rules that will mould it? The safest answer is probably not. True, in retrospect it is evident from practically all of these studies that path dependence has been one of the most powerful influences over the secular course of relations between financial activity and the regulatory responses they elicit. Yet it is also clear that at each turn in this historical process there is much also that is far from being time-invariant. New,

---

[51]   C. Borio and P. Lowe, Asset Prices, Financial and Monetary Stability. Exploring the Nexus, BIS Working Paper no. 114, 2002; and C. Borio and A. Filardo, Back to the Future? Assessing the Deflation Record, BIS Working Paper no. 152, 2004.

never experienced circumstances incessantly arise thanks to human ingenuity in devising ways of reducing risk, gaining informational advantage, combining resources and creating and exploring technology. As society moves along its course, at each crisis the combination of conditions is never the same as before and the defensive response of markets, of institutions and of society as a whole is therefore always likely to be unexpected and even unexpectable. Past patterns of financial regulation consequently do not evolve in linear fashion and extrapolation from earlier experiences is a risky exercise.

In trying to grasp the future state of global and national financial systems, delving into the past need not, however, be pointless. The chapters in this volume, although unlikely to supply a basis for rigorous projection from past trends and exact predictions, still provide useful and thought-provoking indications. They can suggest the sorts of events that trigger off the critical situations which eventually give rise to the necessity for regulatory swings – wars, of course, but, more frequently, jumps in technology, productivity changes, shifts in paradigms and perceptions, to name a few. Knowledge of previous experiences will point to the probable shape of corrective actions that may be expected from a particular conjugation of circumstances. It will also show that these political outcomes are not just the result of a cool analysis of the facts, even when these are fully known. They can be powerfully shaped also by the heat and indignation released by public debate and by changing popular perceptions of what is admissible behaviour in the realm of finance. In this perspective, it is not difficult to imagine that the coming wave of regulation will not only be appropriate to current problems but will probably go too far and last longer than necessary, as well as following paths which a dispassionate analyst would not have recommended.

A final strand of thought suggested by this volume is that the financial world may be about to be entering waters less known to us than on similar occasions before. For the ills of globally integrated markets, obviously only global remedies will work. This means that in dealing with markets which have overreached themselves, the past is not a particularly helpful guide, a fact that is demonstrated by these studies, all of them essentially national in character. Financial regulation and de-regulation has always been the work of sovereign states, even though it has often been replicated across borders, as a result either of the inclination to emulate best practices or of the need to compete institutionally with rival systems in other countries. An intense reversal of the vast sweep of de-regulation of the last two decades, such as is now expected, is therefore a novel experience. The scarcity of significant precedents for supra-national solutions in a domain where sovereignty has always dominated points to a large area of uncertainty ahead and to a considerable scope for regulatory and political creativity. It is likely that what is in store then is an entirely new regulatory era, which, on past showing, will undoubtedly last for at least one or two generations before another Great Reversal makes its presence felt.

CHAPTER 1

'Conservative abroad, liberal at home': British Banking Regulation during the Nineteenth Century

Philip L. Cottrell

The British government was the first to encounter the 'modern' problem of banking regulation. Two aspects – what should constitute the cover for banknotes, coupled with which institutions should be permitted to have circulations – led to the stipulations of the Bank Charter Act of 1844. The preceding debate between various protagonists of the 'Currency School' and the 'Banking School' has been well explored by economists and historians.[1] Far less scholarly attention has been paid to the equally substantial parallel discussion concerned with regulating both the formation and business of joint-stock banks, which also ultimately resulted in legislation by Sir Robert Peel in 1844 – the Joint Stock Banking Act.[2] This chapter considers the path leading to that statute, which involved some transfer of the authorities' growing experience of regulating chartered colonial banks during the 1830s to joint-stock banks in the metropolitan economy. It also reviews why the authorities gave up the regulation of domestic joint-stock banks between 1857 and 1862, and the ultimate consequences that this surrender had for the colonial banking regulations.

The central issues that came to the fore from the early 1820s were: establishing resilient banks, and providing safeguards for their proprietors and those amongst their customers who held their notes but increasingly were their depositors.

From 1711 until 1821 the British State stood back from intervening in the burgeoning formalized provision of banking services.[3] Its benign stance was

---

[1]   The classic study is F.W. Fetter, *Development of British Monetary Orthodoxy 1797–1875* (Cambridge MA, 1965), to which should be added L.S. Pressnell, 'Gold Reserves, Banking Reserves and the Baring Crisis of 1890', in C.R. Whittlesey and J.S.G. Wilson (eds), *Essays in Money and Banking in Honour of R.S. Sayers* (Oxford, 1968).

[2]   There have been only two major scholarly considerations: S.E. Thomas, *The Rise and Growth of Joint Stock Banking*, vol. 1, *Britain: to 1860* (London, 1934); and K.S. Toft, 'A Mid-century Attempt at Banking Control', *Revue Internationale d'Histoire de la Banque*, 3 (1970), pp. 149–67.

[3]   The authorative analysis is that of L.S. Pressnell, *Country Banking in the Industrial Revolution* (Oxford, 1956); but see also R. Cameron, 'England 1750–1844', in R. Cameron

radically changed by the experiences of severe financial crises in Ireland in 1820 and in England in 1825–26.[4] Resultant legislation passed in 1821, 1824, 1825 and 1826 substantially circumscribed the corporate monopoly privileges of, first, the Bank of Ireland, and, then, the Bank of England, by enabling the ready formation of commercial joint-stock banks.[5] This fundamental change followed from the diagnosis that substantial numbers of private banking houses had failed in both Ireland and England during the first half of the 1820s because they lacked solidity, lacked capital. Legislators had accepted the argument, based upon perceived solidity of Scottish joint-stock banking, that banking instability could be quelled by allowing banks to have more than six partners.[6] However, joint-stock banks were only allowed to be established beyond a 65-mile radius of either Dublin or London in continuing deference to the two established corporate banks.

The introduction of a legal framework permitting what came to be called 'joint-stock banking' was hurried; hence the need for three Irish banking measures between 1821 and 1825. The English Act of 1826 was equally a product of pressure,

---

et al., *Banking in the Early Stages of Industrialization* (New York and Oxford, 1967); and H.V. Bowen and P.L. Cottrell, 'Banking and the Evolution of the British Economy', in A. Teichova et al. (eds), *Banking Trade and Industry. Europe, America and Asia from the Thirteenth to the Twentieth Century* (Cambridge, 1997).

For developments in London, see D.M. Joslin, 'London Private Bankers, 1720–1785', *Economic History Review*, 2nd ser., 7 (1954), pp. 167–86; and idem, 'London Bankers in Wartime, 1739–84', in L.S. Pressnell (ed.), *Studies in the Industrial Revolution Presented to T.S. Ashton* (London, 1960); together with I.S. Black, 'Money, Information and Space. Banking in Early Nineteenth-century England and Wales', *Journal of Historical Geography*, 21 (1995), pp. 398–412; idem, 'The London Agency System in English Banking, 1780–1825', *London Journal*, 21, 2 (1996), pp. 112–30; idem, 'Private Banking in London's West End, 1750–1830', *London Journal*, 28, 1 (2003), pp. 29–59. C.G.A. Clay, 'Henry Hoare, Banker, his Family and the Stourhead Estate', in F.M.L. Thompson (ed.), *Landowners, Capitalists and Entrepreneurs. Essays for Sir John Habakkuk* (Oxford, 1994); F.T. Melton, 'Robert and Sir Francis Gosling. 18th Century Bankers and Stationers' in R. Myer and M.R.A. Harris (eds), *Economics of the British Book Trade, 1605–1939* (Cambridge, 1985); and idem, 'Deposit Banking in London, 1700–90', *Business History*, 28, 3 (1986), pp. 40–50.

[4]   For the Irish crisis, see G.L. Barrow, *The Emergence of the Irish Banking System 1820–1845* (Dublin, 1975), pp. 17–23.

[5]   Barrow, *Irish Banking System*, pp. 61–83.

[6]   For the early development of joint-stock banking in Scotland, see R. Cameron, 'Scotland, 1750–1845', in R. Cameron et al., *Banking in the Early Stages of Industrialization* (New York Oxford, 1967); S.G. Checkland, *Scottish Banking. A History, 1695–1973* (Glasgow, 1975); C.W.Munn, *The Scottish Provincial Banking Companies 1747–1864* (Edinburgh, 1981); idem, 'The Coming of Joint-stock Banking in Scotland and Ireland 1820–25', in T.M. Devine and D. Dickson (eds), *Scotland and Ireland* (Edinburgh, 1983); idem, 'The Emergence of Joint-stock Banking in the British Isles. A Comparative Approach', *Business History*, 30, 1 (1988), pp. 69–83; and R. Saville, *Bank of Scotland. A History 1695–1995* (Edinburgh, 1996).

of a government 'fire fighting' in the midst of an acute financial and monetary crisis.[7] The measure went through parliament in a matter of 98 days, members of both houses being as alarmed as government ministers by continuing banking turmoil. Largely modelled on the 1825 Irish statute, it placed no restrictions upon joint-stock banks formed under its stipulations in England and Wales with regard to how they were to be constituted, managed or the capitals that their directors were to embark. Its permissiveness was only counterbalanced to a degree by clauses that placed some ill-considered restraints upon their business operations with respect to the transfer of funds between the provinces and the metropolitan area. Otherwise, joint-stock banks' affairs were subject to a degree of publicity through the Act requiring their officers to make returns to the Stamp Office, while every shareholder or, rather, co-proprietor was fully liable for discharging a bank's debts, should it fail.

An opportunity for considering at greater leisure how the State might regulate joint-stock banks arose in spring 1832, by when some 25 were conducting business in England and Wales. It was occasioned by a parliamentary review of the conditions to be laid down for renewing the Bank of England's charter, undertaken by a Committee of Secrecy chaired by the Chancellor of the Exchequer, Viscount Althorp. And his committee inquired into whether 'checks could be provided to secure for the public a proper management of banks of issue, and especially whether it would be expedient and safe to compel them to publish their accounts'.[8]

The view that joint-stock banks were superior to private banking houses, which had so strongly shaped the State's introduction of legislation between 1821 and 1826, had gained further ground by the early 1830s. As a result, some witnesses before the parliamentary committee argued that joint-stock banks should be further encouraged. This was most hotly contested by Samuel Gurney, the leading London bill broker. He maintained that the 'new' banks offered 'less security' to the public than their private counterparts. As a consequence, the public lost, should they be shareholders, and also more generally through destructive speculation in their shares and by what Gurney considered to be their incompetent management.[9]

Gurney's strictures arose out of a wider concern generated by what was considered to be the speculative nature of joint-stock companies, whether banks or not. It was commonly held that business was best conducted personally by those whose entire fortunes were at risk, an opinion that was to be held in many quarters for much of the nineteenth century. This view of what was the most appropriate

---

[7]   7 Geo. IV c. 46. For the most recent published study of the English 1825–26 crisis, see B. Hilton, *Corn, Cash, Commerce. The Economic Policies of the Tory Governments 1815–1830* (Oxford, 1977), pp. 202ff, 207–10, 215ff.

[8]   British Parliamentary Papers [henceforth BPP], 1831–2, VI, *Report from the secret committee on the renewal of the charter of the Bank of England with minutes of evidence ...*, p. 3.

[9]   BPP, 1831–2, VI, *Report from the secret committee on ... the Bank of England, minutes of evidence*, S. Gurney, qq. 3738, 3748.

way for organizing business also maintained that, should the State permit joint-stock companies to operate, their very nature made them only suitable for areas of enterprise characterized by routine, so not requiring continuous personal attention.

Possibly to meet the hostility to the new joint-stock banking, directors of two interrelated Lancashire joint-stock banks – the Bank of Liverpool and the Bank of Manchester – had already approached Althorp over the government regulating their formation.[10] They also put their *Propositions* before the 1832 parliamentary committee.[11] Like Gurney, they were concerned that the 1826 Act allowed the formation of sham banks. To meet this defect, they took further the remedy arising from the contemporary diagnosis of the cause of both the Irish banking 1820 crisis and the English 1825–26 crisis. Banking stability would not simply be ensured through banks having unrestricted numbers of partners; the government also needed to require minimum levels of capitalization. The Lancastrian joint-stock bankers thought that new banks being established in small towns and the rural shires should have nominal capitals of at least £0.3m., with £0.1m paid up. In the case of major towns, like Liverpool and Manchester, they maintained that this 'floor' capitalization should be higher – £0.5m. – and as much as £1m. for joint-stock banks in London, if the government was persuaded to allow their formation within the Bank of England's privileged metropolitan area. It was put forward that this objective of the *Propositions* could be achieved by joint-stock banks henceforth being established by the grant of individual charters. Each application would give the government the opportunity to use its discretion over the required capitalization, as well as other matters where it might be thought necessary to be applied.

Minimum capitalizations went with other stipulations in the *Propositions* that were considered to be required for safeguarding the public against any abuse of the unfettered ability to form joint-stock banks. It was put forward that such banks should have at least 100 proprietors, 20 of whom would have individual shareholdings of at least £1,000. This, it was maintained, would ensure that these banks had 'capitalists' amongst their proprietors, individuals of strength and respectability suitable to act as their directors. Furthermore, a bank's board was to be made responsible for their institution's affairs by requiring the annual election, or re-election, of every director. Answerability was to be coupled with publicity, directors producing an annual report, registered publicly, that contained a full list of the bank's proprietors, so making it clear exactly who stood behind it. Further public confidence was to be secured by the bank providing ample security for its

---

10   For the Bank of Liverpool during the early 1830s, see G. Chandler, *Four Centuries of Banking*, vol. 1, *The Grasshopper and the Liver Bird. Liverpool and London* (London, 1964), pp. 238–61. For the Bank of Manchester, L.H. Grindon, *Manchester Banks and Bankers* (Manchester, 1877), pp. 242f; and T.E. Gregory, *The Westminster Bank through a Century*, vol. 2 (London, 1936), p. 52.

11   BPP, 1831–2, VI, *Report from the secret committee on … the Bank of England, minutes of evidence*, J.B. Smith, q. 4310.

note issue. Lastly, and probably in a hostile reaction to the recent development of 'district' branching joint-stock banks in north-west England, the directors of the Bank of Liverpool and the Bank of Manchester argued that joint-stock banks should not be allowed to have branches beyond a 20-mile radius of their respective head office, with these offices only permitted to discount bills and accept deposits.[12]

The pioneering joint-stock banker, Vincent Stuckey, agreed that their affairs should be conducted on the basis of sizeable paid-up capitals and publicity. Furthermore, if a system of chartered banks was introduced, he thought that their capitals should be invested in government securities, or comparable assets, as was the case with the Bank of England. And he wanted to go further, arguing that a major defect of the 1826 Act was that it had not introduced limited liability for shareholders. He considered that this omission had deterred investment in the 'new' banks, particularly from 'people of property' whose presence amongst their proprietors would significantly improve their management.[13] Stuckey was to be almost a lone voice on this particular issue, despite his accumulated experience as a major banker in the South-West, through first heading a number of related private houses, and then bringing them together as one of the first joint-stock banks. It quickly became orthodoxy that shareholders in joint-stock banks should not enjoy the privilege of limited liability, it being considered until the late 1870s that unlimited liability provided 'safety' for both those holding a joint-stock bank's notes and those who placed deposits with a joint-stock bank.[14]

There was no consensus amongst the 22 witnesses questioned by the parliamentary committee over the question of reforming the 1826 Act, as was equally the case with regard to other matters of concern to its members. It was doubtful whether any accord would have been forthcoming since the committee's hearings provided the forum for three opposing interested parties to defend their respective ground: the Bank of England, the private bankers and the new joint-stock bankers. As a result, it was left to the Chancellor, Althorp, to negotiate charter

---

[12]   For context, see F.S. Jones, 'Instant Banking in the 1830s. The Founding of the Northern & Central Bank of England', *Bankers' Magazine*, 211 (1971), pp. 130–35; idem, 'The Manchester Cotton Magnates' Move into Banking, 1826–50', *Textile History*, 9 (1978), pp. 90–111; and idem, 'The Cotton Industry and Joint-stock Banking in Manchester 1825–1850', *Business History Review*, 20, 2 (1978), pp. 65–85.

On the general question of branching, see C.W. Munn, 'Banking on Branches. The Origins and Development of Branch Banking in the United Kingdom', in P.L. Cottrell et al. (eds), *Finance in the Age of the Corporate Economy. The Third Anglo-Japanese Business History Conference* (Aldershot, 1997); and L. Newton and P.L. Cottrell, 'Joint-stock Banking in the English Provinces 1826–1857. To Branch or not to Branch?', *Business and Economic History*, 27, 1 (1998), pp. 115–28.

[13]   BPP, 1831–2, VI, *Report from the secret committee on ... the Bank of England, minutes of evidence*, V. Stuckey, q. 1203.

[14]   For contemporary views on the question of bank shareholders' liability, see T. Joplin, *An Examination of the Report of the Joint Stock Bank Committee* (London, 2nd edn 1837), pp. 2f; and J.W. Gilbart, *A Practical Treatise on Banking* (London, 1828), pp. 54, 56–61.

renewal with the Bank of England's directors, which he attempted to undertake on the basis of the evidence received by the committee.

With respect to the question of altering the statutory basis for establishing note-issuing joint-stock banks, Althorp took up some of the *Propositions'* recommendations, putting forward that they should be chartered, albeit that their shareholders were not to enjoy the privilege of limited liability, and publish their accounts. Their solidity was to be further assured by requiring that half of their nominal capitals be paid up, the funds so amassed invested in government securities. With regard to joint-stock banks not issuing notes, his one requirement was that these should have a minimum share denomination of £100. However, his scheme for a chartered note-issuing joint-stock bank met with fierce opposition in the House of Commons on 31 May 1833, and consequently was not introduced.[15] No change was therefore made to the permissive 1826 Act, which remained on the statute book until 1844.[16]

The greater possibility of chartering commercial banks had been opened up by the 1825 measure that had repealed the Bubble Act of 1720.[17] It also empowered the Crown to prescribe the extent of a shareholder's responsibility in a 'corporation' through the grant of Letters Patent.[18] This royal prerogative was administered by the Board of Trade; but its officials employed it merely in one respect – the ability to sue and be sued in the name of a company's officer. Furthermore, the Board of Trade took a very conservative attitude when bestowing even this aspect of incorporation, solely considering favourably approaches from a restricted grouping of companies: charitable or educational bodies and public utilities, although also mines.[19]

The question of how banks might be treated arose in July 1830 with the proposal from Reid, Irving & Co., leading East India merchants, for establishing a chartered

---

[15] Althorp's scheme for chartered, note-issuing joint-stock banks was only finally abandoned in February 1834. The threat of its onerous conditions halted the promotion of the Hull, East Riding & North Lincolnshire Banking & Co., and caused the management of the York City & County Bank to attempt to rally opposition. See P.L. Cottrell and Lucy Newton, 'Banking Liberalisation in England and Wales, 1826–1844', in R. Sylla et al. (eds), *The State, the Financial System and Economic Modernization* (Cambridge, 1999), p. 87.

[16] A declaratory clause of the 1833 Bank Charter Act (3 & 4 Will. IV c. 98), permitted joint-stock deposit banks to be established within the Bank of England's privileged metropolitan area. Being merely a declaration of a legal interpretation of the Bank's charter, the London joint-stock banks subsequently founded were consequently operating within a 'grey' legal context, to cause their managements and shareholders considerable difficulties. The 1833 statute explicitly repealed clauses of the 1826 measure that prevented provincial joint-stock banks from undertaking certain forms of financial transfers between their respective business areas and London.

[17] 6 Geo. IV c. 91.

[18] So called because the sovereign's grants are not sealed up, but exposed to view with the great seal pendant at the bottom.

[19] P.L. Cottrell, *Industrial Finance 1830–1914. The Finance and Organization of English Manufacturing Industry* (London, 1980), pp. 42f.

bank in Mauritius. Their application came to the Board of Trade and the Treasury in London, with support from the Colonial Office, albeit on the condition that the bank gave proper security for its notes. Advantage was seen in the project since it was foreseen that the bank could provide liquidity in place of either the colony's local government or 'individual capitalists', should the island colony experience a financial crisis.

The Board of Trade and the Treasury were prepared to charter the proposed bank if it had 'an ample capital subscribed and an adequate preparation of such capital actually paid up and governed by certain regulations and restrictions as to the conduct of their [sic] business'. The regulations, the germ of the colonial banking regulations, were agreed by the two ministries to be, first, that its shareholders bore 'personal responsibilities … not less than twice the amount of shares held by each' *pace* that as members of a chartered corporation they had the privilege of limited liability. This stipulation was coupled with that for a published, detailed half-yearly balance sheet, of which a copy was to be submitted to the colony's local government, while its governor could at any time require 'similar accounts'. Furthermore, the regulations restricted the business to be undertaken to 'Banking, viz: advances upon commercial paper or Government securities, and general dealings in moneys and Bills of Exchange', but from which 'loans or advances upon land or other property not readily convertible into money nor in the purchase of any such property' were specifically excluded. Eventually, the bank was chartered not by the metropolitan government but by the colony's governor under a special arrangement. Nevertheless, its terms replicated and developed what had been put forward earlier by the Board of Trade and the Treasury.[20]

The issues posed by the chartering of the Bank of Mauritius appear to have led within months to the Treasury attempting to take the leading place in grants of colonial banking charters on the grounds that its 'opinion … is more particularly charged with questions relating to the finances and currency of the Empire'. Its officials pointed to the government's then-growing interest in chartering domestic joint-stock banks. This accompanied concerns within the Treasury caused by the problems of developing a sterling-exchange standard in the Empire, largely managed through the conduct of official payments between London and the colonies. The major anxiety was over the safety of public funds, particularly ensuring that none were employed, directly or indirectly, in unwise private lending. There was also

---

[20] A.S.J. Baster, *The Imperial Banks* (London, 1929), pp. 29ff. The other major consideration of the colonial banking regulations is provided by a contemporary 'official' historical review; see The National Archives, Public Record Office, Kew, London: T[reasury] 158/83, [E.W. Hamilton], [Confidential] *Memorandum on chartered banks*, Apr. 1877, with bound-in subsequent, updating notes in manuscript [hereafter, Hamilton, *Memorandum*]. See also F.H.H. King, 'Structural Alternatives and Constraints in the Evolution of Exchange Banking', in G. Jones (ed.), *Banks as Multinationals* (London, 1990), p. 87; and idem., *British Multinational Banking 1830–1990* (Oxford, 1993), pp. 19f.

concern over there being no partiality in the choice of agents undertaking official remittances. These issues went with that of 'administrative tidiness' –

> the extreme importance that all bank charters should be framed upon a settled and consistent principle, and of the difficulty of attaining this result if charters were to be granted indiscriminately by various independent departments of the state without reference to the Treasury.[21]

However, within 16 months, the Treasury had accepted that no decision over granting a colonial banking charter was to be taken until it had received 'a distinct report' from the Board of Trade 'both on the merits of the case and on the provisions necessary to be introduced in every such charter'.[22] The equal roles of the two ministries of state were established during the lengthy, precedent-setting discussions that eventually led to the chartering in London of the Bank of Australasia.

This colonial banking scheme had achieved some definite shape amongst its London promoters by April 1833. The upshot was the decision to establish the bank as a corporation – a joint-stock company with limited liability – through gaining a royal charter for a venture that they were then calling the Royal Bank of Australasia & South Africa, planned to be a bank for the Empire in the southern hemisphere. The project had already been aired with the Board of Trade and the Treasury. One of the promoters' past associates, Spring Rice, involved in their previous ventures – the Provincial Bank of Ireland and the National Provincial Bank of England – was now Secretary of the Treasury. He was receptive to the proposed imperial banking scheme, and, in the very preliminary discussions, the only condition stipulated by the Treasury was that the bank's shares, amounting to £0.3m. nominal, should all be taken up within two years of its formation.[23]

Following initial approaches proving positive, a memorial for a charter was submitted to the Treasury on 18 May 1833. While awaiting the outcome, the promoters legally established their nascent bank as an unincorporated body – a co-partnership, or joint-stock company with unlimited liability – through the signing of a deed of settlement. Nonetheless, their aspirations remained clear, since the bank's board of directors rapidly became called its 'Court', following the

---

[21]   Hamilton, *Memorandum*, p. 18.

[22]   Baster, *Imperial Banks*, p. 25; and Hamilton, *Memorandum*, pp. 18f. Baster's research was a considerable achievement, deserving full recognition, since, as Hamilton wrote in 1877, 'Owing to the defective Treasury records, and owing to some Charters being granted on the advice of the Treasury, and others being granted on the advice of the Board of Trade, considerable difficulty has been experienced in ascertaining to what Banking Companies Charters have been granted, and with how many of those Charters are still operative.' Hamilton, *Memorandum*, p. 3.

[23]   S.J. Butlin, *Australia and New Zealand Bank. The Bank of Australia and the Union Bank of Australia Limited 1828–1951* (London, 1961), pp. 22ff.

nomenclature of both the Bank of England and Bank of Ireland. From the outset, they were seeking to give their embryonic institution all the prestige and status of a chartered bank, well aware of the consequent positive public impact, as was to be later acknowledged.[24]

Despite the personal connections between the promoters and Spring Rice, no response was received from the Treasury until 18 December 1833. The seven-month delay was due to the charter application being the first for a London-based colonial bank, and the authorities had come to regard its grant as likely to set precedents. Indeed, the submission for incorporating the Royal Bank of Australasia & South Africa had put further into motion the framing of the colonial banking regulations, not to be fully developed until 1840.[25]

News that a charter would be granted finally came in mid-December 1833, but its provisions failed to meet the promoters' aspirations. It was to have a term of only 21 years. Furthermore, the Board of Trade would not permit the bank to operate outside of Australia, and separate banks for colonies 'at a great distance from and having no natural connection with each other' came to be a basic tenet of the colonial banking regulations. Alongside this 'territorial principle' went a number of others that also became planks of the regulatory code. As with the terms of the charter for the Bank of Mauritius, its shareholders were to shoulder 'double' limited liability through each being liable for the bank's debts to the extent of twice the nominal value of their respective shareholding.[26] The bank's soundness was to be further assured through all its shares being taken up within 18 months, by when half of their nominal value was to be paid up. Thereafter, its debts were not to exceed triple the aggregate amount of its equity and deposits.

In the authorities' further development of a code for chartered colonial banking, it was also stipulated that the Australian bank's notes were to have a minimum denomination of £1, all payable on demand at not only the respective issuing office but also the bank's principal colonial branch. This requirement went with any suspension of cash payments for either a continuous period longer than six days or of more than 60 days in total within any 12-month period automatically leading to the charter's abrogation. Furthermore, the bank's business, like that of the Bank of Mauritius, was to comprise solely 'the legitimate operations of banking, namely advances upon commercial paper or government securities, and dealings in money, bills of exchange, or bullion'. Land was not be to taken as security for loans, the Treasury considering it an unsuitable asset for a note-issuing bank, but this stipulation created a significant problem for developing banking in Australia, and subsequently in other colonies. Other restrictions upon business included advances involving a director, or staff member, not collectively totalling more than a third of extended accommodation. As a chartered body, the Australian

---

[24]   See Baster, *Imperial Banks*, p. 21.

[25]   See Baster, *Imperial Banks*, pp. 32–46.

[26]   This regulation was to require special legislation for its enforcement – 6 Geo. IV. Cap. 91; see Baster, *Imperial Banks*, p. 21.

bank's business was to be generally publicized through half-yearly statements, displaying averages of specified weekly returns of assets and liabilities sent to the London head office by its branches. Lastly, dividends were only to be paid from realized profits.[27]

Settling the terms of the charter for the Australian bank in conformity with the unfolding colonial banking regulations was to take two further years. However, the promoters were unable to make much ground on major issues in dispute. The few major concessions gained, often resulting from divisions of opinion between the Treasury and the Board of Trade, were over the duration of any suspension of cash payments and the bank's equity capital. It was eventually conceded that cash payments could be suspended for no more than 130 days within any 12-month period, the authorities finally accepting that this longer period was required because of the time required to obtain coin from south Africa, the nearest point of supply to Australia. Second, with the bank obliged to have all of its shares taken up within 18 months of their issue, when half their nominal value was to be paid up, the Treasury agreed to its nominal capital being reduced to £0.2m. This could be increased subsequently to £0.6m., as had been envisaged by the promoters, but only with the Treasury's explicit consent. In all this, as the Board of Trade insisted, the charter would not bestow a monopoly of either the note issue or conducting official business.[28]

A charter for a London-based bank – the Bank of Australasia – was settled with the Treasury by March 1834.[29] This enabled the circulation of a prospectus.[30] However, the bank was not to be incorporated until May 1835, by when some of its staff and specie were already on the high seas bound for Australia. The final delay arose from a dispute between the Treasury and the Attorney-General. The Attorney-General idiosyncratically maintained that no charter under the great seal could have a finite term – 21 years – that the Treasury had stipulated for the bank's note-issuing powers. In his opinion, this could only be specified in a charter granted by Letters Patent, as allowed by recently enacted legislation.[31] The bank's founders were initially prepared to accept the Attorney-General's opinion, although it meant their project's further postponement, caused by having to fulfil a public-notice requirement of three months. Yet that was not to be endured, as the directors had also obtained sound legal opinions directly contradicting the Attorney-General's novel interpretations. These proved sufficient for the Treasury's solicitors to commence drafting the Bank of Australasia's definitive charter in January 1835. When received, it was uniquely, and advantageously, a

---

[27]   Butlin, *Australia and New Zealand Bank*, pp. 24f.

[28]   Baster, *Imperial Banks*, p. 23.

[29]   Butlin, *Australia and New Zealand Bank*, pp. 26f.

[30]   Baster, *Imperial Banks*, pp. 51f; and Butlin, *Australia and New Zealand Bank*, p. 29.

[31]   4 & 5 Will. IV c. 94, Trading companies Act; and Baster, *Imperial Banks*, pp. 51–2.

perpetual charter as opposed to one having a finite term. No other colonial bank was to gain a comparable charter.[32]

Hamilton concluded in 1877 in an internal Treasury memorandum that charters of a finite term were henceforth granted to colonial banks presumably: (1) to limit royal protection to the infancy and development of the undertaking only; (2) to avoid saddling colonial dependencies indefinitely with banking companies possessed of independent powers and capable of abusing those powers; (3) to make it easy to give greater freedom of action to the colonies themselves in matters of internal concern; (4) to prevent these banking companies from being hampered by provisions which, in the course of some years after they were granted, might become ill-adapted to the circumstances of the day; and (5) to afford an opportunity of reviewing the policy of granting the charter.[33]

The chartering of the Bank of Australasia set the pattern for what subsequent promoters of chartered colonial banks were to endure – long-drawn-out, grinding negotiations with the Board of Trade, the Treasury and sometimes the Colonial Office, with, on occasions, helpful, or otherwise, interjections from colonial governors. In the case of the Colonial Bank, they produced one exception to the solidifying colonial bank regulations. Its shareholders were not called upon to bear the burden of 'double liability', a concession granted exceptionally by the authorities because of the bank's very sizeable initial nominal capital – £2m. – which eventually became £7m.[34]

The regulations were sent out to colonial governors for their guidance when dealing with applications to establish banks under a locally-granted charter. Until 1840 they were strictly enforced, resulting in bank acts passed by colonial governments being disallowed by the metropolitan authorities and in schemes for London-based chartered colonial banks being drastically changed during negotiations with the Board of Trade and the Treasury. Of the two ministries of state, it was the Board of Trade that generally sought the most rigid application of the regulations' stipulations in colonial banking charters. Nonetheless, the metropolitan authorities displayed some elasticity, especially to meet particular local circumstances, either economic or political.

By the close of 1840, the metropolitan authorities had the accumulated experience of chartering nine London-based colonial banks, of intervening in the chartering by local colonial governments of at least a further six banks, and of being deeply involved, along with the Colonial Office, in the opening discussions for the chartering of a further London-based colonial bank.

During 1839 the regulations had begun to be codified, undertaken by the Treasury in response to the Colonial Office's request for their general circulation to all colonial governors. The Board of Trade put forward two additions to the

---

[32]   Butlin, *Australia and New Zealand Bank*, p. 29; and Hamilton, *Memorandum*, p. 20.

[33]   Hamilton, *Memorandum*, p. 21.

[34]   Baster, *Imperial Banks*, p. 68.

Treasury's draft abstract. The first was a requirement that a shareholder's individual 'double' liability for a bank's debts should continue for six months after any transfer of shares, seen as a necessary check against the formation of speculative concerns and associated share trading. Second, experience had shown that the inclusion in charters of very complicated details of management made the overall document 'unintelligible', and caused subsequent grave difficulties for the boards of some chartered banks. However the exclusion of this problematic material from future charters resulted in the banks concerned having longer deeds of settlement, sometimes supported by supplementary deeds. Lastly, the Board of Trade restated its commitment to the Treasury of ensuring that the regulations were fully adopted in any further colonial banking charters. The regulations were eventually issued to the colonies in March 1840.[35]

The colonial banking regulations were further amended in 1846, so as to bring them broadly into accord with the principles underlying the 1844 Bank Charter Act. The extent of a chartered colonial bank's circulation was henceforth restricted to its paid-up capital, and required to be covered one-third in specie. Two Treasury officials, Pennington and Arbuthnot, undertook the drafting of subsequent banking charters, and came to be regarded within the department as 'the principal authorities on Colonial banking'.[36]

While the colonial banking regulations were being developed, the formation of joint-stock banks in England and Wales under the 1826 Act mounted, culminating in the outbreak of a 'mania' in spring 1836, a feverish speculative episode comparable to the canal 'mania' of the 1790s. Joint-stock bank promotions had averaged ten a year during the mid-1830s, but in 1836 prospectuses for at least 59 were put before the public. By March, these flotations were being 'stagged', with shares on which a deposit of merely 1s. had been paid being traded at 25s., and even the chances of an allotment of bank shares offered on the markets at a price. The gloomy predictions that Gurney had made to the 1832 parliamentary committee had come about.

Alarm bells had already rung, the directors of the Bank of Liverpool and Bank of Manchester having once more publicized their *Propositions* at a meeting in November 1834. Their recommendations for greater regulation had been recast in an even more stringent form. They now called for a minimum share denomination of £50, and for branches of joint-stock banks to be separately constituted banking companies, located no further than 12 miles from their respective parent institutions.[37] However, their campaign had no impact, and the need to consider the matter was not acted on till May 1836, when William Clay obtained a Commons select committee to investigate the new joint-stock banks. At the beginning of what was to prove to be five years of almost continuous inquiry, Clay favoured joint-

---

[35]   See BPP, 1845, VIII, Select Committee on Accounts of Colonial Receipt and Expenditure, *Report*, Appendix N.

[36]   Hamilton, *Memorandum*, pp. 19, 50.

[37]   *Circular to Bankers*, 333 (5 Dec. 1834).

stock banks having limited liability, albeit that their capitals were to be fully paid up and the greatest publicity given to their affairs.[38] Clay could command some authority, being a significant London merchant, chairman of the Grand Junction Railway and also of the Southwark and Vauxhall water companies. He had entered the House as a Liberal in 1831, campaigning for reform as a philosophical radical not only with regard to banking but also land and London's government. Clay's speech in the House was published with an addendum containing his *Reflections*.

Clay's parliamentary committee of inquiry adopted the stance of the *Propositions* but found that the problems presented by some of the joint-stock banks, the sham and near sham, were not just those posed by inadequate capitals but also ineffective management, which could only be overcome by growing experience as opposed to a regulatory law.[39] Mismanagement was plainly abundant and notorious in the cases of the failures of the Agricultural & Commercial Bank of Ireland, the Northern & Central Bank of England, the North of England Banking Co. and the Norwich & Norfolk Banking Co. The flaws detected in joint-stock banking by Clay's committee between 1836 and 1838, publicized through the publication of the substantial evidence that it had taken, were amplified by a further two parliamentary inquiries during 1840 and 1841, occasioned by the monetary panic of 1839.[40]

Legislation reforming the 1826 Act was finally passed in 1844, one of three parallel measures by which Peel attempted to meet the problems of financial and monetary instability. The Act to regulate the Joint Stock Banks in England went alongside the year's Bank Charter Act and Joint Stock Companies Act.[41] The banking measure's stipulations melded some of the various proposals for more stringent regulation that had been put forward since 1832, while also being informed by the Treasury's experience of chartering colonial banks over the past decade and more. Furthermore, its requirements were framed to be a corrective response to how some bank promoters had exploited the permissiveness of the 1826 Act, revealed in the copious evidence collected by the parliamentary committees of 1836–38.

The Act totally changed how further joint stock-banks were to be founded, but made no major demands of those already formed under the legislation of 1826, of which some 126 were carrying on business in England and Wales. Although radical,

---

[38]   Cottrell and Newton, 'Banking Liberalisation', pp. 96–7.

[39]   See BPP, 1836 IX, Select committee on the establishment of joint stock banks, *Report, minutes of evidence etc*; BPP, 1837, XIV, Select committee on the establishment of joint stock banks, *Report, minutes of evidence etc*; BPP, 1837–8, VII, Select committee on the establishment of joint stock banks, *Report, minutes of evidence etc.*

[40]   See BPP, 1840, IV, Select committee on banks of issue, *Report, minutes of evidence etc*; BPP, 1841, V, Select committee of secrecy on banks of issue, *First report, minutes of evidence etc*; and BPP, 1841, V, Select committee of secrecy on banks of issue, *Second report, minutes of evidence etc.*

[41]   7 & 8 Vict., c. 113.

it did not introduce some of the reforms that had been urged on the government, particularly by Clay. Limited liability continued to be denied and, furthermore, banks formed under the Act were not required either to have fully paid-up share capitals or to publish balance sheets in a specified common form.

The unfettered ability to establish joint-stock banks was superseded in 1844 by a system of individual chartering, undertaken not by the Treasury but by the Privy Council, whose members had the freedom to impose any conditions thought required. The Board of Trade was given a role in the chartering process – that of approving a projected joint-stock bank's deed of settlement – and came to replace the Privy Council as the prime body responsible for chartering of new joint-stock banks. However, the opinions of the government's law officers were also sought, including specifically those of the Lord Advocate for Scotland and the Solicitor-General for Scotland in the cases of applications for Scottish banking charters. As with securing colonial banking charters, obtaining a domestic bank charter came to be a process of bank promoters conducting prior negotiations with the State, although greatly simplified since these needed to be undertaken primarily with only one ministry – the Board of Trade – rather than three. Nonetheless, the Treasury's continuing interest in banking charters, domestic as well as colonial, continued, as shown by its interventions in establishing the terms of their clauses. The 1844 Act had given powers of discretion to the Privy Council over charters' terms. It was applied specifically in the case of that for the Royal British Bank by the requirement for a special meeting of shareholders if the bank lost its reserve fund and a quarter of its equity capital, although this proved to be a safeguard of no substance.

Charters, the durations of which were limited to 20 years, were to be granted in response to petitioning, undertaken by holders of at least half of a bank's shares who had already paid up 10 per cent of their respective nominal value. This requirement went along with those for a minimum nominal capitalization of £0.1m., consisting of shares of a nominal denomination of no less than £100.

The bank's deed of settlement, signed by at least seven shareholders and attached to the petition, was required to specify its trading title and where it was to undertake business. These matters were to be accompanied by identifying information, at some length, about every shareholder. The petition not only had to display clearly the basis for establishing the bank but also provide details of its governance – the election of its directors, their qualifying shareholdings and how their board was to conduct its management. There was to be an annual general meeting of shareholders, whereas nine shareholders collectively holding 21 shares could summon an extraordinary meeting of the bank's proprietors. Furthermore, a bank was forbidden to extend advances against its own shares, and required to have its books audited by at least two independent persons, chosen by the shareholders. The shareholders were given some further protection through receiving annually both a balance sheet and a profit-and-loss account, amplified by the auditors' report, albeit that the Act did not specify their form. The public in general had the safeguard of the mandatory publication of a monthly statement of assets and liabilities, together with that provided by banks making to the Stamp Office various annual returns identifying all those involved in their equities, directorates and middle managements.

Charters bestowed on banking companies consisted of the respective petition and the bank's deed of settlement together with a few further clauses. The principal points contained in the latter were:

1. The incorporation of the Bank 'one body politic in name and deed', with power by its name to 'sue and be sued, implead and be pleaded, in all courts whether of law or equity' in the United Kingdom and elsewhere, with 'perpetual succession' and a 'common seal'.
2. Power to hold lands of a certain value for business purposes but no other (except as a security for debt, and then for five years only); sale and purchase of such lands to be notified to the Board of Trade.
3. Business to be carried on according to provisions of the deed of settlement, and clauses of that deed, and of the Act of 1844, to be the Company's regulations.
4. Power to revoke the Charter in the case of its provisions or those of the Act not being observed.
5. Charter to be void on dissolution of Company, and to be valid in all courts of law.[42]

These provisions agreed with those contained in charters granted to colonial banks that had the colonial banking regulations as their template.

Following the receipt of a charter, conferred by the grant of Letters Patent, a bank could only commence business once all its shares had been taken up, every shareholder had signed its deed of settlement and half of its nominal capital had been paid up in cash. A full list of named shareholders, with their respective addresses, had also to be supplied to the Stamp Office within three months of a bank's being chartered. This return, completed in the form laid down by the Act, had further to specify the directors and officers. Thereafter, the return, signed by a manager and director and validated by a Justice of the Peace, had to be made annually, and delivered to the Stamp Office between 28 February and 25 March. A comparable return was required for detailing any changes amongst either the bank's directorate or its shareholders. The latter return followed from requirements concerned with maintaining share-transfer books and with transfer of shares.

Peel's code for the establishment of new joint-stock banks was extended to Ireland and Scotland in 1846.[43] Although only applying to new institutions, Peel

---

[42] Hamilton, *Memorandum*, p. 12.

[43] 20 & 21 Vic. c. 49. See Checkland, *Scottish Banking*, pp. 454–8; and Barrow, *Irish Banking System 1820–1845*, p. 188.

hoped that the requirements of his Act would lead to existing joint-stock banks adopting their spirit and principles.[44]

Peel had intended the 1844 Act should not contain harsh or inconvenient stipulations, and had conducted prior consultations with sections of the banking community, although their representatives were more anxious to secure changes in the 1826 measure's clauses that would clarify the existing law and further remove petty restrictions. However, there were immediate complaints about the onerous regulation imposed by the 1844 Act, and these were subsequently followed by criticism of particular aspects. Whether intended or not, the 1844 banking code halted the promotion of new joint-stock banks in the United Kingdom, only 12 being established under its provisions, of which two were in the process of being founded when the Act became operative and so became subject to its stipulations.

One new development was that the 1844 Act's provisions were to be turned to for attempting to form chartered colonial and foreign banks, beginning with the London & Eastern Banking Corporation in 1853–54, followed by the short-lived London & Paris Joint Stock Bank and the Agra & United Service Bank. This was paralleled by the colonial banking regulations being brought to bear upon banks that were to operate in areas beyond the formal sway of the British State, as in the cases of the Chartered Bank of Asia, the Chartered Bank of India, Australia & China, the Bank of Egypt and the Ottoman Bank.[45]

Clay's committees of inquiry of 1836 to 1838 had concluded that the basic problems of the new joint-stock banking arose from inadequate capitals and ineffective management. One of the objectives of Peel's 1844 Act was to secure by legislation that new banks had sufficient capital. However, promoters quickly found ways round the Act's apparently rigorous provisions. In order to meet the one requiring petitioners for a charter to have already paid up 10 per cent of the nominal value of the shares they held, the founders of the Royal British Bank had its manager sign a promissory note for £4,300. Mismanagement was compounded by inexperience and, in the cases of the Royal British Bank and the London & Eastern Bank, outright fraud. Consequently, the 1844 Act not only stopped bank formations, leading to the view by the early 1860s that England was 'under-banked', but also failed to ensure the solidity of most of those formed under its provisions. One, the London & Paris, failed to open for business, and a further three had failed by 1858, followed by yet a further five over the ensuing eight years. Only three of the 12 banks established under the 1844 code were to have totally untrammelled business 'lives'.

Peel's 1844 banking code sat alongside that which he had had established for non-banking joint-stock companies. Indeed, initially he had looked during 1843–

---

[44]   Toft, 'Banking Control', p. 152.

[45]   With regard to the latter two banks, see A.S.J. Baster, 'The Origins of British Banking Expansion in the Near East', *Economic History Review*, 5, 1 (1934), pp. 76–86; and P.L. Cottrell, 'The Coalescence of a Cluster of Corporate International Banks, 1855–1875', *Business History*, 33, 3 (1991), pp. 31–52.

44 to the introduction of an umbrella measure regulating all joint-stock companies. However, by the early 1850s the Board of Trade's legal counsel for corporate matters, Bellenden Kerr, was irked by, and dissatisfied with, various governments' attempts since 1825 to address the problems continually posed by joint-stock companies of various kinds. In his opinion, legislation had merely introduced 'useless machinery' while constituting a 'mass of confusion'. His views were part of a groundswell, still not completely comprehended by historians, which led in 1855 and 1856 to the total liberalization of British company law.[46] With some prescience, Robert Lowe maintained in February 1856 that the State had not the power to prevent the formation of fraudulent companies. With regard to joint-stock banks, this was to be abundantly shown in the cases of the collapses of the Royal British Bank and the London & Eastern Banking Corporation during 1857. These financial disasters swayed public opinion against Peel's 1844 code.

In 1857 Lowe partially assimilated joint-stock banks into the 1856 permissive code for establishing limited-liability companies, Peel's regulatory provisions only continuing primarily in terms of banks having to continue to have shares with a nominal value of no less than £100, and their shareholders not enjoying limited liability.[47] However, within a year, joint-stock banks could be established with limited liability, and the last remaining vestiges of Peel's 1844 code disappeared with the passage of the Companies Act in 1862. One major financial feature of the ensuing decade was the numerous promotions of limited-liability banks for operating either in the domestic economy or overseas.[48]

The freedom given by the 1862 Companies for establishing joint-stock banks with limited liability resulted in the Treasury advising that no further colonial banks should receive royal charters. This counsel was accepted with one exception – the chartering of the Asiatic Banking Corporation in 1864. Nonetheless, the policy was not taken to its ultimate conclusion, the Treasury permitting the renewal of the Oriental Bank Corporation's charter in 1872 because of the uncertainties arising from 'a Chartered Bank being loosed from the "leading strings" of a Charter, and left to shelter itself as best it could under the provisions of Imperial and Colonial

---

[46] Cottrell, *Industrial Finance*, pp. 45–52. See also R.A. Bryer, 'The Mercantile Laws Commission of 1854 and the Political Economy of Limited Liability', *Economic History Review*, 50, 1 (1997), pp. 37–56; R. Ingham, 'Mill on Limited Liability Partnerships', *Journal of Liberal Democrat History*, 23 (1999), pp. 16 and 28 seguitur; S. Jones, 'The Professional Background of Company Law Pressure Groups', *Accounting, Business and Financial History*, 7, 2 (1997), pp. 233–42; and D. Loftus, 'Capital and Community. Limited Liability and Attempts to Democratize the Market in Mid-nineteenth Century England', *Victorian Studies*, 45, 4 (2002), pp. 93–120.

[47] 20 & 21 Vict., c. 49.

[48] Baster, *Imperial Banks*, pp. 124–30; Cottrell, *Industrial Finance*, pp. 52f; and idem, 'Credit, Morals and Sunspots. The Financial Boom of the 1860s and Trade Cycle Theory', in P.L. Cottrell and D.E. Moggridge (eds), *Money and Power. Essays in Honour of L. S. Pressnell* (Houndsmill, 1988).

Acts of Parliament regulating banking business and Joint Stock Companies'.[49] The question of the continuance of the system of chartered colonial banking was finally formally considered in 1880, the government introducing the Chartered Banks (Colonial) Bill, which was referred to a select committee, the membership of which included two distinguished bankers – Sir John Lubbock and Sampson Lloyd.

By the late 1870s the Treasury was imbued with laissez-faire, while its officials had been concerned for some years about the regulatory duties imposed upon them by the terms of colonial banking charters but 'which [they] cannot suitably or conscientiously undertake'. However, an abrupt cessation of the chartered system might cause a loss of confidence in any, or all, of the banks that had been established under its regulations. Furthermore, it would end the special privileges that they enjoyed for some areas of their businesses, such as note issuing, and, in turn, call for legislation being passed by the respective local imperial government. The option of continuing the 'life' of a chartered bank through its registration under the 1862 Companies Act was equally fraught. The main issue in this respect was the consequently arising substitution of 'single' liability for the 'double' liability that shareholders in chartered colonial banks bore. It involved the interests of the bank's creditors and shareholders alike.[50] The Treasury was well aware of these difficulties, Hamilton having aired them at length in an internal printed *Memorandum* in 1877.

The evidence-collecting sessions of the 1880 select committee were brought to an abrupt end by parliament's dissolution. As a result, the Treasury introduced a 'model charter' scheme in place of the 1880 bill's provisions. This was to be applied when chartered banks requested a new charter in place of one shortly to expire. New charters, with ten-year terms, relieved the Treasury of its supervisory functions and replaced them by the bank being required to pass special resolutions, while its directors were to have any discretionary powers formerly exercised by the Treasury. If the bank had needed the Treasury's consent to increase its note issue or open a new branch, it now had to obtain that of the requisite local colonial governor or, in the case of India, the Secretary of State. Furthermore, the bank was in future to conduct its business in accordance with the laws of the colony in which it operated.[51]

The 'model charter' scheme failed to resolve all the difficulties facing the chartered colonial banks from the late 1870s. Two had to apply immediately for private acts of parliament in order to be able to extend their business fields in responses to changes in the scope and techniques of overseas banking. A precedent was established by the Oriental Bank Corporation in 1884; its management was only able make good losses by surrendering a restrictive charter and reconstructing their institution under the various Companies Acts. The same somewhat complex procedure had to be followed by three further colonial banks in 1893: English,

---

49   Hamilton, *Memorandum*, p. 3.

50   Baster, *Imperial Banks*, pp. 134f; and Hamilton, *Memorandum*.

51   Baster, *Imperial Banks*, pp. 135f.

Scottish & Australian Chartered Bank, London Chartered Bank of Australia and the Chartered Mercantile Bank of India.[52]

The late 1870s proved to be equally a turning point for domestic joint-stock banks that had been established under either the 1826 Act or the 1833 Bank Charter Act's declaratory clause. The shock to domestic commercial banking caused by the City of Glasgow Bank's second and fatal collapse in autumn 1878 led to the realization that unlimited liability was untenable for bank shareholders. Those of the ill-fated Glaswegian bank were called upon twice to meet its debts, resulting in severe personal financial distress to the extent that some were forced into bankruptcy. Shareholders in other unlimited banks pressed immediately for legal safeguards to cover their own positions, legislated for by the 1879 Companies Act's introduction of reserved liability. During the early 1880s, 27 unlimited joint-stock banks took advantage of the 1879 Act's provision, and by the 1890s there was hardly a bank operating as an unlimited concern.

Some textbook writers have attributed the growing stability of British banking over the nineteenth century to the ascendancy of joint-stock banks and their growing branch networks from the 1860s. Their number had increased to 1880, by when there were 128. Certainly, joint-stock banks became the major players, since in 1884 there were only 160 private country banks and 40 London private banking houses. Within a further 40 years, private commercial banking had almost disappeared, represented by merely 17 houses in the provinces and 12 in the metropolis.[53] Nonetheless, domestic joint-stock banks continued to fail, although not in crisis-induced numbers after 1866.

Joint-stock banking's growing robustness from the mid-century was due to a range of factors, although not including its regulation by the State through legislation; that had come to an end in 1862. The state nearly legislated again and was almost forced to by the Baring crisis of 1890, caused by the collapse of a leading acceptance and issuing house rather than of a domestic commercial joint-stock bank. In late January 1891, Goschen, the Chancellor of the Exchequer, trailed the possibility of legislation containing measures that would both economize on the public's use of gold coinage and establish a second gold reserve. It was never enacted. More importantly for what subsequently occurred, he called upon commercial banks to hold greater cash reserves and to publicize this by publishing their balance sheets more frequently .[54]

---

[52]   Baster, *Imperial Banks*, pp. 130f.

[53]   S. Nishimura, *The Decline of Inland Bills of Exchange in the London Money Market 1855–1913* (Cambridge, 1971), table 1, pp. 80–81.

[54]   Pressnell, 'Gold Reserves', pp. 208–9.

CHAPTER 2

Lobbying, Institutional Inertia, and the Efficiency Issue in State Regulation: Evidence from the Evolution of Bankruptcy Laws and Procedures in Italy, England, and the US (c.1870–1939)

Paolo Di Martino*

Analysis of the causes and consequences of the state's direct intervention in the economic sphere is a very rich field in economic history. Topics such as increasing state control over firms and banks after the Great Depression, as well as the state's 'retreat' in the 1980s and the 'revenge' of the market, have generated long-standing and strong debates among economic historians and economists alike. Less attention has been paid to the role of the state's indirect intervention in the economy, in particular to the provision and enforcement of commercial law and practices. Recent findings in economics about the strategic role that institutions and laws play in fostering and supporting long-term economic performance indicate the importance of filling this gap in the literature.[1]

Among the most neglected subjects is the evolution and impact of bankruptcy laws and procedures. The development of bankruptcy legislation is a very interesting historical case of institutional regulation of the economic sphere during the nineteenth and the twentieth centuries, and of the state's ability (and inability) to provide institutions able to sustain economic performance. During this period, deep changes in the structure of industry, trade, and finance forced governments to rethink old bankruptcy laws and to provide new ones. In general, more tolerant remedies took the place of rigid and punitive legislation, in order to address

* I wish to thank the participants in the Annual Conference of the European Association of Banking and Financial History (Lisbon 2006), F. Carnevali, and an anonymous referee for their useful comments. Usual disclaimer applies.

[1] R. Laporta, F. Lopez-de-Silanes et al., 'Law and Finance', *Journal of Political Economy*, 106, 6 (1998), pp. 1113–55; and R. Levine, 'The Legal Environment, Banks, and Long-Run Economic Growth', *Journal of Money, Credit and Banking*, 30, 3 (1998), pp. 596–620.

the new problems emerging in the economic environment.[2] Despite the general phenomenon of convergence towards similar principles and instruments, this evolution was not uniform across countries. Diversity did not necessarily manifest itself in the formal characteristics of the various laws, but more often either in the use of specific counterbalances, or in the timing of the introduction of various pieces of legislation. In terms of the efficiency of various bankruptcy systems, these differences were not neutral. In fact, specific procedures or norms failed to be adopted, or were introduced with a substantial lag, even when substantial agreement among contemporaries existed on their superior level of efficiency.

Explaining why in a sort of 'free market for institutions' the most efficient set of rules did not emerge, or at least not at the same time, is an issue for economic historians. As a matter of fact, in theory nothing stopped governments from copying from other countries' experiences and trying to implement the best rules possible. Why did this not happen? Along general lines, the difficulty of defining exactly the features of 'the' efficient bankruptcy legislation is one of the most straightforward explanations for the lack of homogeneity of insolvency legislation across countries. Bankruptcy law has to deal with a number of conflicting aims requiring toughness and softness at the same time; it is therefore not easy to indicate which mix of the two elements is in theory expected to work best.[3] In practice, matters become even more complicated because theoretical issues such as fostering entrepreneurship or enforcing credit contracts take different forms depending on the structure of the real economy and the working of the credit market. There is no doubt that the history of the evolution of bankruptcy and insolvency laws in various countries, and the persistence of differences, cannot be separated from the study of the features of national industrial structures, the idiosyncratic functioning of various banking systems, the emergence and transformation of country-specific formal and informal commercial rules and habits, and so on. However, even if these general explanations are convincing, nonetheless they are not complete; they do not fully explain, for example, the failure to adopt specific legal devices whose efficiency was unanimously recognized.

The aim of this chapter is to provide explanations for this historical puzzle by focusing on three cases: England, Italy, and the US. However, rather than a full study of the political economy of the evolution of bankruptcy and insolvency laws in the various cases, this chapter focuses on three specific issues: the differences between the workings of the debt-discharge system in England and the US, the

---

[2]   Examples of this trend can be found in the abolition of imprisonment for debt or the easing of friendly agreements between creditors and debtors. For a comprehensive analysis of 19th to early 20th century evolution of bankruptcy laws in Europe, see J. Sgard, 'Do Legal Origins Matter? The Case of Bankruptcy Laws in Europe 1808–1914', *European Review of Economic History*, 10, 3 (2006), pp. 389–419.

[3]   For a more detailed analysis of these problems, see P. Di Martino, 'Approaching Disaster. A Comparison between Personal Bankruptcy Legislation in Italy and England (c.1880–1939)', *Business History*, 47, 1 (2005), pp. 23–43.

length of the time necessary for Italian lawmakers to adopt English-style 'official' management of bankruptcy procedures, and the differences between friendly debtor-creditor agreements ('compositions') in the two countries.

We argue that two forces prevented the 'market for bankruptcy legislation' from being a real 'free market' and thus enabling the most efficient solutions to emerge. The power of lobbying groups to interfere with the process of institutional change is one cause. 'Path-dependency' in the process of institutional change is the other.

The chapter is structured as follows. Section one provides an analysis of the most significant differences in bankruptcy laws in Italy, England, and the US between c1800 and the 1930s. Section two focuses on the most important phases of the evolution of bankruptcy legislation in the three examples, analysing the role played by lobbying groups. Section three addresses the same issue and looks at historical accidents and path-dependency. Section four concludes.

I

During the 1930s European and American scholars, although starting from very different perspectives, converged on an explicit and implicit consensus on the superior degree of efficiency of some of the elements of the English bankruptcy system.[4] American commentators, in particular, emphasized the advantages of the English debt discharge mechanism, and indirectly of English 'officialism'. These aspects were also praised by Italian scholars, who also appreciated the positive results of the more relaxed English approach to friendly compositions as an alternative to bankruptcy and liquidation, vis-à-vis the tightly but inefficiently regulated Italian equivalent.

Introduced in England as early as the beginning of the eighteenth century, debt discharge had passed through a long phase of experimentation until changes finally introduced in 1914 eventually transformed the original institution into a fundamental instrument to support economic activity, via selection of debtors and the provision of the 'fresh start' option to the 'worthy' ones. 'Officialism' was a much more recent institution. At the end of a controversial reform process culminating in 1883, 'officialism' de facto meant that the working of personal-bankruptcy procedure relied to a very large extent on a figure called the *official receiver*, who was an employee of the Board of Trade and not a creditors' representative. Before the actual bankruptcy hearing, official receivers were in charge of collecting information about debtors' conduct, and they operated alongside creditors in running the so-called *public examination*. This was a public

---

[4]   See in particular, C. Del Marmol, *La faillite en Droit Anglo-Saxon. Etude de législation et de jurisprudence faite dans le cadre de la loi anglaise de 1914* (Paris et Bruxelles, 1936), and M. Radin, 'Discharge in Bankruptcy', *New York University Law Quarterly Review*, 9, 1 (1931), pp. 39–48.

meeting in which debtors had to answer on oath to creditors' questions about their business conduct, the reasons for insolvency, and so on. Receivers were also put in charge of the actual management of bankruptcy procedures in all cases in which courts were not satisfied with the representative chosen by creditors.[5]

American scholars admired the results of English debt discharge procedures. In the first instance, they appreciated the wide spectrum and variety of outcomes, which included conditional and suspended forms of discharge. The former, which imposed extra payment on top of what had already been obtained via liquidation, could be used by creditors to secure the collection of further share of debt, while the latter operated as a disciplinary device and supposedly effected debtors' behaviour ex ante. During the 1930s the American debt-discharge system, regulated by the 1898 law, did not contemplate the variety of solutions available in England, and judges could only either grant or deny immediate discharge on the basis of a set of relatively rigid criteria. As a consequence, debtors could not be disciplined by suspended discharge or forced to pay additional money by conditional discharge. Furthermore, the American system was seen as open to exploitation by debtors, who were far too easily granted absolute discharge.[6]

The possibility for the English system to hand down a wider spectrum of sentences, and the fact of being less open to exploitation by debtors, was in part the consequence of the articulated legislation, but also the result of the reliance on accurate information. 'Officialism', with the extended powers of inquiry given to the receiver and the public examination process, ensured this result. Although the US system was subject to a form of 'officialism' too, meaning that courts and not creditors had the power to accept or deny discharge, nothing like the richness of information available to English judges was in the possession of their American counterparts. It is clear that, although the lack of availability of instruments such as suspended and conditional discharge and the poor level of information available to judges were in theory separate problems, in fact the two issues were two faces of the same coin. As Boshkoff argued, 'It would be possible to have conditional/ suspended discharge system without an Official receiver – but it would not be the same system'.[7]

Interestingly, European scholars shared this point, but from the opposite perspective; it was seen as positive that the English system did not have the too

---

[5]   On the evolution of bankruptcy and insolvency law in England, see I.P.H. Duffy, *Bankruptcy and Insolvency in London during the Industrial Revolution* (New York and London, 1985), V.M. Lester, *Victorian Insolvency. Bankruptcy, Imprisonment for Debt, and Company Winding-up in Nineteenth-Century England* (Oxford, 1994), and Di Martino, 'Approaching Disaster'.

[6]   Radin 'Discharge in Bankruptcy', and D.G. Boshkoff, 'Limited, Conditional, and Suspended Discharge in Anglo-American Bankruptcy Proceedings', *University of Pennsylvania Law Review*, 131, 1 (1982), pp. 69–125.

[7]   Boshkoff, 'Limited, Conditional, and Suspended Discharge', p. 103.

conservative, punitive, and creditor-supportive features of many Continental laws which simply did not contemplate the debt discharge option.[8]

Italian scholars also explicitly recognized that the English legislation, in particular debt discharge, was an efficient system to avoid business instability overshooting into macro 'domino effect' and the consequential uncontrolled waste of companies and entrepreneurs.[9]

The praise of this specific element of the English system was in fact only one aspect of a more general critical view of Italian bankruptcy law and procedures and their limited effectiveness in terms of 'restarting' instruments. In this regard, Italian scholars were as unhappy with the excessively lenient and unregulated extra-judicial friendly agreements,[10] as they became unsatisfied with the too rigid judicial alternatives (*concordato preventivo*) after they appeared in 1903.[11]

In the view of Italian scholars, the excessive rigidity of formal norms was to blame for the disastrous conditions of the whole system, together with the inefficient functioning of procedures. While bankruptcy law lacked useful instruments, on the other hand courts were accused of having done the very best to use the available devices in the worst way possible; procedures, so scholars maintained, were long, expensive, unfair and open to corruption. An odd power-sharing between creditors and public bodies was indicated as the cause of trouble.[12] Paradoxically, the *concordato preventivo*, criticized on the one hand for being too strictly regulated in its formal structure, was also stigmatized as too poorly and loosely administered in practice.[13] Indirectly, then, Italian scholars showed appreciation for the general principle of 'officialism' as a form of power redistribution from creditors to a central authority. Eventually, a radical reform went in this direction and the management of procedures was passed to public officers, more or less as happened in England. This reform, however, only occurred in the early 1930s, half a century after the introduction of 'officialism' in England.

From this analysis, it appears very clear that some of the elements of the English legislation, either explicitly or as an implicit alternative, looked very appealing to both American and Italian scholars. The idea of more closely imitating English instruments remained, however, a theoretical option. The American system retained its pro-debtors orientation (including its ultra-lenient and little-scrutinized debt discharge system), while in Italy 'officialism' was eventually implemented

---

[8]   Del Marmol, *La Fallite.*

[9]   J. Rezzara, *Il concordato nella storia, nella dottrina, nella giurisprudenza. Studio di diritto commerciale* (Turin, 1901).

[10]   L. Bolaffio, *Il concordato preventivo secondo le sue tre leggi disciplinatrici* (Turin, 1932).

[11]   G. Bonelli, *Del Fallimento. Commentario al codice di commercio* (Milan, 1907).

[12]   U. Pipia, *Del Fallimento* (Turin, 1932).

[13]   In 1930, Minister Rocco noticed 'the lack of any rigorous check on *concordati*.' A. Rocco, 'Il disegno di legge sul fallimento e sul concordato preventivo', *Rivista di Diritto Commerciale*, 28 (1930), p. 216 (author's translation).

(although only in the 1930s), but reforms of friendly agreement or the introduction of discharge were ignored.

The persistence of sub-optimal legal institutions represents an historical puzzle; the next two paragraphs provide two explanations for it, not necessarily mutually exclusive.

II

The analysis conducted above suggests that laws, procedures and institutions more generally can be exchanged in a sort of 'free market', and consequently inefficient solutions should disappear as the result of 'competition'. A possible alternative view is that, in fact, obstacles to the working of the 'market' were strong enough to block its theoretical beneficial action. In order to understand which kind of obstacles might have been at work, we must turn our attention to the theoretical explanations of the problem of the existence and persistence of inefficient institutions.

In general scholars are divided into two fields. On the one hand, there are authors who believe that institutions evolve because of the action of selfish forward-looking insiders (political entrepreneurs). In this literature, inefficiency emerges because insiders are motivated by their own interest and not inspired by the search for macroeconomic efficiency, because distorted or imperfect knowledge and computational ability strongly constrain their action, or because of a combination of the two problems.[14] In the second field, scholars believe the inertia of institutional change is strong enough to limit (if not to nullify) such an element of human agency. Historical accidents, so the argument runs, might start paths of institutional development that, once established, simply perpetuate themselves, giving human agency a marginal role or even no role at all (a concept called path-dependency). In this case, inefficiency is not the result of miscalculation or opportunism of specific agents, rather of the inner anarchic character of institutional evolution.[15]

---

[14]   Among others, see, in particular, D.C. North, *Institutions, Institutional Change and Economic Performance* (Cambridge, 1990).

[15]   See, in particular, R.R. Nelson and S.A. Winter, *An Evolutionary Theory of Economic Change* (Cambridge MA, 1982), and P. David, 'Why Are Institutions the "Carriers of History"? Path-dependency and the Evolution of Conventions, Organizations and Institutions', *Structural Change and Economic Dynamics*, 7, 5 (1994), pp. 205–20. For a survey on theories of institutional evolution, see A. Greif, *Institutions and the Path to the Modern Economy. Lessons from Medieval Trade* (Cambridge, 2006). Interestingly, North uses the concept of path-dependency as well. In this case, however, the idea is that institutions are trapped in an inefficiency path because political entrepreneurs are not interested or unable to change them. In this approach there is thus still a room for human

In this section, we consider the most important transitions that marked the evolution of bankruptcy and insolvency laws in Italy, England and the US, looking at the impact of human agency. In the next section, we analyse the role of path-dependency.

As we stressed above, three main elements attracted the attention of non-English commentators: soundly regulated debt discharge, efficient use of friendly compositions (deeds of arrangement), and the public nature of procedures. Each of these three elements was introduced in a distinctive phase of reform of English bankruptcy legislation: discharge at the beginning of the eighteenth century, deeds of arrangement in the 1820s, and 'officialism' in the 1880s. Our study must thus necessarily start from the analysis of these three distinctive periods.

The introduction of discharge was the result of the combination of human intentionality and specific historical circumstances. At the beginning of the eighteenth century, wars and particularly bad weather had caused severe interruptions to trade, with the consequent failure of a high number of what were perceived as honest traders, who fled Britain to avoid the harsh consequences of bankruptcy. It is in this climate that parliament legislated on the first embryonic idea of debt discharge as part of a wider ad hoc reform aimed at supporting non-fraudulent debtors who decided to cooperate. The same principle was behind a more general re-design of bankruptcy law, which was eventually passed in 1732.[16]

At the end of the century, however, changes in the economic structure of the country made the law inadequate and, in particular, rising levels of bankruptcy – the result of a more complex and risky economic environment – could not be addressed with old instruments. However, it took rather a long time for Parliament to be able to understand and solve the problem, despite the abundance of theoretical solutions provided by various politicians. Parliament did not seem to have the will or the interest to proceed, and the whole institutional process was blocked. However, petitions from the City and its active lobbying activity ended the 'parliament resistance to legal reform'.[17] The 1825 Act, which included the possibility of friendly yet regulated agreements between the parts, was eventually approved. The 1825 Act was, however, only the beginning of a phase of deep institutional change that took place in the 1830s. As Lester noticed, the 1825 law had settled the macro norms, but not the set of micro legal instruments and structures necessary to implement the law. Efforts of strongly motivated political entrepreneurs coming from the English bar, in particular Lord Brougham, resulted in 1831 in the introduction of the first form of 'officialism', i.e. the attempt to transfer administrative power from creditors to public bodies.[18] 'Officialism' was, however, suspended in 1869 under the accusation coming from the business community that

---

agency, while path-dependency à la David implies a much stronger role for historical accidents to trigger a mechanical process.

[16]   Duffy, *Bankruptcy and Insolvency*, pp. 10f.
[17]   Duffy, *Bankruptcy and Insolvency*, p. 47.
[18]   Lester, *Victorian Insolvency*, pp. 40–59.

the new system was slower and more expensive than the previous one. In the early 1880s, 'officialism' was introduced again. Two major elements were behind the approval of the new law. The 1869 Act, strongly supported by the business community, proved to be a disaster in terms of costs and length of procedures; therefore the strength of this lobbying group was severely undermined. On the other hand, the action of motivated civil servants such as Joseph Chamberlain and the staff of the Board of Trade proved fundamental.[19]

By the end of the process of institutional change taking place between 1705 and 1883 English bankruptcy law had acquired the distinctive features envied by non-English law scholars in the 1920s and 1930s. According to the evidence provided, it is hard to disagree with Lester, who maintained that 'two groups helped to shape the system …: the legal profession and the business community. Later in the [nineteenth] century, civil servants can be added to this list.'[20] In practice, the whole pattern of development of English bankruptcy and insolvency legislation was engineered by groups of insider political entrepreneurs, whose aims eventually coincided with the issue of providing efficient rules. Civil servants simply aimed at producing fair rules, while the legal profession and the business community, even if motivated by a direct vested interest, ended up pushing for the implementation of efficient solutions. In general, the pressure coming from various interest groups went consistently in the same direction of re-balancing the bargaining power between creditors and debtors and introducing sound screening devices. Exceptions to the rule existed; the 1825 Act was the victory of the business community against the apathy of Parliament, while the fundamental introduction of 'officialism' in 1883 was due to the effort of civil servants against the interests of the business community.

In conclusion, it seems that the English experience gives credit to the idea that institutions were transformed by the action of insiders and that inefficiency was the result of 'bounded rationality'. However, in the next section we shall see that not all the results achieved by the English system can be directly linked to the action of some pressure group.

Before turning to analysing this issue, it is necessary to look at the problem of why other systems did not use the English model as an example to imitate, and in particular at the extent to which the action of political entrepreneurs can be blamed for this. The study of this problem starts with the US. In this regard the key point of the story is the emergence in 1898 of a new national bankruptcy law. Contrary to its numerous predecessors,[21] this piece of legislation survived for a long period and remained the standard for personal bankruptcy well into

---

[19]   For a detailed reconstruction of the passage of the 1883 Act, see Lester, *Victorian Insolvency*, pp. 170–221.

[20]   Lester, *Victorian Insolvency*, p. 11.

[21]   Federal bankruptcy laws were in existence between 1880 and 1883, 1841 and 1843, and 1867 to 1878. See C.J. Tabb, 'The History of Bankruptcy Laws in the United States', *American Bankruptcy Institute Law Review*, 3, 1 (1995), pp. 5–51.

the 1930s. Also, the 1898 Act represents a fundamental landmark as, for the first time, American norms about debt discharge, included in the law, broke with the English tradition.[22] First, while the previous laws contemplated the possibility of granting conditional and suspended discharge, this option disappeared in the new act. Second, contrary to what was established by the English 1883 law, the formal enquiry into a debtor's conduct of affairs, and anything resembling the public examination, found no equivalent in the American legislation. In other words, all the problems in the American debt-discharge system originated from the 1898 act, and it is to the process of approval of this law that we must turn our attention to understand the reasons for the existence of a relatively inefficient institution. The established view stresses that the law matured in a deeply pro-debtor environment. Boshkoff, for example, claims that the absence of clauses about suspended or conditional discharge was part of a deal that creditors had to accept in order to obtain approval for a national bankruptcy law at a time of debtors' dominion. In 1898, Boshkoff argues, creditors 'abandoned the conditional discharge principle without the slightest expression of regret'.[23] Similarly, Skeel maintained that low creditor bargaining power was the reason why the 1898 Act did not include the possibility of investigating the claimants' conduct of affairs, as was the case under the English system.[24] If the pro-debtor character of the legislation is the key to explaining its limitations, it then becomes important to understand where this feature came from. The general argument is that traditionally American bankruptcy laws were the result of economic shocks, and therefore approved at times when the issue of discharge of debtors was relatively more urgent and relevant than the protection of creditors' rights. This was certainly the case with the 1898 law, passed in the aftermath of the 1893 crisis. Also, by the time of the approval of the Act, the nature of the instruments conceived to deal with corporate insolvency had already contributed to creating a pro-debtor cultural environment.[25] At first glance an argument thus seems to emerge that the pro-debtor character of the 1898

---

[22]   C.J. Tabb, 'The Historical Evolution of the Bankruptcy Discharge', *American Bankruptcy Law Journal*, 65 (1991), pp. 325–71; and Boshkoff, 'Limited, Conditional, and Suspended Discharge'.

[23]   Boshkoff, 'Limited, Conditional, and Suspended Discharge', p. 110.

[24]   D.A.J. Skeel, *Debt's Dominion. A History of Bankruptcy Law in America* (Princeton, 2001).

[25]   While a national law was still vacant, a series of bankruptcies hit the American economy during the 1880s, namely a wave of failure of railways companies. At the time, various pressure groups competed for the provision of institutional solutions to the problem. Creditors, not surprisingly, pushed for companies' liquidation, while debtors wanted to raise new capital and keep businesses as ongoing concerns. The two forces were very much in balance, but the dispute was solved by government intervention; in response to government pressure, courts gave a seal of approval to new credit contracts that, de facto, advantaged debtors and disallowed companies' liquidation. See P. Tufano, 'Business Failure, Judicial Intervention, and Financial Innovation. Restructuring US Railroads in the Nineteenth Century', *Business History Review*, 71, 1 (1997), pp. 1–40.

law depended on historical accidents fitting into an already established trend, in other words a path-dependency-based explanation. However, the idea that the pro-debtor character of the 1898 bankruptcy law should be connected to the shock produced by the 1890s crisis, or the persistence of a cultural element, is far from being fully supported in the current debate.[26] Skeel for example suggested that the crisis had an impact, if any, only in terms of accelerating the demand for a national law, and its character derived completely from the stronger bargaining power of the pro-debtor lobby vis-à-vis the pro-creditor one.[27]

During the 1930s, attempts were made to correct the unbalanced nature of the 1898 law, in particular to reintroduce some forms of conditional discharge. However, with the depression already on the horizon and the number of bankruptcies growing, 'creditors' timing was bad'[28] and the project failed.

According to this analysis, the debtor-friendly character of the law emerged because of the action of political entrepreneurs, and relative inefficiency must be seen as the result of the mismatching between macro aims and specific interests. However, a different, path-dependency-based, explanation also exists, and we will turn to it in the next section of the chapter.

In Italy, after the introduction of the code of commerce in 1882, bankruptcy law[29] faced two major transformations; the first one in 1903 with the introduction of the *concordato preventivo*, the second one in the 1930s when the Italian version of 'officialism' was implemented. In the former case, the change was driven by the increasing awareness, among both policy-makers and academic scholars, of the problem of the lack of suitable alternatives to company liquidation. The *concordato* never, however, emerged as a credible alternative to the official bankruptcy system centred around the idea of liquidating companies rather then keeping them as ongoing concerns. Italian law established particularly strict conditions of implementation, with the result that this institution never took off,[30] and its usage remained well below that of its English counterpart.[31] In the case of

---

[26]   Berglof and Rosenthal believe that the 1893 economic crisis was the fundamental engine of the process leading to the approval of the law. See E. Berglof and H. Rosenthal, The Political Economy of American Bankruptcy. The Evidence from Roll Call Voting, 1800–1978, Mimeo, Princeton University (1998). Hansen, however, downplays the impact of the economic shock. See B. Hansen, 'Commercial Associations and the Creation of a National Economy. The Demand for Federal Bankruptcy Law', *Business History Review*, 72, 1 (1998), pp. 86–113.

[27]   Skeel, *Debt's Dominion*, pp. 23–43.

[28]   Tabb, 'History of Bankruptcy Laws', p. 27

[29]   In Italy there is no distinction between personal bankruptcy and corporate insolvency.

[30]   In order to reach *concordato preventivo*, Italian debtors had to guarantee the payment of 40 per cent of unsecured debt; in England, for example, the percentage was only 25 per cent. Di Martino, 'Approaching Disaster'.

[31]   Statistics can be found in Di Martino, 'Approaching Disaster'.

the introduction of 'officialism', the action of Minister Rocco, in the framework of an attempt by the fascist regime to build up its own legal environment, was the most important force behind the institutional change.

In both cases, then, political entrepreneurs had a fundamental role in shaping the legislation. However, while in the case of 'officialism' the lag in the introduction of a necessary reform can be explained in terms of absence of a context able to allow political entrepreneurs to make the right decisions, in the example of the limits of friendly arrangements other explanations are necessary.

III

In broad terms, path-dependency means that the past is important in shaping the availability of present options. This idea applies to all possible economic decisions such as the implementation of different technologies, decisions about alternative consumption choices, etc. In practice economic agents are not fully free to choose according to a given utility function, as the decisions taken in the past limit the spectrum of current possibilities, cutting off alternatives or making them too expensive. Usually, but not necessarily, the result is a sub-optimal decision, as in the famous examples analysed by David.[32]

The path-dependency effect can help to explain the relative inefficiency of bankruptcy laws in Italy and America vis-à-vis England. It may be the case that the implementation (or the lack of implementation) of specific institutions was the result of the legacy of decisions taken in the past. Specifically, the presence of a given institutional set-up (laws already operating; the working of the court system, etc.) may have constrained the action of the lawmakers and reduced the possibility of introducing alternative instruments. The presence of idiosyncratic cultural elements – which is a component of the informal institutional environment – can be included in the list of elements potentially able to limit the action of the political entrepreneurs.

This definition of path-dependency helps to understand the character of the Italian legislation and some of its flaws, in particular the inability to provide efficient alternatives to liquidation. In practical terms this problem manifested itself in the absence of debt-discharge mechanisms, and in the peculiar strictness of conditions to file for amicable settlement. Together, these two elements suggest a relatively harsher view of bankruptcy and insolvency problems. Among other possible explanations, it could simply be the case that Italian lawmakers were less free from anti-debtor moral bias than their English counterpart. Evidence of this problem can be found in the language and arguments used by contemporary Italian lawyers and lawmakers in discussing issues such as the possibility of making friendly composition easier. In the period up to the 1930s scholars and politicians

---

[32]   P.A. David, 'Clio and the Economics of QWERTY', *American Economic Review*, 7, 2 (1985), pp. 332–6.

recognized the advantages of the tolerant approach of English law, but at the same time they were adamant in suggesting that in Italy such a soft approach would have been counter-productive. This position was, however, supported not by a deep analysis of the working of the two economic systems, but instead by either reference to the alleged inferior moral strength of Italian traders vis-à-vis an idealized form of progressive and honest Anglo-Saxon merchant, or a generic moral antipathy towards debtors. For example, the lawyer Vivante justified the fact that the English legislation facilitated friendly debtor–creditor settlements by arguing that Anglo-Saxon people were 'honest and strong', while the Italian environment was 'morally slack.'[33] In 1897, in expressing his negative opinion about the possibility of making settlements easier to reach, Minister Gianturco stated: 'sentimentalism towards the debtor is ... morbid and harmful to the public interest'.[34]

If the problem was in the moral bias, this certainly had a path-dependent nature. According to various scholars, the influence of the Napoleonic code, even stricter and more creditor-oriented than medieval laws, was fundamental in shaping the approach and mentality of Italian lawyers and lawmakers.[35] In other words, it was the Napoleonic code, via its strong influence on the Italian laws of the 1860s and 1880s, which helped to forge and preserve a particularly strict and punitive idea of debts and bankruptcy.

Path-dependency also helps in understanding the specificities of the American case. In the previous section we stressed how the dominant view sees in the bargaining power among different political entrepreneurs the force that shaped the structure of the law. An alternative interpretation, however, suggests that at the time when it was approved, the 1898 law was not at all a debtor-friendly piece of legislation; it was actually a pro-creditor one. This explains why the management of procedures remained in the hands of creditors, and 'officialism', although adopted in Canada and proposed in alternative drafts of the law, was not contemplated, with negative consequences in terms of accuracy in the management of debt discharge. In other words, 'ironically, the ease of discharge arose directly from the system of creditor control.'[36] According to the same explanation, it was only during the following period that the law became debtor-friendly, and this was largely because of path-dependent elements.[37] During the 1930s the same forces made it impossible to reintroduce limitations in the debt-discharge mechanism. At

---

[33] C. Vivante, 'Il fallimento civile', in P. Ascoli et al. (eds), *Il codice di commercio commentato* (Turin, 1909), p. 327.

[34] Quoted in G. Bonelli, *Del Fallimento. Commentario al codice di commercio* (Milan, 1907–09), p. 22.

[35] Di Martino, 'Approaching Disaster'.

[36] B.A. Hansen and M.E. Hansen, The Role of Path-dependency in the Development of US Bankruptcy Law, 1880–1938, American University, Department of Economic Working Paper Series, 2005, p. 20.

[37] Hansen and Hansen, Role of Path-dependency, p. 23. It must be noted that lobbying power from pressure groups that became interested in not altering the structure of the Act

this point this interpretation converges with the one suggesting that the 1898 Act was from the very beginning a debtor-friendly law: attempts to change the law in the 1930s were frustrated by debtors' strength.

The story of discharge option in England – and of the way in which it turned to be an efficient device to support entrepreneurship – is another example of the impact of path-dependency in shaping bankruptcy laws. Debt discharge was introduced in eighteenth-century England as a device to increase debtors' co-operation, and as part of English law was then exported to America. During the 1880s, English debt-discharge procedure was affected by the more general changes that were occurring in the English law, in particular the introduction of 'officialism'. This meant that the administration of discharge also benefited from the increased accuracy and decreasing corruption that characterized the new regime's procedures. In particular, judges who had to decide on applications for discharge could use the information provided by *official receivers* who ran independent inquiries into the bankrupt's activity. It is this combination of tolerance (the existence of discharge itself) and rigour (typical of 'officialism') that 1930s scholars praised as the major advantage of English discharge as a support to entrepreneurship. This combination was, however, the result of the historical development. Its possible beneficial impact in terms of efficient support to risk-taking was not even remotely in the mind of the 1880s law-reformers. Lester is adamant in this regard when he argues that: 'The possibility that more stringent bankruptcy laws might have an adverse effect on the willingness of entrepreneurs to take risks did not seem to concern the Victorians .... The question was never publicly discussed'.[38] A similar judgment is provided by Tabb, who argues that the 1705 law was not at all a pro-debtor system.[39] In this case, path-dependency 'created' efficiency: after the 1880s an already existing instrument (debt discharge) proved to be the best empirical solution to a problem (supporting entrepreneurship) that was not the reason why that device was introduced.

IV

The provision of bankruptcy and insolvency law and procedures is a fundamental component of government indirect intervention in the economic sphere. During the course of the nineteenth and twentieth centuries these institutions have been dramatically transformed in the Western world. Despite a general convergence towards certain principles, between the 1880s and the 1930s legal systems were not totally homogenous and relative degrees of inefficiency survived.

---

once it was approved is one of the path-dependent elements. This explanation is more in line with the concept of path-dependency as used by North than with David's.

[38]   Lester, *Victorian Insolvency*, p. 3.

[39]   Tabb, 'History of Bankruptcy Laws', p. 110.

This chapter provides two explanations for the survival of inefficient regulations. First, political entrepreneurs – forward-looking agents – played a large role in the evolution of bankruptcy legislation, and in some cases their action was not motivated by the search for macro efficiency, or it was constrained by bounded rationality. This, however, is only one side of the coin. The other one is that institutional development was not totally under the control of political entrepreneurs; historical accidents and lock-in effects were at work too, and inefficiency (but also efficiency) emerged out of the largely unpredictable combination of old institutions and new ones.

This result has some policy implications for contemporary issues. Even today enormous differences still exist among various countries' legislation, and there is a fierce debate on how to harmonize legislation across various systems so as to provide the best possible set of legal instruments. Borrowing form historical developments, this chapter shows that limiting the impact of interested lobbying groups on the process of institutional change is a necessary condition, but it does not suffice. Bankruptcy legislation is part of a complex institutional matrix which involves both formal elements – such as the role of court decisions in the formation of laws and the involvement of public bodies in the procedures – and informal, less tangible, cultural elements. The harmonization of modern bankruptcy laws and the search for efficient solutions therefore also require the building of wider suitable institutional support. This might prove a very hard task for modern policy-makers.

CHAPTER 3

Regulation and Governance: A Secular Perspective on the Development of the American Financial System

Eugene N. White

What accounts for the trajectory of financial regulation in the United States? In this chapter, I argue that the underlying forces driving regulation are the upsurges in productivity growth, rather than periodic crises. More precision can be given to the timing and direction of regulation by treating the financial system as primarily a provider of information rather than liquidity or diversification. During the twentieth century, two productivity surges – one in the first three decades and the other in the 1990s – increased the demand for finance that widened the information asymmetries facing the financial sector. The market responded to these challenges by innovating to provide solutions. Business-cycle shocks then tested institutional governance and the capacity of the market to adequately screen and monitor borrowers. The limitations of the innovations, often constrained by the pre-existing regulations, were highlighted, leading to regulation. Whether this regulation correctly treated a problem or was hijacked by interest groups depended how the political equilibrium was upset by productivity surges.

The most widely accepted explanation of why governments intervene in the market is the economic theory of regulation, which had its genesis in George Stigler's 1971 article.[1] Although the model has been found to be useful in analysing existing regulation, the theory offers limited predictions about the timing of regulation and deregulation.[2] In its basic version, legislators are self-interested maximizers who legislate to ensure their re-election. Politicians provide regulation to rent-seeking groups that offer the best electoral resources in exchange. The ability of any group to deliver resources to politicians depends on the information and organization costs it faces. A relatively small group will be able to reduce free riding, and higher per capita stakes will help it to cohere. Once a regulatory regime is established, politicians will seek to preserve a politically optimal distribution

---

[1] G.J. Stigler, 'The Theory of Economic Regulation', *Bell Journal of Economics and Management Science*, 2, 1 (1971), pp. 3–21.

[2] S. Peltzman, The Economic Theory of Regulation after a Decade of Deregulation, *Brookings Papers in Economic Activity, Special Issue: Microeconomics*, 1989, pp. 1–59.

of rents within the regulated industry, changing regulations as demand or cost conditions alter.

In his influential survey, Sam Peltzman argued that regulation is likely to be repealed if there are large wealth-reducing deadweight losses, which reduce the potential political payoffs, or if the gap between the regulated equilibrium and a competitive equilibrium narrows so much that there are few rents to be captured and distributed.[3] To this literature, I would add that wealth-increasing events are just as important because long-term increases in productivity growth create potential sources of rents. For the financial system, the key feature of a productivity boom is that it spawns new industries, where it is much more difficult to screen and monitor firms, thereby posing challenges to the existing institutions and financial techniques.

Productivity upsurges pose new problems not only for financial institutions and markets but also for the ultimate investors. In the absence of financial intermediaries, lenders must directly determine whether borrowers are capable of repaying funds and monitoring them afterwards, to avoid, first, the perils of adverse selection, and secondly, moral hazard. Financial institutions help to solve these problems because they specialize in the collection of information, and economies of scale enable them to reduce costs. Combining various types of financial services which require complementary information gives intermediaries the added advantage of economies of scope that reduce cost. Very generally, if acquisition and dissemination of information is not costly, then markets, aided by various agents, may handle intermediation; but if there are high costs that require long-term investment, then financial institutions will be more likely to manage the intermediation. The ultimate lenders will now face the problem of monitoring the financial institutions and agents in the markets because of conflicts of interest. Given the nature of this information-intensive business, conflicts of interest are rife in every part of the financial system. Most frequently, conflicts of interest arise because (1) a financial service provider has multiple lines of business and there may be incentives to benefit one line at the cost to another, or (2) management may benefit at the expense of the financial intermediary.[4] Thus, correctly aligned incentives are essential for good governance.

The problem that surges in productivity create is that the financial system will face increased information asymmetries that augment opportunities to exploit the conflicts, while the creation of new wealth increases temptations to do so. In these circumstances, business cycle shocks – recessions – that may be accompanied by panics or stock-market crashes highlight any failures of the financial system to identify weak borrowers and control the exploitation of conflicts of interest. When the consequences of productivity waves are added, the traditional economic

---

[3]   Peltzman, *Economic Theory*.

[4]   A. Crockett, T. Harris, F. Mishkin, and E.N. White, *Conflicts of Interest in the Financial Services Industry. What Should We Do About Them?* (London, 2004).

theory of regulation helps to better explain the long swings in regulation and deregulation.

Long Swings in Productivity Growth

Virtually all research ascribes regulation as a consequence of governmental responses to business-cycle shocks, including unanticipated inflation or deflation, wars, or even the relative openness of the economy.[5] Most often banking panics and stock-market crashes get centre stage. What is omitted are long swings in productivity growth. Cyclical forces are important, but in the long run it is the successful or less-than-successful efforts of the financial industry to meet the shifting structure and growth of the economy that generate problems resulting in regulatory responses.

In this chapter, I will, for the most part, treat productivity and economic growth as an exogenous factor driving the evolution of the financial system. However, as is well known, causality flows in both directions. Confirming an old tradition that identified financial development as a key to growth, current research has corrected modern growth theory's omission of finance. Empirical evidence from international panel data has established that well-developed banking systems and stock markets exogenously stimulate economic growth.[6] More recently, historical studies have shown that the very beginning of American economic growth was driven by the formation of financial intermediaries and markets.[7] Furthermore, Richard E. Sylla asserts that independence from Britain permitted the US to design a superior financial system and implement policies that fostered economic development.[8]

Over the course of the twentieth century, there have been two long upward swings in productivity growth, separated by a slowdown at mid-century. The first of these upswings began at the very end of the nineteenth century; it was driven

---

[5]   R.G. Rajan and L. Zingales, 'The Great Reversals. The Politics of Financial Development in the Twentieth Century', *Journal of Financial Economics*, 69, 1 (2003), pp. 5–50.

[6]   R. King and R. Levine, 'Finance and Growth. Schumpeter Might Be Right', *Quarterly Journal of Economics*, 108, 3 (1993), pp. 717–37; R. Levine and S. Zervos, 'Stock Markets, Banks, and Economic Growth', *American Economic Review*, 88, 3 (1998), pp. 537–8.

[7]   P. Rousseau and R.E. Sylla, 'Emerging Financial Markets and Early US Growth', *Explorations in Economic History*, 42, 1 (2005), pp. 1–26; H. Bodenhorn, *A History of Banking in Antebellum America. Financial Markets and Economic Development in an Era of Nation-Building* (Cambridge, 2000).

[8]   R.E. Sylla, 'U.S. Securities Markets and the Banking System, 1790–1840', *Federal Reserve Bank of St Louis Review* (May/June, 1998), pp. 83–98; R.E. Sylla, Comparing the UK and US Financial Systems, 1790–1830, mimeo, April 2006.

primarily by the increase in the labour input.[9] In spite of cyclical fluctuations, growth was relatively stable, with real GDP rising to 3.92 per cent for 1800–40 and 4.10 per cent for 1840–1900. Labour input accounted for 54 per cent and 45 per cent of this growth. However, capital inputs and technological change, measured as total factor productivity, were becoming more important by the latter period, rising from 29 per cent to 35 per cent and 10 per cent to 18 per cent, respectively. Thus, growth in the late nineteenth and early twentieth centuries slowly became more capital-intensive and technology-driven.

The rapid rate of economic growth persisted into the twentieth century; Robert Gordon calculates output growth for 1870–1913 at 4.42 per cent.[10] Moses Abramovitz and Paul David located the peak years of the first wave of productivity growth as 1929–48 and Robert Gordon as 1928–50.[11] For 1890–1927, the former find that output per capita was driven primarily (70 per cent) by total factor productivity, and secondly by capital intensity (27 per cent). However, Alex Field emphasized that this peak should not be associated with any increase in productivity during the Second World War.[12] In a careful parsing of the data, he found that it was actually in the 1930s that productivity for the non-farm sector reached its zenith, with total factor productivity rising from 2.02 per cent in 1919–29 to 2.31 per cent for 1929–41.

The long decline in productivity growth eventually drove down economic growth after the Second World War, in spite of the increases in human capital and man-hours. Gordon's data finds productivity growth falling to 1.47 per cent in 1950–64 and reaching a nadir of 0.16 per cent for 1972–79. Although it began a slow rise, the recovery of productivity growth only became evident in the 1990s, with total factor productivity reaching 1.79 per cent by 1995–99. The brevity of this period makes any estimation of the trend difficult, and Field estimated total factor productivity growth for 1995–2000 at a more modest 1.14 per cent per annum, although more recent studies have confirmed the continuing higher rates of total factor productivity growth.

---

[9]   R.E. Gallman, 'Economic Growth and Structural Change in the Long Nineteenth Century', in S. Engerman and R.E. Gallman, *The Cambridge Economic History of the United States* (Cambridge, 2000), vol. 2, pp. 1–56.

[10]   Gallman, 'Economic Growth'.

[11]   M. Abramovitz and P.A. David, 'Growth in the Era of Knowledge-Based Progress', in S. Engerman and R.E. Gallman, *The Cambridge Economic History of the United States*, vol. 3 (Cambridge, 2000), pp. 1–98; and R.J. Gordon, 'Does the "New Economy" Measure up to the Great Inventions of the Past?', *Journal of Economic Perspectives*, 14, 4 (2000), pp. 49–74.

[12]   A.J. Field, 'Technical Change and US Economic Growth. The Interwar Period and the 1990s', in P.W. Rhode and G. Toniolo, *The Global Economy in the 1990s. A Long-run Perspective* (Cambridge, 2006), pp. 89–117.

Central to the upswings in both periods was the arrival of 'general-purpose' technologies.[13] Not limited to a narrow industry or one problem, these technologies are identifiable by the fact that they (1) spread to most sectors, (2) are continually improved over time and (3) lead to many new products or processes. Peter Rousseau demonstrated that electricity in the first half of the twentieth century and computers in the last quarter of the century share these features.[14] In addition, if new technologies are more easily adopted by new firms because they are not held back by sunk costs of old technologies and old firm-specific capital, then there should be a wave of new listings. Rousseau found that there were surges in IPOs between 1895 and 1929 and after 1977, which match the dates for the adoption of the general-purpose technologies, with the value of IPOs constituting the dominant share of total investment. In addition to electricity and computers, it has been argued that the internal combustion engine and the chemical industry general-purpose technologies helped to drive growth in the first half of the century, while biotechnology similarly contributed to the boom of the 1990s.

Two periods thus stand out as periods of exceptionally high growth. The first began at the end of nineteenth century and crested just before the Second World War, while the second began no later than the last decade of the century. Because of more rapid economic growth and the need for new finance for new firms, these booms placed extraordinary demands on the financial system. The challenges forced major changes in the system, whose flaws were highlighted with crises and scandals, thereby inducing a regulatory response.

The Nineteenth-Century Inheritance

The financial system that twentieth-century America inherited from the nineteenth century had served the financing needs of the nation reasonably well. Its structure was determined by both financial technology and state and federal intervention. The key structural feature of American banking was the predominance of narrowly-defined, single-office commercial banks.

The commercial bank was the premier financial institution. Of all financial intermediaries, it accounted for 63 per cent of all financial intermediaries' assets in 1880. If mutual savings banks at 23 per cent are included, banks generally defined had 86 per cent of assets.[15] Both of these institutions had narrowly-defined activities that produced liquidity and diversification services. They provided

---

[13]   T.F. Bresnahan and M. Trajtenberg, 'General Purpose Technologies. Engines of Growth?', *Journal of Econometrics*, 65, 1 (1995), pp. 83–108.

[14]   P.L. Rousseau, 'General-purpose Technologies. Then and now', in P.W. Rhode and G. Toniolo, *The Global Economy in the 1990. A Long-run Perspective* (Cambridge, 2006), pp. 118–38.

[15]   E.N. White, 'Were Banks Special Intermediaries in Late Nineteenth Century America?', *Federal Reserve Bank of St. Louis Review* (May/June 1998), pp. 13–32.

depositors with liquidity in the form of demand and savings deposits backed by a portfolio of longer-term assets, primarily short-term commercial loans for banks and construction and home loans for savings banks. Little changed over the next twenty years and in 1900 commercial banks still had 63 per cent of assets, with savings banks slipping to 15 per cent.[16]

The inherited system of regulation in 1914 had changed little since the middle of the nineteenth century. The National Banking Act of 1864 defined the essential character of the banking industry. Based on the antebellum free banking laws of the states, the 1864 Act permitted free entry subject to minimum requirements. These federally chartered banks competed with state-chartered banks. Consequently, entry into banking was easy – facilitated by the 'competition in laxity' of the dual banking system, where state regulators eased their regulations to induce banks to take out state instead of federal charters. As a result, the minimum capital required to open a bank was quite small. Coupled with the almost universal prohibition on branch banking by the federal and state governments, there were thousands of small banks, rising from 2,696 in 1880 to 8,100 in 1900 and finally 22,030 in 1914.[17]

The creation of a uniform currency in the form of US bond-backed national banknotes had been a centrepiece of the Civil War legislation, but these liabilities were gradually bypassed by the emergence of deposit banking. High reserve requirements that did not discriminate between demand and time deposits constrained the issue of liabilities, which were primarily demand deposits. State and federal law and good banking practice, as guided by the real bills doctrine, pressured commercial banks to keep the asset side of their balance sheets invested in short-term commercial loans. In practice, many of these credits were rolled over at the discretion of the banker; but the maturity mismatch was limited.

As late as 1870, the typical American manufacturing firm was relatively small, with modest fixed and working capital requirements. For example, the minimum efficient scale of firms in terms of value added was $128,000 in cotton textiles, followed by $64,000 in big iron and millinery.[18] McCormick's farm machinery, a contemporary giant firm, had $407,000 of value added. What were the demands for finance placed by this relatively small-scale American industry? In his study of New England, Lance Davis found that loan size varied from $68 to $50,000.[19] Another study for 1879 found that the average size of loans was $3,962 in New

---

[16]   E.N. White, 'Banking and Finance in the Twentieth Century', in S.L. Engerman and R.E. Gallman, *The Cambridge Economic History of the United States*, vol. 3 (Cambridge, 2000), pp. 743–802.

[17]   E.N. White, *The Regulation and Reform of the American Banking System, 1900–1929* (Princeton, 1983).

[18]   J. Atack, 'Industrial Structure and the Emergence of the Modern Industrial Corporation', *Explorations in Economic History*, 22, 1 (1985), pp. 29–55.

[19]   L.E. Davis, 'The New England Textile Mills and Capital Markets. A Study of Industrial Borrowing, 1840–1860', *Journal of Economic History*, 20, 1 (1960), pp. 1–43.

York and $2,224 in Chicago.[20] The regulatory constraint on national banks limited loans to an individual firm to 10 per cent of capital; and state-chartered banks had similar constraints. In 1900, there were 3,731 national banks, with a total capital of $1.0 billion – which included capital and surplus. For the average bank this would have implied total capital and surplus of $272,000. Even if it was all capital, the maximum-size loan would have been $27,000, but more likely it was about half that given the importance of surplus. Given that the more numerous state banks were smaller, the 'average' bank could offer no loan in excess of $10,000 as late at 1900.

In this environment, the dominance of these banks among intermediaries is attributable to what modern theory has described as their 'special' character.[21] While many other intermediaries today provide transaction services and diversified portfolios, banks are delegated by depositors to screen and monitor borrowers that the market cannot. Banks develop relationships with individual borrowers, acquiring non-marketable information and monitoring them through their transactions within the bank and by covenant enforcement. Thus, banks are central to solving important information asymmetries, screening and monitoring borrowers. In the nineteenth century, information asymmetries loomed much larger and few firms had direct access to financial markets.

While money and capital markets grew rapidly in the nineteenth century, most businesses were relatively small and found it difficult to produce and transmit information that would yield marketable assets. Neither the accounting nor financial information industries were well-developed. Accountancy was in its infancy with few standards, and the first professional society of accountants in the US was organized in New York in 1887.[22] There were credit agencies, notably R.G. Dun and Company, but their reports were usually based on estimates of a firm's worth by lawyers and other businessmen, who provided information about the character of the proprietors rather than financial statements.[23]

In this world, the specialized knowledge of a banker was paramount. Forming a long-term relationship with a customer where the banker could personally monitor a business was important to reduce the basic information asymmetry between borrower and lender. Thus, loans were typically referred to as 'character loans'. Bankers did buy commercial paper, but authorities advised them only to accept notes that were endorsed by men of wealth and good reputation or by ample collateral. Banks operated with very modest-sized staff. It is striking that the first

---

[20]   J.A. James, *Money and Capital Markets in Postbellum America* (Princeton, 1978).

[21]   S. Bhattacharya and A. Thakor, 'Contemporary Banking Theory', *Journal of Financial Intermediation*, 3, 1 (1993), pp. 2–50.

[22]   Crockett et al., *Conflicts of Interest*, Chapter 3.

[23]   N. Lamoreaux, *Insider Lending. Banks, Personal Connections, and Economic Development in Industrial New England* (Cambridge, 1994).

credit departments appeared first in the late 1880s and only slowly spread. By 1899, there were only ten banks in New York with formal credit departments.[24]

In the absence of a well-developed market for information on borrowers, banks performed a special service by screening potential borrowers and monitoring those to whom they had given credit. However, the same information asymmetries made it difficult for bank stakeholders to monitor the management of the bank. The management of most banks was relatively small, even for fairly large banks. Markets for bank stock were thin and often non-existent. Little is known about the actual structure of pre-1913 bank ownership, but the assumption is that most banks were closely held, which would reduce the free-rider effects. Nevertheless, it appears that there was concern that stock owners were not sufficiently attentive, and federal and many state laws prescribed double liability; if a bank failed, shareholders not only lost their initial investment but were also compelled to provide funds equal to the par value of their stock. Banknote holders, whose liabilities were a declining fraction of total liabilities, had been given one hundred per cent insurance in the form of backing with US government bonds. Depositors had no such protections, except the very limited remedy of reserve requirements and capital requirements. They could monitor the performance of the bank only through the limited published balance-sheet statements, and perhaps rumours.

City banks had another level of monitoring. The clearing houses required banks to submit weekly information that proved they would be able to make good on the collection of funds for the clearing of cheques. Failure of this weekly audit raised alarms and could trigger a run on a bank. Withdrawals and runs were the instrument of discipline for depositors. High reserves, in excess of required reserves, were one means that banks could signal their liquidity, and high capital and surplus ratios signalled solvency. These market mechanisms were supplemented by government oversight from national and state bank examiners. Their job focused largely on whether a bank's accounts were correct rather than whether its assets were sound.[25] Their infrequent inspections made them a weak monitor of banks, compared to the clearing houses.

The fragmented structure of the American banking system, dominated by single-office unit banks, did not prevent the formation of unified money and capital markets. The correspondent banking system and commercial-paper houses system helped to knit together the system, gradually equalizing interest rates.[26] However, the pyramided structure of reserves and correspondent balances linked thousands of small banks with incompletely diversified loan portfolios and left the financial

---

[24]   White, *Regulation and Reform*.

[25]   R. Robertson, *The Comptroller and Bank Supervision. A Historical Appraisal* (Washington DC, 1968).

[26]   L. Davis, 'The Investment Market, 1870–1914. The Evolution of a National Market', *Journal of Economic History*, 25, 3 (1965), pp. 355–99; H. Bodenhorn, 'The More Perfect Union. Regional Interest Rates in the United States 1880–1960', in M.D. Bordo and R.E. Sylla, *Anglo-American Finance* (New York, 1995), pp. 415–54.

system particularly subject to shocks. Jeffrey Miron has documented how increases in seasonal demands for credit drove up interest rates and increased the probability of banking panics.[27] The frequent runs and panics were regarded as one of the key weaknesses of the financial system. Yet, in spite of the apparent susceptibility of the system to shocks, the banks were relatively well protected. Banknote holders never suffered any losses, and depositors' losses were kept relatively minimal by the double liability of stock and the high capital-to-asset ratios.[28]

One is tempted to argue that the system was in a macro sense relatively fragile but relatively sound in a micro sense. A lender of last resort – a central bank, capable of injecting emergency liquidity – was absent. Nevertheless, the market responded to this problem even if it could not provide a complete private substitute. The clearing houses devised a temporary form of high-powered money for interbank settlements in the form of clearing house loan certificates that reduced the need for system-wide suspensions of payment.[29]

Overall, the American banking system compares well with other systems. Michael Bordo, Angela Redish and Hugh Rockoff offer an instructive comparison with Canada, whose economy was similar in structure to the US but whose banking system with nationwide branching and high barriers to entry was subject to criticisms of oligopoly.[30] They find that as far back as data can be pushed, the two countries had roughly the same interest rates on loans, although deposit rates were slightly higher in Canada. The key difference was that the rate of return for Canadian banks was higher due to leverage, permitted because of the ability of the branching banks to achieve greater diversification of loans and deposits. The risk of bank failure appears to have forced American banks to keep higher capital-to-asset ratios and lower loan-to-asset ratios. Thus, at the end of the nineteenth century, the financial system dominated by commercial banks lending short-term had served the economy reasonably well. However, the usefulness of that system was being rapidly undermined in the late 1890s with the emergence of the vertically-integrated manufacturing firm, applying newly developed technologies.

---

[27] J. Miron 'Financial Panics, the Seasonality of the Nominal Interest Rate and the Founding of the Fed', *American Economic Review*, 76, 1 (1986), pp. 125–40.

[28] C.A. Calomiris and E.N. White, 'The Origins of Federal Deposit Insurance,' in C. Goldin and G.D. Libecap (eds), *The Regulated Economy. A Historical Approach to Political Economy* (Cambridge, 1994), pp. 145–88.

[29] M. Friedman and A.J. Schwartz, *A Monetary History of the United States, 1863–1960* (Princeton, 1963); G. Gary and D. Mullineaux, 'The Joint Production of Confidence. Endogenous Regulation and Nineteenth Century Commercial-bank Clearinghouses,' *Journal of Money Credit and Banking*, 19, 4 (1987), pp. 457–68.

[30] M.D. Bordo, H. Rockoff and A. Redish, 'The US Banking System From a Northern Exposure. Stability versus Efficiency,' *Journal of Economic History*, 54, 2 (1994), pp. 325–57.

The Decline of Commercial Banking, 1895–1929

The technological changes that originated at the end of the nineteenth century created large vertically-integrated firms that challenged the limits of postbellum American bank finance. Rising productivity manifested itself in the development of continuous-process technologies, first in the 1880s in cigarettes, matches, flour milling, oil refining and metals. A merger wave from 1897 to 1902 created even larger firms, including United States Steel, International Harvester, American Can, United Fruit, Du Pont and Anaconda Copper. Given the modest size of even the largest banks, bank finance under the regulations established in the mid-nineteenth century proved to be insufficient to assist these firms with funding. A panel study of 266 firms for 1911–22 found that larger firms invested more and had higher growth rates, reaffirming that technological innovation was driving the development of large vertically-integrated companies.[31] Regression analysis found that the higher the size of a firm the more sensitive its investment was to cash flow, indicating that larger firms faced greater external finance constraints than small firms, attributed to the limits placed on branching and lending.

Banks' share of credit was shrinking on all levels. Between 1900 and 1929, banks' share of all financial intermediaries' assets shrank from 68 to 50 per cent. Insurance companies and other lenders were not constrained by size like banks, and they replaced banks loans. Thus, in 1900 banks had 57 per cent of all loans to corporations, tumbling to 41 per cent by 1929. Only for unincorporated business, where firms were smaller, did banks' share hold at just below 90 per cent in these thirty years.[32] In terms of total funding, banks provided only 23 per cent of a total of $17.9 billion of external funds to non-financial corporations for 1901–12. Stocks provided 31 per cent and bonds 46 per cent of all financing. After excluding the war years and the distortions caused by government finance, banks had roughly the same share, 26 per cent out of $39 billion of total funds for 1923–29. But there was an important compositional shift, with securities shifting from bonds with 31 per cent to stocks with 43 per cent. This development boded ill for the banks because the established law prohibited them from directly owning or handling stocks, because they were not 'evidences of debt', like loans or bonds.

Under this pressure, the financial industry began a period of rapid innovation aimed at satisfying the needs of manufacturing. Commercial banks sought to modify the regulations governing their operations, while other markets and institutions expanded to provide alternative forms of financing. The key elements of the national banking regulatory regime that limited the financing of industry were restrictions on (1) the ten per cent of capital limit on the maximum loan size, (2) branching, which limited the geographic spread and hence the size and lending

---

[31] D.C. Giedeman, 'Branch Banking Restrictions and Finance Constraints in Early Twentieth Century America,' *Journal of Economic History*, 65, 1 (2005), pp. 129–51.

[32] R.W. Goldsmith, *Financial Intermediaries in the American Economy* (Princeton, 1958).

capacity of banks and (3) product mix, preventing banks from owning or handling stocks.

The effects of the ten-per-cent rule are illustrated in the history of the Philadelphia National Bank, one of the nation's largest banks.[33] The bank sought out the business of Swift, B.F. Goodrich, Westinghouse, and Sears Roebuck. In 1903, the Comptroller of the Currency charged that the bank had exceeded the 10 per cent of capital rule for the size of loans it had made. The bank responded that it had kept the loans below ten per cent of its capital accounts that included capital and surplus. Congress stepped into this debate and clarified the law so that the maximum loan size was ten per cent of capital and surplus, but no more than thirty per cent of a bank's capital. Many firms shopped the nation trying to find larger loans. Gulf Oil found the Houston banks too small to assist with anything but payrolls and checking; and the company turned to the few large banks in New York and Pittsburgh to obtain credits for its oil pipelines in 1906 and 1907.[34] However, the constraints imposed by the maximum loan size were better remedied by increasing the size of a bank, as no bank wanted too high a fraction of its capital or assets invested in a few firms.

The obvious solution was a relaxation of the prohibition on branch banking. But here, the well-entrenched unit-banking lobby, fearful of competition from larger banks, successfully fought off most challenges to the status quo. In 1900, only 87 commercial banks operated 119 branches, at a time when there were 8,100 commercial banks. The branching banks held a scant 1.8 per cent of all banks' loans and investment. By 1925, when there were 27,858 banks in the nation, branching was just beginning to emerge, with 720 banks operating 2,525 branches, with 35.2 per cent of all loans and investments.

Growth from branching was restrained at both the federal and the state level. National banks were forbidden to operate more than one office. In 1909 only 9 states allowed some form, often limited, of branching. By 1924, this number had crept up to ten.[35] The impact on the structure of the banking system was minimal, with the sole important exception of California, where branching systems were beginning to form. However, as already seen, this development did not prevent an erosion of banks' role in the financial system. Not only did small-town bankers block states from changing their branching laws, they lobbied for the adoption of deposit insurance at the state and federal level, recognizing that insurance would make them more attractive to potential depositors, as they could not offer the same degree of safety as much larger diversified banks.[36]

---

[33]   N.B. Wainwright, *The History of the Philadelphia National Bank* (Philadelphia, 1953).

[34]   W.L. Buenger and J.A. Pratt, *But Also Good Business. Tax Commerce Banks and the Financing of Houston and Texas 1886–1986* (College Station, 1986).

[35]   White, *Regulation and Reform*, Chapter 3.

[36]   Calomiris and White, 'Origins'.

The Rise of Market-Based Finance and the Regulatory Response before the First World War

Given these constraints on the growth of banking, other intermediaries and markets expanded to supply finance to rapidly growing industry. However, for the market to meet the new financial demands of industry, the information asymmetries needed to be tackled. A broader investing public had to be reassured that investments were properly screened and management adequately monitored as the volume of new securities rose. The most influential firm, J.P. Morgan, had built a reputation for identifying high-quality securities. Having carefully screened new issues, Morgan wanted to protect its reputation among investors who in this information-limited age were unable to adequately monitor companies that had issued these securities. To ensure that management acted in the interests of its bond and stock holders, Morgan placed his partners on the boards of companies whose securities Morgan had underwritten, a signal that was favourably appreciated by the market.[37]

Morgan's solution was, however, a limited one, as partners of investment banks could not be dispatched to every company. Instead a market for information arose that helped to mitigate the problem of monitoring management by investors. The accounting profession continued to develop in this period and the small New York association of accountants evolved to become the American Society of Certified Public Accountants in 1921.[38] Nevertheless, by the 1920s, the reforming accountant Arthur Anderson railed against the failures of the accounting profession.

Investors had relied on the New York Stock Exchange's listing requirements as a standard quality that induced firms to disclose information. However, with the growth of new industries, many new issues were not listed on the NYSE. There was little standardization of the information that was delivered, and some firms – like the Standard Oil companies – refused to cooperate and were thus unwilling to list on the NYSE, preferring to remain on the Curb Exchange where there were weaker rules. Other exchanges had very limited listing and reporting rules. 'High tech' firms of the day were more likely to appear on the less demanding New York Curb market and the regional exchanges. Consequently, the exchanges' listing requirements were tempered by their need to compete with one another. For bonds, investors found a new source of information in the modern rating agencies that arose in this period. Poor's Publishing Company began the publication of its *Poor's Manual* in 1900 to analyse various types of investments. As the number of investors increased, a demand arose for some comparative analysis and ranking of the quality of securities. The first ratings were developed in 1909 by John Moody, who translated measures of credit quality into a single rating symbol. Moody's

---

[37]   J. Bradford De Long, 'Did J.P. Morgan's Men Add Value. An Economist's Perspective on Financial Capitalism', in P. Temin (ed.), *Inside the Business Enterprise. Historical Perspectives on the Use of Information* (Chicago, 1992).

[38]   Crockett et al., *Conflicts of Interest*, Chapter 3.

Investors Services was incorporated in 1914, followed by Poor's, the Standard Statistics Company and the Fitch Publishing Company.[39]

As marketed information on borrowers improved, the investment-banking industry was able to expand and increase its financing of American industry. The leading industries of the new wave of technological change combined, via first trusts and then mergers, culminating in the first merger wave of 1897–1902, financed by issues of securities. The key problem that investment banks faced was finding customers for the flood of new issues. Their old networks of wealthy investors were inadequate, and perhaps the most natural partners, commercial banks, were constrained by size and their inability to handle stocks. A more ready partner was the insurance industry, where cooperation was made easier as the insurance industry was highly concentrated, unlike the banking industry. Three firms, the Mutual, the Equitable and the New York Life Insurance companies, had half of all policy sales. Each of these companies had close ties to important investment banks. New York Life worked closely with J.P. Morgan, while the Equitable had strong ties with the Harriman and Kuhn Loeb investment banks. The portfolios of the insurance companies were soon dominated by the bonds and stocks that their partners had underwritten. In turn, insurance companies helped to provide the investment banks with short-term financing. To coordinate their activities, the investment banks and insurance companies developed interlocking directorates.[40]

This restructuring of the financial industry challenged the governance structures, creating arrangements with conflicts of interest that could be exploited because of the lack of transparency in the activities of company officials. The close alliance of life-insurance companies with investment banks led the officers of the former to violate their fiduciary responsibilities. As firms in the insurance industry were typically organized as mutuals, the incentive for individual policyholder-owners to monitor management was extremely diluted by free-rider problems. Consequently, some insurance-company officials took advantage of information asymmetries to personally benefit at the expense of their holders from private partnerships in syndicates, while permitting investment companies to benefit at the expense of the life-insurance companies. Although they were members of issuing syndicates, evidence arose that insurance companies had purchased securities for their portfolios at higher prices and did not participate in the syndicate's profits. There was no institutional development or market response to these problems. Some investment banks were concerned but did not take strong action. When George W. Perkins, a vice-president of New York Life was invited to become a partner of J.P. Morgan, it was recommended that he resign from the insurance company so that there would not be any conflict of interest, as the firm was a

---

39 Crockett et al., *Conflicts of Interest*, Chapter 3.

40 D. North, 'Life Insurance and Investment Banking at the Time of the Armstrong Investigation of 1905–1906', *Journal of Economic History*, 14, 3 (1954), pp. 209–28; and V.P. Carosso, *Investment Banking in America. A History* (Cambridge, 1970).

regular purchaser of Morgan-sponsored issues. However, when Perkins refused, he was still permitted to become a partner.[41]

The exploitation of the conflicts of interest between insurance and investment banking came to light after the stock-market crash of 1903. As insurance was regulated at the state level and concentrated in New York State, the legislature created the Armstrong Committee to investigate. The committee found that investment banks and officials of the insurance companies had profited from their position at the expense of the insurance companies. The New York State legislature took up their recommendations and passed a bill in 1906 that required that the two financial industries be separated. Life-insurance companies were prohibited from underwriting securities, they were forbidden to hold any significant quantity of equities, and they were compelled to dissolve interlocking directorships and other relationships with investment banks. This law then served as a model for 19 additional states, making it nearly universal.[42]

Although largely forgotten, this early episode is instructive. The need for institutions to develop governance structures for new environments was not answered. Consequently, state legislatures responded with regulations that took the most extreme form of complete separation and restricted asset portfolios. Legislators appear to have become convinced that only the most narrowly-defined financial institutions could be safe from conflicts of interest that would injure investors and imperil the soundness of financial intermediaries. This reaction then became an ingrained American response to similar issues.

The stock-market crash of 1903 and then 1907 revealed problems not only with the governance of financial intermediaries but also with the distribution of securities. As securities were marketed to a broader less-sophisticated public, complaints arose about fraud. Regulation of securities sales was first addressed by Kansas's Blue Sky Law in 1911, which required prior approval by the state bank commissioner of any securities issued or sold in the state. Many additional states adopted these laws, apparently at the behest of local banks who wanted to suppress competition for lending to business by out-of-state securities firms. But these laws had limited effects as they were never adopted by the states with the big securities markets. Like complete separation of the financial industry by function, the Blue Sky laws represented an extreme solution, as only securities approved by government officials could be issued.

The panic of 1907 was transmitted by the fragmented banking system and the absence of a lender of last resort. The panic of 1907 identified the limits of private cooperative arrangements in the clearing houses to contain panics in increasingly integrated domestic and world capital markets. Because of the need to provide incentives to a club to monitor and control, the New York Clearing House had excluded trust companies, where the panic was born. In terms of the banking system, the establishment of the Federal Reserve System was a limited reform

---

[41]   Carosso, *Investment Banking*.

[42]   Carosso, *Investment Banking*.

conditioned by the economic interests. The unit bankers would not tolerate any increase in branching. While reformers favoured the establishment of a central bank upon a European model, there was fear among the bankers that this would be controlled by a few bankers in New York. Instead, the Fed was modelled on the clearing houses with the Federal Reserve banks as more centralized agencies for the clearing and collection of cheques and a source of discount for banks in need of temporary liquidity. There was no real reform of the underlying structure of the banking system. Small units remained dominant though branching was growing, and the future of corporate finance lay outside the banking system.

The Boom of the 1920s and the New Deal

After investment banks could no longer cooperate with insurance companies to obtain short-term financing and distribute new issues, they began to develop and expand their relationship with commercial banks. Early on, banks sought to provide complementary services to investment banks and assist with placement and short-term financing. National City Bank, the largest bank in the US in 1905 with capital of $50 million and assets of $308 million, worked with Kuhn Loeb to finance and distribute new issues.[43] However, commercial banks faced a major obstacle to directly engaging in investment banking or to even cooperate with investment banks. By law, banks were only permitted to hold or trade in 'evidences of debt', which by definition excluded equities. Commercial banks had bond departments that could engage in investment-banking activities but they could not directly touch stocks. The solution that commercial banks hit upon to circumvent this restriction was the formation of separate security affiliates to take over their investment-banking operations. The first affiliate was founded by the First National Bank of New York in 1908, followed by the National City Bank, which created the National City Company in 1911. These affiliates grew quickly in number from 10 in 1922 to 114 in 1931, although bond departments also expanded from 62 to 123 in number.[44] These subsidiaries even permitted the banks to overcome their geographic confinement, and in 1930 National City Company had 60 branches and Chase Securities Corporation had 26. These changes allowed these commercial banks to successfully compete in investment banking and brokerage, gaining 45 per cent of all bond originations.

By creating a securities affiliate, a commercial bank gained economies of scope that gave it advantages over investment banks, with large potential customer bases and sources of short-term financing. Commercial banks gained information about firms by making and monitoring loans that was complementary to the information obtained by investment bankers for a new issue by a firm. However, because these intermediaries now combined these distinct services, there were increased

---

[43]   H.B. van Cleveland and T.F. Huertas, *Citibank. 1812–1970* (Cambridge, 1985).

[44]   W.N. Peach, *Security Affiliates of National Banks* (Baltimore, 1941).

risks of conflicts of interest. Some banks tried to correctly align incentives so that managers would seek to maximize shareholder value and not exploit conflicts of interest. At National City Bank and its affiliate, National City Company, there was a management fund where the earnings of the bank and its affiliate were pooled. Owners and management were granted a minimum return of eight per cent in dividends or salaries, with the remaining profits distributed to owners and managers in a ratio of four to one. The underlying objective was to ensure that managers would not favour one line of business and its customers over another and thereby not exploit the inherent conflict of interest.[45]

Far from damaging banking, recent research has shown that the market believed that universal banks used their superior information to certify a higher quality of securities rather than exploit conflicts of interest. The market was convinced and accepted a lower yield on equivalent securities that were underwritten by universal banks in comparison to those underwritten by independent investment banks. Furthermore, there were fewer defaults among the securities originated by universal banks and the losses sustained by the securities were no different between universal and independent investment banks.[46] Investors appear to have been very sensitive to potential exploitation of conflicts of interest and banks found that they could reassure the market by creating an independent securities affiliate, providing greater transparency. Consequently, investors accepted lower yields for securities that were underwritten by intermediaries with more carefully designed controls. The result was a shift of activity from internal bond departments to securities affiliates.

This alternative path for financing business was brought under intense scrutiny when the stock market crashed in October 1929 and then failed to recover. Unfortunately, the massive economic decline, when even otherwise good investment and sound financial intermediaries suffered, made it difficult to identify the real problems of the financial system, and left the door of reform open to adroit political entrepreneurs with their pet schemes. Regulation took aim at the apparent failures to solve the information asymmetries and in governance. Some of these regulations were the product of politicians working closely with special-interest lobbies, but some seem to have been designed to suit the public interest.

When Congress approached the issue of 'unsound' and 'risky' securities, it eschewed the approach of the Blue Sky laws that had been favoured by small-town banks to keep investment banks off their turf. Instead, the goal of the Securities Act of 1933 and the Securities and Exchange Act of 1934 was to increase disclosure, which did not favour any one interest group. Investors would not be protected from making mistakes, but government would ensure that they did not make them on the basis of insufficient or misleading information. The 1933 Act subjected all new publicly offered securities to registration. Specific information on the issuer and the securities was made available to the public and no sales

---

[45]   G. Benston, *The Separation of Commercial and Investment Banking. The Glass-Steagall Act Revisited and Reconsidered* (Oxford, 1990).

[46]   Crockett et al., *Conflicts of Interest*, Chapter 4.

could be made until twenty days after the filing, to allow investors to examine the information. Underwriters were held liable for the information. The 1934 act imposed disclosure requirements on securities traded on all exchanges, obliging them to register and file periodic reports. This approach aimed at the difficulty the market had of imposing uniform standards. The Act of 1933 also required that the regular financial statements that companies had to submit to the public be certified by an independent public or certified public accountant, while the 1934 Act gave the Securities and Exchange Commission jurisdiction over the accounting profession and its rules. The SEC then delegated the determination of standards to the American Society of Certified Public Accountants.[47]

While treatment of the problems of information asymmetries between companies and investors focused on mandating disclosure of information, more radical treatment was applied to the structure and governance of financial institutions. This regulation was much more clearly driven by rent-seeking interest groups. In Congressional hearings universal bankers were blamed for exploiting conflicts of interest by selling excessively risky issues to their customers, converting bad loans into securities issues and conducting pool operations, where the officers of the banks conducted speculation by private participation with insider information. Recent scholarship has shown that except for a few cases these abuses were very limited.[48] Some experts recommended relatively modest remedies to prevent the exploitation of conflicts of interest. W. Nelson Peach favoured making it illegal for officials of a bank to participate individually in the business of their affiliates.[49] He also promoted prudential supervision of banks and affiliates, with compulsory combined periodic examinations by federal officials.

Commercial banks would probably have retained their affiliates if the head of the Senate Committee on Banking and Currency, Senator Carter Glass, had not used his position to block any reform without a complete separation of commercial and investment banking. Sections 16, 20, 21 and 32 of the Banking Act of 1933, known as the Glass-Steagall Act, restricted banks to dealing in some government securities; no bank could be affiliated with any dimension of investment banks. No officer of the bank could be associated with any of these activities, and it became illegal for investment banks to accept deposits. The Act forced a virtually complete separation of commercial and investment banking. This remedy mirrored the solution that the states had employed to control the exploitation of conflicts of interest between the insurance industry and investment banking. And like that solution, it forsook any benefits from economies of scale in favour of annihilating the conflicts of interest. This Act also served to benefit the investment bankers, who subtly lobbied to drive the securities affiliates out of business.

---

[47] Crockett et al., *Conflicts of Interest*, Chapter 2.

[48] Crockett et al., *Conflicts of Interest*, Chapter 4.

[49] Peach, *Security Affiliates*.

The banking panics gave the advocates of deposit insurance a chance to trade support with Senator Glass for separation of commercial and investment banking.[50] Rather than permit branch banking and thereby create larger, more diversified institutions, small unit banks obtained protection in the form of insurance with the Federal Deposit Insurance Corporation. Perversely, it subsidized the small banks at the expense of big banks, many of whom would have preferred a market solution of branching to gain diversification of loan portfolios and deposits. In addition, the weak profitability of commercial banks was enhanced by limits on the entry of new banks and limits on interest rates on deposits. The Banking Acts of 1933 and 1935 did not alter the basic structure of the banking industry, and created a loosely organized cartel with barriers to entry and price controls. A century of 'free' entry was terminated and bank regulators were given discretionary authority to determine whether a community needed a new bank. The only modification of the restrictions on branching was to give national banks the same privileges as state banks. Interest on demand deposit was prohibited and the rates on time deposits regulated. Although the small-town banks had been battered by the depression, they were able to exert enough influence, and jumped on the anti-big-business and anti-big-banking bandwagon.

Although small banks did not regain the level of prominence they had enjoyed at the outset of the early twentieth century, they were able to prevent any further rapid shrinkage. The collapse of the stock market and the economy, coupled with new securities regulations, both contributed to the decline of public issues. Underwriters disliked the cooling-off period, which increased their risk; issuers objected to public disclosure, and parties that signed registration statements were concerned about liability. The result was an increase in private placements. Banks took up part of the slack by increasing their term loans, a shift in their historic emphasis on short-term credit; and regulators altered the rules to encourage this development. The regulation of the financial system that arose out of the Great Depression was a mixture of standards and disclosure requirements designed to improve the flow of information from borrowers to lenders and a restructuring of financial institutions engineered by rent-seeking segments of the financial industry and true believers in the real-bills doctrine. As such, they represent a potential for improvement, but at the same time corseted the financial system until the shocks of the 1970s and 1980s.

The Great Inflation and the Further Decline of Banking

The Second World War was an unanticipated shock that served the interests of those fathers of the New Deal banking system, who had wanted to freeze the nineteenth-century structure of banking. The race for liquidity during the decade of the 1930s was satisfied by the vast increase in the federal debt that was absorbed

---

[50]   Calomiris and White, 'Origins'.

not only by individuals but also by financial institutions. By the time that shares of government bonds in intermediaries' portfolios had diminished, the pace of productivity growth had levelled off. The highly constrained system worked satisfactorily without challenges, given the absence of serious macroeconomic shocks in the 1950s and 1960s. With high barriers to entry, limits on geographic and product-line competition and interest controls, there were substantial rents to be harvested by the groups who lobbied to support the New Deal regime. Although changing economic conditions gradually eroded the rents, regulations were adjusted to best preserve a balanced distribution among interest groups, thus conserving the New Deal's essential anti-competitive features.

The Great Inflation beginning in the mid-1960s and exploding in the 1970s hit the financial system hard, for the simple reason that it had by design encouraged a substantial maturity mismatch for most financial institutions and limited the creative response of institutions. Inflation, begun by jumps in the prices of primary commodities, which eventually collapsed, created major regional shocks. Given the fragmented nature of the banking system, the concentration of lending on primary commodities in those regions yielded banking failures. Inflation played havoc with the maturity mismatch of financial intermediaries, and most severely where it was greatest, in the savings and loan associations. Combined with the morally hazardous character of deposit insurance, many regional banks and virtually all of the S&L industry met their demise. When unanticipated inflation appeared, the deadweight losses increased and modifications to preserve the regulations and the political distribution of rents among vying interest groups reduced the regulated equilibrium to a point where it was close enough to the competitive equilibrium so that deregulation resulted. Slowly, controls on entry, both geographic and product-diversity, and controls on pricing were undermined.

The interest-rate controls in Regulation Q that prohibited payment of interest on demand deposits and set a maximum rate on time deposits in commercial banks were non-binding until inflation hit in the 1960s. Savings and loans were not subject to the same constraints and expanded, protected by lobbying with the homebuilding industry. The commercial-bank lobby fought back and restricted savings and loan rates to a small additional premium. However, the unexpected surge of inflation left both commercial banks and savings and loans open to disintermediation when mutual funds, whose rates were unregulated, jumped in. Modifying the rules to allow banks to compete with mutual funds for deposits made the difference between the regulated and competitive equilibrium vanish with the rents that banks had enjoyed, leading to a complete deregulation of interest rates that began in 1980.[51]

The McFadden Act of 1927 that limited national banks to the same branching rights as state-chartered banks gave the states control over the geographic expansion of banks. Coupled with vigorous federal anti-trust policy through mid-century that restricted concentration using very narrow market definitions, regulation left the

---

[51] Peltzman, 'Economic Theory'.

United States with some very large banks but a great hinterland of small town banks. Narrowly-defined banking continued to decline. As a share of all financial intermediaries' assets, commercial banks dropped from 50.8 per cent in 1950 to 27.0 per cent in 1990, while mutual savings banks dropped from 7.6 to 2.1 per cent. Yet change was very slow. Fought out at the state level, the easing of branching impediments was blocked wherever small banks and insurance firms were strong relative to large banks.[52] Technological innovations, like ATMs, lowered the costs of using more distant banks. The widespread regional commercial-bank failures and the implosion of the financial industry eased the constraints on branching as states sought out white-knight banks to rescue native banks in distress and small banks' influence faded. Regional interstate branching compacts began to accelerate the process; and many small town bankers found themselves with the decision of whether to sell or face competition from a banking giant. The barriers to branching and universal banking finally tumbled at the century's end. In 1994 the Riegle-Neal Interstate Banking and Branching Efficient Act effectively erased all federal and state barriers, permitting full-scale nationwide branching to begin in 1997.[53] Nevertheless, while there has been a wave of mergers and total banking assets have become quite concentrated, there are still thousands of small banks.

The spirit of Senator Glass lived on for over fifty years after the barriers to universal banking were erected in 1933. Commercial banks lobbied heavily to expand their range of activities, desirous of providing a complete range of financial services to both individual depositors and corporate borrowers. However, they met with vigorous lobbying by all protected industries, which feared they could be able to provide lower-cost services from economies of scope. Insurance agents, small investment banks and many other types of financial and non-financial services stymied efforts by the commercial banks. But even these supporters of Glass-Steagall expanded the scope of their operations as competition within their industries increased. Finally, in 1987, the Federal Reserve permitted commercial banks to enter investment banking via a bank holding-company subsidiary whose gross revenue from underwriting was limited to ten per cent. The types of activities were very slowly expanded but the revenue limit was only at 25 per cent by 1996. The Graham-Leach-Bliley-Leach Financial Services Modernization Act of 1999 finally repealed the strict separation of financial intermediaries, enabling commercial banking, investment banking and insurance companies to combine within a financial holding company.

The re-emergence of universal banking was not without its vocal critics, but it has not been accompanied by any significant exploitation of conflicts of interest. On the other hand, significant benefits have been gained. Banks' investment subsidiaries have underwritten relatively smaller issues compared to independent

---

[52]   R.S. Kroszner and P.E. Strahan, 'What Drives Deregulation? Economics and Politics of the Relaxation of Bank Branching Restrictions', *Quarterly Journal of Economics*, 114, 4 (1999), pp. 1437–67.

[53]   White, 'Banking and Finance'.

investment banks, benefiting smaller companies and regaining part of the special role of commercial banks in assisting firms with the greater asymmetric information hurdles.[54] Commercial bank subsidiaries have provided greater certification for investors, often signalled by a lending stake in the firm, and the market has rewarded these issues with lower yields compared to similar issues from independent investment banks. The reappearance of commercial banks in the investment banking market has led to a decline in concentration and lower spreads. The management structures of separated subsidiaries that signalled the best incentives for controlling the exploitation of conflicts of interest in the 1920s have been effectively replicated in the 1990s. Perhaps, in full awareness of the earlier history, this form of universal banking has not led to scandal and demands for new regulation, even as the market boomed and opportunities to exploit conflicts of interest abounded.

It is interesting to speculate whether or how long the New Deal regime would have endured in the absence of the inflationary shocks, and if the problems of the late 1990s would have appeared. The New Deal system showed very few signs of change by the mid-1960s and probably would have endured or at least experienced comparatively minor changes to those that were forced on the system by the banking disasters of the 1980s. How would an untouched New Deal regime have met the increased demand for finance in the productivity upsurge of the 1990s? The answer, I think, is that the same problems would have emerged even without the deregulation of the financial system because the *loci* of the conflicts of interest were centred on the parts of the financial system least affected by New Deal regulations.

The Second Productivity Surge and its Consequences

Like the first thirty years of the twentieth century, the 1990s witnessed a remarkable rise in productivity and economic growth. While the resultant economic growth created considerable wealth, it also challenged the newly deregulated financial system by the widening information asymmetries. The incentives to exploit conflicts of interest, which had always been present, grew enormously.

Productivity growth in the 1990s produced a surge in IPOs, concentrated in new industries, particularly exploiting the new computer and information technologies. This explosion of the market has a close parallel with the 1920s.[55] By many measures, the general-purpose technologies that appeared in the 1990s produced even more rapid change. Peter Rousseau compared the arrival of electrification in the first four decades of the twentieth century with the arrival of information

---

[54]   Crockett et al., *Conflicts of Interest*, Chapter 2.

[55]   E.N. White, 'The 1990s in the Mirror of the 1920s', in P. Rhode and G. Toniolo, *The Global Economy in the 1990s. A Long-run Perspective* (Cambridge, 2006), pp. 193–217.

technologies beginning in 1971.[56] Although he found that the share of households adopting novel information technologies was slightly faster than for electricity, the price decline for computers was much faster. In addition there was a more rapid rise in patents. Because the new technologies were largely untested, with many potential false leads, information asymmetry was particularly acute. Managers of hi-tech firms would be exposed to moral hazard because of the difficulty of monitoring untried technologies. Gatekeepers – auditors, investment bankers, financial analysts and rating agencies – who were supposed to select and monitor the firms were tempted to exploit conflicts of interest, given the enormous potential for gain in the booming stock market of the late 1990s.

The banking system was largely bypassed by the new tech industry in raising money. Instead, it used IPOs underwritten by investment bankers, who then had to sell them to the public. Technology firms that had comprised 26 per cent and 23 per cent of IPOs in the 1980s and the first half of the 1990s rose to 72 per cent in 1999–2000. The opportunities that this new technology offered drove the market up, even though many investment banks initially counselled caution.[57] There appears to have been fairly widespread under-pricing of IPOs, enabling underwriters who had discretion in share allocation to favour managers they wanted as future clients. Analysts were accused of being excessively optimistic in promoting telecommunications, technology and media companies to assist underwriters in their firm with the promotion of new issues. Nevertheless, the market was generally sceptical of the positive assessments given by analysts of lead investment-banking houses, discounting their reports relative to independent analysts. There were, however, egregious cases of analysts – notably at Merrill Lynch and Salomon Smith Barney – who promoted securities to their customers while deriding them in private and, in turn, receiving much of their compensation from investment bankers. The misalignment of incentives with investment banks in the absence of any 'walls' between analysts and investment bankers provided an opportunity for the exploitation of conflicts of interest.

Surprisingly, neither the Securities Exchange Commission nor any of the other official market regulators discovered these problems after the stock-market crash of 2000. Instead, it was the New York Attorney General Eliot Spitzer. Disclosures from his office led to public outrage and debate; and he induced the other regulators to join in a 'global settlement' in December 2002. In addition to fines, the ten largest investment banks agreed to sever all links between research and investment banking and put in strict controls whereby contact was effectively eliminated. All firms had to make their recommendations public and had to supply their customers with additional research from independent providers. Effectively, Spitzer engineered a complete within-firm separation of analysis from investment banking, dividing the activities of screening and monitoring the same firms on the buy-side and the sell-side. Because of the added costs imposed by the settlement

---

56 Rousseau, 'General-purpose technologies'.
57 Crockett et al., *Conflicts of Interest*, Chapter 2.

and concern over potential litigation, many firms reduced their research for buying customers.[58]

During the boom of the 1990s, auditors frequently failed – spectacularly in the case of Arthur Andersen and Enron – to provide an independent and true assessment of the accounts rendered by hi-tech firms. There were considerable opportunities for the exploitation of conflicts of interest by the largest accounting firms as they rapidly expanded by increasing related and complementary activities, including taxation, management and advisory services. The combination of these activities enabled them to take advantage of the economies of scope in the collection of information on firms whose accounts they handled. However, there is no significant evidence that these potential conflicts were the source of problems experienced by the industry. Instead, faulty governance structures and incentives wreaked havoc. One of the most important problems was the practice of allowing auditors to be selected by and report to the officers of corporations rather than the board of directors. Reporting to the management that they were entrusted to audit created a very basic conflict of interest. Litigation risk also induced auditors to give less meaningful reports. Increasingly, auditors found themselves exposed to lawsuits when they opined on accounts. The response of the profession was to move away from discretion and towards Generally Accepted Accounting Principles (GAAP) rules-based audits. No longer did an audit determine whether a firm's accounts gave a 'fair presentation' or 'true and fair view' of financial performance, but simply whether the accounts complied with GAAP rules. The result was that the ingenious schemes of Enron, used to enrich officers, were completely consistent with GAAP. Lastly, the partnership structure of many agencies established local offices where there were a few large accounts that made individual partners subject to strong pressure to give favourable reports in order to retain clients' business.[59]

The remedy adopted by the Sarbanes-Oxley Act of 2002 was the establishment of a new agency, the Public Company Accounting Oversight Board (PCAOB). This new regulatory body was charged with the registration of public accounting firms and the establishment of rules for auditing, ethics and independence. One important change was to require that auditors report to the board and not to the CEO or president, thus removing an important conflict of interest. However, it did not substantially change the rules-based auditing that reduced the information content of audit reports. Although conflicts of interest between lines of business within accounting firms were not implicated in the scandals, the Act also imposed a rigid separation of activity, making it unlawful for a public accounting firm to provide virtually any non-audit service to an issuer contemporaneously with the audit.

Unlike the 1930s, the economy recovered from the crash in 2000, although many hi-tech firms disappeared and the NASDAQ remained far below its pre-crash heights. Consequently, there was less opportunity for rivals in afflicted financial industries to impose rent-seeking legislation. Otherwise, the post-2000

---

[58] Crockett et al., *Conflicts of Interest*, Chapter 2.
[59] Crockett et al., *Conflicts of Interest*, Chapter 3.

crash responses were very much like those of 1903. Again as in the New Deal, some legislation appeared to be in the public interest, particularly the efforts to increase the flow of information. Some of the problems of governance have also been addressed. Although not forcibly splitting firms apart, the remedy of separation by function was again used to create walls thick enough within firms to eliminate any economies of scale in information collection. More seriously, central problems of governance have not been addressed.

Conclusion

The financial system plays a key role in fostering economic growth. Nevertheless, it is one of the most heavily regulated sectors. This chapter has focused on the origins of the regulatory impulse over the course of the American century. Contrary to the conventional story that explains regulation as a response to panics, crashes and depressions, I have emphasized the importance of productivity surges. By creating new technology industries, fast productivity growth widened the information gap between borrowers and lenders, forcing the financial system to innovate. However, by increasing the information asymmetries while generating greater wealth, productivity growth also created incentives to exploit conflicts of interest in firms where issues of governance and alignment of incentives had not been resolved. The general demand by the public for intervention to correct these flaws in the wake of crashes and panics has sometimes produced legislation that has improved standards and flows of information, but it has also permitted special-interest groups to cohere and lobby for regulatory advantage against their competitors, thereby setting the stage for new problems in the future.

CHAPTER 4

The London Stock Exchange and the British Government in the Twentieth Century[1]

Ranald C. Michie

The precise role played by the securities market within the financial system is little understood by most of those in government, because it was indirect. It was bankers who provided governments with the loans they required, either directly or through the issue of bonds, while stock exchanges simply provided a market where such securities could be subsequently bought and sold. In addition, there was always pressure for the government to act from those who had lost money either in the aftermath of speculative excesses or through the occasional abuses committed by professionals and insiders. This meant that the stock exchange was always exposed to the threat of government intervention aimed at curbing or controlling its activities.[2] Even to the economist securities markets were not worthy of serious study, being more symbols of popular capitalism than the substance of complex and sophisticated financial systems. What mattered was the process through which savings were generated, collected, mobilized and used for productive purposes by governments and business rather than financial-market activity that produced no obvious or measurable gain for society.[3] The Oxford-trained economist, and British prime minister in the 1960s and 1970s, Harold Wilson, publicly denounced

---

[1]   This chapter has benefited from comments made when delivered at the Lisbon conference of the European Association for Banking History in May 2006 and at a seminar organized by Yago Kazuhiko at Tokyo Metropolitan University in July 2006. I am very grateful for the advice received. For the general history of the London Stock Exchange see R.C. Michie, *The London Stock Exchange. A History* (Oxford, 1999). For the relationship between the British government and the financial centre of which the London Stock Exchange was a key component see R.C. Michie and P.A. Williamson (eds), *The British Government and the City of London in the Twentieth Century* (Cambridge, 2004). For the global securities market as a whole see R.C. Michie, *The Global Securities Market. A History* (Oxford, 2006).

[2]   J.P. Raines, *Economists and the Stock Market. Speculative Theories of Stock Market Fluctuations* (Cheltenham, 2000), p. 1, cf. pp. 1f, 23, 28, 45, 54–7, 69, 73, 92f, 99, 106, 109, 111, 149.

[3]   R.J. Schiller, *Irrational Exuberance* (New York, 2001), pp. 9, 12, 35, 38, 60f, 182, 188f, 193, 195, 228, 233, 246; P.J. Drake, *Money, Finance and Development* (Oxford, 1980), pp. 34ff, 192f, 215; N. Dimsdale and M. Prevezer (eds), *Capital Markets and Corporate Governance* (Oxford, 1994), pp. 14, 71f, 80, 179–83, 191, 295–9.

the 'casino mentality' of the City of London and declared that the stock exchange was a 'spiv's paradise'.[4] That this was no isolated attack delivered by a left-of-centre politician can be seen from the comments made in a recent popular work by the British economist and *Financial Times* columnist, John Kay. Though arguing the case for markets rather than government direction of the economy, he makes an exception for the stock exchange. In his opinion, 'Most transactions in securities markets are not about sharing or spreading risks: they are like transactions in the betting shop'. In his view, 'Securities markets are better described as arenas for sophisticated professional gambling than as institutions which minimize the costs of risk bearing and allocate capital efficiently among different lines of business'. Finally, in referring to the dot.com speculative boom, his verdict was equally scathing: 'It is impossible to have lived through that period and believe that the securities markets allocate capital efficiently'.[5]

Whether in popular opinion or expert advice, government intervention in securities markets was seen to be necessary in order to rectify the damage inflicted on the economy as a whole through the flawed signals they delivered and the volatility they generated.[6] Conversely, those operating in the securities market saw no need for government intervention, believing firmly that self-regulation was all that was required. According to Gordon Pepper, an experienced broker in the government bond market in London, 'Left alone, a market provides its own stabilising mechanism'[7] Any attempt by the government to control the market would lead to it becoming more and more chaotic.

By the beginning of the twentieth century, securities markets were playing a key role in the financial systems of most advanced economies and had also established a niche position within many less developed countries. In turn, these markets existed in the shape of stock exchanges, as these provided the organizational structure required to cope with a large and diversified turnover conducted by numerous brokers on behalf of even more numerous investors. As the American economist Huebner noted in 1910:

> The enormous mass of corporate stocks and bonds, the wide distribution of their ownership among hundreds of thousands of persons of all classes, together with the increasing tendency to use such securities as collateral for loans, has necessitated the creation of a large number of stock exchanges in

---

[4]   B. Pimlot, *Harold Wilson* (London, 1992), pp. 58, 87, 222. A spiv was a person who bent rather than broke the law but was generally untrustworthy.

[5]   J. Kay, *The Truth About Markets* (London, 2004), pp. 10, 223, 249, 268, 335, 337, 339, 353, 357f, 362f, 370, 373.

[6]   Michie and Williamson, *British Government*, pp. 67ff (Capie), 97 (Whiting), 120 (Peden), 161f, 171 (Green), 174ff, 191 (Tomlinson).

[7]   G. Pepper, *Official Order – Real Chaos* (London, 1990), p. 2.

every important commercial country, where securities can be marketed with the greatest convenience and promptness.[8]

Though these stock exchanges all fulfilled the same basic function of providing a permanent and orderly market where securities could be bought and sold, there did exist considerable differences between them in the precise role they performed, their relationship to other components of the financial system, and the way each operated.

Helping to create these differences before 1914 were such factors as whether they were located in a major financial centre, whether banks were members, whether there was an established investor culture, and the nature of the relationship that existed between each of them and their national government. One clear divide among stock exchanges was between those where the State exerted a major influence and those left free to regulate their own affairs. At one extreme were those in Britain, where stock exchanges remained totally unregulated by government and at the other extreme Germany, where government supervision, regulation and taxation were very much in evidence. In between existed a number of different practices. These included relative freedom from government intervention in Belgium and the Netherlands, government control only over the main stock exchanges as in France and Spain, and the use of regional legislation in Switzerland.

Outside Europe the British practice of non-intervention by government tended to prevail, being followed not only throughout its extensive empire, including such places as Australia, Canada, India, New Zealand and South Africa, but also in Japan and the United States. There was little sign before the First World War that governments in general were beginning to exercise growing control over stock exchanges. Even in the face of popular pressure most governments were reluctant to intervene, as the prevailing economic orthodoxy was economic liberalism. There continued to be a faith in the ability of markets to deliver the greatest good to the greatest number and this extended to the securities market, where stock exchanges were largely left to regulate themselves.[9] It was only in Central Europe that government intervention made a significant impact on the operation of the securities market. In those countries a mixture of attempts to outlaw speculation and tax turnover from the 1890s did distort the development of their domestic financial system, giving greater prominence to banking than elsewhere, and encouraging investors there to trade through foreign stock exchanges.[10]

---

[8]   S.S. Huebner, 'The Scope and Functions of the Stock Market', *Annals of the American Academy of Political and Social Science*, 35 (1910), pp. 1–23, p. 5.

[9]   See Report of the Select Committee on Loans to Foreign States, 1875; Royal Commission on the London Stock Exchange, 1878.

[10]   W.J. Greenwood, *American and Foreign Stock Exchange Practice, Stock and Bond Trading and the Business Corporation Laws of all Nations* (New York, 1921), pp. 259, 273, 629, 640, 657, 661, 754, 783, 823, 907, 916, 923, 926f, 953; D. Waldenstrom, *A Century of Securities Transaction Taxes. Origins and Effects* (Stockholm, 2000), pp. 1f.

However, all this was to change from the First World War onwards. Through an examination of the relationship between the London Stock Exchange and the British government over the course of the twentieth century, it becomes possible to trace the changes that took place, suggest the reasons for them and identify what the position was at particular times. Prior to the First World War, the London Stock Exchange had emerged as the central component of a global market for corporate stocks and bonds, attracting investors, issuers and members from around the world. One illustration of the change was that whereas in 1853 the British National Debt comprised 70 per cent of the value of all securities quoted, in 1913 that had fallen to a mere 11 per cent, with railways emerging as the largest single category at 43 per cent. US railways alone comprised 18 per cent of the total (see Table 4.1). As the British government operated balanced budgets, adhered firmly to the Gold Standard and devolved control over the management of the National Debt and the setting of interest rates to the privately owned Bank of England, it had little reason to intervene in the securities market as a matter of economic policy. Conversely, as the London Stock Exchange was able to operate in an environment free from government controls over either capital or credit, it had little reason to try to influence government policies, especially as so much of its business was in international securities. Consequently, on the eve of the First World War almost no direct or indirect relationship existed between the London Stock Exchange and the British government.

Table 4.1   UK Government Securities and the London Stock Exchange, 1853–1990 (Nominal Values)[11]

Year	Nominal Value of UK Government Securities	UK Government Securities as a % of all securities quoted on the London Stock Exchange
1853	£ 854 million	70
1913	£ 1,013 million	9
1920	£ 5,418 million	33
1939	£ 6,923 million	35
1945	£ 11, 864 million	54
1950	£ 14,669 million	64
1960	£ 18,260 million	58
1970	£ 21,638 million	46
1980	£ 74, 652 million	60
1990	£128,808 million	34

[11]   Michie, *London Stock Exchange*, pp. 88f, 175, 184, 276, 278, 320ff, 360f, 419ff, 440, 473, 521f, 589f.

As with all stock exchanges around the world, the realization that a war was imminent caused a panic on the London Stock Exchange in late July 1914. With so much buying and selling being for forward delivery, and often on international account, and financed on credit with securities as collateral, members of the London Stock Exchange faced bankruptcy because of the sudden collapse in prices and the inability to either repay the loans being recalled by banks or deliver the securities that had been sold. The response was to close the London Stock Exchange. This averted the immediate crisis, as members could not be forced to pay or deliver if the market was not open. The decision to close was taken without advice from or consultation with the British government. As it was, the government did implement emergency measures that stopped the banks from calling in their loans, and so ruining numerous brokers and dealers. This was done as part of a financial package that was required if a general financial collapse was to be avoided, especially among the banks, rather than as a special arrangement for the London Stock Exchange.[12] This intervention gave the government power over the London Stock Exchange, as it was now providing the ultimate guarantee of solvency for both the entire financial system and stockbrokers in particular. As well as appealing to the patriotism of the London Stock Exchange and its members in the interests of the war effort, the government now possessed the sanction that any resistance to its wishes could result in the banks being permitted to call in their loans. With depressed prices in many stocks, and problems of obtaining both payments and securities from foreign clients, such a move could spell disaster for many members through the web of buying and selling interconnections that existed in the market. Only the realization that the resumption of formal trading was necessary for the financing of the war effort, along with the growth of an increasingly active outside market, persuaded the government to permit the re-opening of the London Stock Exchange. This was delayed until January 1915, and even then there was to be no forward market and all transactions had to be for cash, so as to limit speculative activity, while a regime of minimum prices was introduced in order to preserve the value of securities held by banks as collateral. International business was also virtually prohibited so as to deny foreigners access to the London market and to stop British investors placing money abroad.

This government control over the London Stock Exchange was exercised jointly through the administrative arm of the Treasury, under the control of the Chancellor of the Exchequer, and the Bank of England, which remained independent but operated as a central bank. During the four years of the war a strong working relationship developed between the Treasury, the Bank and the Stock Exchange. The outcome was a gradual recognition among the membership of the London Stock Exchange that they had to take into account the interests of the government and the opinions of the public more than ever before. This meant in practice a greater willingness to intervene in the operation of the market they provided in order to control activities and excesses that had previously been tolerated. The First World

---

[12]   J.E. Meeker, *Short Selling* (New York, 1932), pp. 107, 112–16, 216.

War thus left a legacy of control and caution in the London Stock Exchange that would not be easily dispelled once the hostilities ended. At the same time, the First World War boosted the power of the government over the London Stock Exchange, as the National Debt was now a dominant influence in the market. Between 1913 and 1920 the nominal value of the National Debt quoted on the London Stock Exchange rose by £5.4 billion, or from 9 per cent of all quoted securities to 33 per cent (see Table 4.1). Even this figure significantly understated the importance of the government's own debt, as many foreign securities continued to be quoted even though they had been sold or repudiated. By 1919 foreign securities with a value of over £1 billion had been sold by UK investors.[13]

Though hostilities ended in November 1918, the London Stock Exchange was too important an element within the money and capital markets to be left unsupervised in the difficult monetary and financial conditions that followed. Even without the imposition of any statutory authority or formal control, the London Stock Exchange and its membership accepted the maintenance of wartime restrictions in peacetime partly out of a sense of patriotism but also because they were reluctant to antagonize the government and provoke the imposition of direct control. As a result, it was not until towards the end of 1922, or eight years after the war had begun, that normal trading practices finally resumed on the London Stock Exchange.

Even then, the London Stock Exchange was not left free of government intervention. Behind the scenes the Treasury and the Bank of England, either singly or jointly, continued to exert an influence in the manner they had become accustomed to during the war. This was especially so before the return to the Gold Standard in 1925, when the government remained concerned about the effects of speculation upon the value of the pound. To that end the government sought the assistance of the London Stock Exchange, owing to the authority it possessed over its membership, in order to restrain foreign investment, as this put a strain on the pound as well as reducing the funds available for the purchase of its own debt. The London Stock Exchange cooperated by making its market less attractive to foreign issues of stocks and bonds. In return for this cooperation the London Stock Exchange received few, if any, privileges from the government. In fact the government, in desperate need of revenue to pay interest on its huge war debt, taxed stock-exchange turnover in the 1920s and ignored pleas that this drove business abroad. Consequently, in the 1920s, the London Stock Exchange suffered as a result of its relationship with the government. Some business was driven into the hands of those in London not subject to the rules and regulations of the London Stock Exchange or even to stock exchanges abroad, as was the case with trading in a number of foreign securities.

---

[13]   E.E. Spicer, *The Money Market in relation to Trade and Commerce* (London, 1924), 4th edition, pp. 183, 196f, 202f; C.T. Hallinan, *American Investments in Europe* (London, 1927), p. 12.

Nevertheless, the London Stock Exchange and its members were willing to accept the restrictions and disadvantages that the government imposed, for they were left with the freedom to regulate their own affairs and operate as they wished. This was valuable in itself, especially after the return to the Gold Standard in 1925. With the currency situation stabilized and the government running a balanced budget there could be some kind of a return to the prewar situation in the late 1920s. Though much international business had been lost, with the market in dollar securities never to return, other international opportunities re-appeared, such as providing a market for stocks and bonds from throughout the Empire or even central Europe, where hyperinflation had destroyed savings. At the same time, there was a growing market for domestic corporate securities as the investing public had expanded enormously, due to subscriptions to war loans, while British business sought new sources of finance at a time of high personal taxation. Under conditions such as these, the restrictions and taxes imposed by the government were neither particularly onerous nor intrusive. However, this situation was to change again in 1931.

When Britain left the Gold Standard on 20 September 1931, the London Stock Exchange had been consulted beforehand but only as to whether it intended to remain open on the day of the announcement, and then only by the Deputy Governor of the Bank of England. The London Stock Exchange did close but only briefly, re-opening on 24 September 1931. Under pressure from the government to limit speculative activity, dealings were only for cash and no forward market operated. Dealing for the account was not restored until 16 November, while options trading reopened on 18 December 1931. Even then, the London Stock Exchange remained under government pressure to control activity in foreign securities, given the weakness of sterling, and so it restricted the business undertaken by its own members in this area. As a result, trading in foreign securities in London in the 1930s fell more and more into the hands of non-members of the London Stock Exchange, especially the large banks with strong international connections. It was they who were well placed to profit from a situation in which organized markets were supervised and policed by governments and capital movements were subject to exchange and other controls. They could train staff to understand the regulations and internalize operations within their branch and agency networks. Instead, the members of the London Stock Exchange turned more and more to domestic securities in the 1930s.

However, even there the London Stock Exchange was subjected to increasing pressure from the government to change the way it operated. In the wake of a number of scandals involving the issue of new shares in the late 1920s, followed by the high–pressure sales techniques employed by a few brokers in the mid 1930s, the London Stock Exchange found itself the focus of unfavourable media attention. With the real possibility that government legislation to curb abuses would follow, the London Stock Exchange was forced to tighten up further its regulations on dealings in new issues. This made it a less attractive market for the stocks of smaller British companies, mining enterprises and new ventures, which gravitated to other markets, such as those provided by the numerous provincial stock exchanges. Conversely, by proving itself responsive to public opinion and co-operating with the national authorities, the London Stock Exchange escaped other fates, such as complete closure, direct government control or close supervision by a statutory body. This did happen in other countries in the 1930s, as with the establishment of the Securities and Exchange Commission in the United States in 1934. Instead, the London Stock Exchange emerged as the one institution capable of exercising some control over securities and investment on behalf of the government. Like the Bank of England, another privately owned financial institution that acted in the public interest, the London Stock Exchange came to occupy a semi-official position as supervisor of the securities market by the end of the 1930s. This had implications for the way it operated, for it no longer responded solely to the needs of the securities market but now to the wishes of government as well. Nevertheless, before the Second World War, the prime role of the London Stock Exchange remained the provision and operation of an orderly securities market on behalf of its members, but within this market UK government securities were highly significant, comprising around one third of the total value (see Table 4.1).

Unlike the First World War, the Second was long expected, with preparations for the conflict beginning years before its eventual outbreak. A set of plans, agreed with the Treasury and the Bank of England, was in place on the London Stock Exchange, which covered both the institutional arrangements and the activities of members. There was thus no panic when war did break out between Britain and Germany in 1939. The London Stock Exchange closed on 1 September 1939, on the declaration of war, but re-opened a week later, on 7 September. Government debt and associated stocks were subject to minimum prices, trading was for cash, immediate delivery was required and options were banned. The government preferred to have the Stock Exchange open, but operating under its supervision, rather than experience an uncontrolled outside market. As the priority of the London Stock Exchange and its members was to keep the market open, and thus available for business, they were willing to agree to the conditions imposed by the government without the need for a formal arrangement. This even extended beyond those measures taken to regulate trading to an acceptance of limitations placed upon access to the market. From the outset, the London Stock Exchange introduced a rule that, if the Treasury objected to any new issue, it would not be traded. This ceding of ultimate power to the Treasury was done voluntarily by the London Stock Exchange and ensured that the government could prevent any serious domestic competition for savings appearing for its own loans, as well as controlling any seepage of funds into foreign securities. The result was that the securities market provided by the London Stock Exchange became ever more dominated by UK government debt, which reached 54 per cent of the total value by 1945 (see Table 4.1).

What the London Stock Exchange wanted from the government, in return for its full cooperation, was legal recognition that it alone constituted the securities market in Britain. The government was reluctant to concede this as the London

Stock Exchange remained a private institution; nevertheless, there was growing government awareness during the war of the need to bolster the authority of the London Stock Exchange. Eventually in 1944, with the passage of the Prevention of Fraud (Investors) Act, the London Stock Exchange was given a degree of official recognition, as this Act restricted the activities of brokers who were not members of the London Stock Exchange. Beginning with the First World War and completed during the Second, an implicit bargain had been forged between the British government and the London Stock Exchange. In return for policing the securities market and supporting national policy, the government would do what it could to reinforce and extend the power of the London Stock Exchange over the securities market, short of official recognition. Such recognition was only possible with state ownership, as happened to the Bank of England in 1946. The London Stock Exchange had in place a set of rules and regulations that could enforce obedience among its members but did not extend to non-members. As long as most of those who bought and sold securities in Britain belonged to the London Stock Exchange, and this was especially the case with domestic stocks and bonds, its authority could be fairly effective, and the Prevention of Fraud Act did bolster its power by making it difficult for non-member brokers to operate.

The result was to make the London Stock Exchange ever more domestically focused, especially as the requisitioning or sale of foreign securities during and after the war had destroyed once important markets such as those in Argentinian, Canadian and Indian railways. In turn, this heavy dependence upon the domestic market made the London Stock Exchange even more susceptible to government influence. The National Debt alone had risen to 49 per cent of the market value of quoted securities by 1945 compared to 36 per cent in 1939, and there was to be no lessening of this in the immediate postwar years. The Labour government nationalized large sections of the economy, including the entire railway system, and compensated investors with further issues of government bonds. Investors did attempt to diversify into the stocks and shares of British industrial and commercial companies, but the issue of these remained under the control of the Treasury, which used its power to favour its own funding operations. At the same time, the prospects of these companies, and the returns they generated, were heavily influenced by government economic and fiscal policies. As a consequence the securities market provided by the London Stock Exchange was now dominated by UK government securities, having reached 64 per cent of the total nominal value (see Table 4.1).

Though the London Stock Exchange retained its nominal independence after the end of the war, that was only an illusion given the power over it that the government had acquired in so many different ways. The London Stock Exchange was not able quickly to restore its peacetime mode of operation and develop new markets, as each step had to be negotiated with either the Treasury or the Bank of England, and faced government suspicion and even hostility to the operation of uncontrolled markets. There was always the worry that speculation could be a disruptive influence on both the fragile foreign-exchange position and the maintenance of a low interest-rate regime domestically. Robert Hall, who was economic adviser to the postwar Labour government, noted in his diary in 1949, that, 'The Stock Exchange is mad anyway and I don't think we should take any notice of them'.[14] It was not until December 1946 that normal trading was resumed, for example, and even then certain activities remained prohibited, such as options, until the 1950s. In addition, the British government retained the power to monitor and prohibit new issues until 1959 and to control external capital movements until 1979, as these might interfere with its own funding operations or destabilize the currency.[15]

Consequently, the British government was able to influence the post-1945 operation of the London Stock Exchange without the need for either statutory controls or even written directives. Instead, it acted via informal and unrecorded meetings, with the implication being ever-present that if the London Stock Exchange did not cooperate the relationship would become both statutory and formal. Though this informal control might appear a more flexible arrangement than direct intervention backed by the power of the law, it also had major disadvantages. The principal one was that it encouraged a high degree of caution. The merest expression of disapproval from the Bank of England, whether acting on its own or for the Treasury, was sufficient to discourage those running the London Stock Exchange from pressing ahead with any contemplated changes. This had the effect of making the Stock Exchange a much more conservative institution than it had ever been in the past, as that was perceived to be the best way of preserving its existence. In exchange for direct access to the Governor of the Bank of England, and thus the ear of the government, the London Stock Exchange was expected to conduct itself in a way that met government approval and fitted in with the direction of financial and monetary policy. Instead of stock-exchange practices being driven by the evolving demands of the market, and the desire to maintain a disciplined trading environment, they were determined by the influence wielded by the government through the Bank of England. However, in the aftermath of a war that had lasted six years and left a weakened and impoverished British economy and a disorganized and unstable international situation, there appeared little for the London Stock Exchange and its members to do other than to accept the position in which they found themselves. At least the situation could be regarded as a temporary one.

By the 1950s the British economy had recovered from the war, the international situation had stabilized and the left-wing Labour government had been replaced by a right-wing Conservative one. However, for the London Stock Exchange little appeared to change. Apart from the steel industry, those areas of the economy taken into public ownership remained there, so depriving the London Stock Exchange of many domestic securities that had been actively traded in the past, especially

---

[14]   Sir Robert Hall, 16 November 1949, in A. Cairncross (ed.), *The Robert Hall Diaries* (London, 1989), p. 96.

[15]   Michie and Williamson, *British Government*, pp. 322 (Schenk), 369 (Goodhart).

railways. Exchange controls remained in place, as successive governments remained worried about the fragile strength of sterling as an international currency. This made it difficult to re-establish the market in foreign securities on the London Stock Exchange. Finally, successive chairmen of the London Stock Exchange relished the power they possessed and acted almost as government officials. They recognized the dependency of the London Stock Exchange on the government, not least through the continuing importance of the market for the national debt, and this influenced their behaviour. The effect of this was to make the London Stock Exchange highly resistant to change and innovation even though new opportunities, such as the development of Eurobonds, were appearing in the securities market. However, the London Stock Exchange did not possess a complete monopoly over the securities market. There did exist other stock exchanges in Britain, located in the major provincial cities, and their members were not covered by the rules of the London Stock Exchange. With improving telephone communications, these provincial brokers could provide a rival national market in certain categories of industrial securities.

Even more serious was the fact that the London Stock Exchange's own rules excluded both banks and foreign-based brokers from membership, and these were often better placed to undertake the trading and selling of securities in the more complex world that existed after the end of the Second World War. This was especially true of the trading in foreign securities, given the maintenance of exchange controls. As a consequence the London Stock Exchange's command over the securities market was to be slowly eroded by outside competition after 1950, because of the role it now played in policing the securities market as a whole. This was an inevitable outcome of a situation in which the London Stock Exchange no longer policed the securities market on behalf of those who used it but as unpaid agent of the UK government. Without the authority of a statutory body, the London Stock Exchange was not immune to competition, though it did possess a very strong position that made it difficult for alternatives to develop.

Apart from inclusion in the loop of advance information emanating from the government, the benefits obtained by the London Stock Exchange in return for the role it played appeared minimal. The tax on transfers of securities had been raised to 2 per cent in 1947 under the postwar Labour government, but it was not until August 1963 that it was lowered again to 1 per cent. That reduction was tied to the introduction in 1964 of a tax on the appreciation in value of securities. Such a tax was deeply unpopular on the Stock Exchange as it dampened demand for securities compared to other investments, especially as no allowance for inflation was introduced until 1982. At 1 per cent the tax on transfers still drove trading abroad, especially that of bearer bonds as these commanded an international market. In 1974 the transfer tax was doubled again to 2 per cent by the new Labour government, and it was not until 1984 that it was again reduced to 1 per cent.

Though it did fall further to 0.5 per cent in 1986, it was not abolished despite that happening in numerous other countries around the world.[16]

However, over the years from 1950 onwards there was a significant change in the importance of UK government securities to the London Stock Exchange, despite the steady growth in their nominal value. Between 1950 and 1990 the quoted debt of the UK government climbed from £14.7 billion in 1950 to £128.8 billion, having risen rapidly in the 1970s. By 1980 this debt comprised 60 per cent of the nominal value of all securities quoted on the London Stock Exchange, before beginning to decline as the government's borrowing tapered away in the 1980s (see Table 4.1). What this suggests is an ever-greater dependency between the London Stock Exchange and the government; but the underlying trend was in the opposite direction, when market values are examined. Due to the steady rise in inflation, investors turned away from the government's own debt and towards corporate shares, which had the capacity to increase in value whereas fixed-interest securities declined in real terms. Thus the real value of UK government debt was continuously eroded by inflation, greatly reducing its importance within the market. Whereas in 1950 the National Debt comprised 55 per cent of the market value of quoted securities, by 1980 it was down to 22 per cent, and then dropped to 6 per cent by 1990 (see Table 4.2). Instead, the London Stock Exchange became, increasingly, a market for the shares issued by British companies.

Table 4.2   UK Government Securities and the London Stock Exchange, 1939–1990 (Market Values)[17]

Year	Market Value of UK Government Securities	UK Government Securities as a % of all securities quoted on the London Stock Exchange
1939	£ 6,598 million	36
1945	£ 12,168 million	49
1950	£ 13,758 million	55
1960	£ 4,353 million	32
1970	£ 16,101 million	15
1980	£ 60,780 million	22
1990	£ 124,173 million	6

In the past, many British companies had been quoted on the provincial stock exchanges rather than in London, as the bulk of their shares were held by knowledgeable investors living in and around the location of their main operations. In the years after 1950, such companies were increasingly replaced by national businesses that attracted investors nationwide. Government policy itself, such as

---

[16]   Michie and Williamson, *British Government*, p. 295 (Thomas).

[17]   Michie, *London Stock Exchange*, pp. 320ff, 360f, 419ff, 440, 473, 521f, 589f.

high personal taxation and limits on dividend payments, encouraged the growth of large national companies, through a process of mergers and acquisitions, as capital gains were taxed less highly than income. In addition, the postwar tax regime also encouraged collective investment via pension funds and insurance policies rather than individual holdings of shares. Thus the British securities market was increasingly dominated from the late 1950s onwards by trading in the issues of large national companies on behalf of fund managers, who largely clustered in London. As the London Stock Exchange provided the deepest and broadest market for securities in Britain, there was a steady drift of business in its direction and away from the once-thriving provincial exchanges. Domestic industrial and commercial stocks comprised 21 per cent of total quoted securities by market value in 1950 but 47 per cent by 1980. Over the same period, financial stocks had climbed from 7 per cent to 13 per cent and those of mining and oil companies from 8 per cent to 16 per cent. The inevitable outcome of this was the merger of the London and provincial stock exchanges in 1973. This delivered to the London Stock Exchange a virtual monopoly of the domestic market for both British government debt and the shares of British-based companies, and was partly the indirect and accidental product of government policy.

Finally, the very exchange controls that had done so much to destroy the London Stock Exchange's business in foreign securities made it difficult for foreign stock exchanges to compete for the business of British investors. At the same time, the support received by the London Stock Exchange from the Bank of England, in the interests of bolstering its ability to police the domestic securities market, meant that domestic rivals were largely absent. What government policy achieved was a centralization of the securities market that was to the benefit of the London Stock Exchange. This was not an intended outcome of government policy but an accidental one, being present throughout the years of not only right-wing Conservative rule between 1951–64 and 1970–74 but also that of left-wing Labour governments between 1964–70, and 1974–79. It was the returning Conservative administration of Mrs Thatcher that destroyed the protection from competition enjoyed by the London Stock Exchange, when it abandoned exchange controls in 1979. That administration also pressed ahead with plans to introduce a greater degree of competition into the domestic securities market, despite the opposition of the London Stock Exchange and its membership, many of whom had actively supported the election of a Conservative government.

Thus, until the 1980s, the London Stock Exchange accepted the restrictions and taxes imposed by the government because of the advantages it and its members enjoyed through the ability to monopolize the domestic securities market. This did not mean that the members of the London Stock Exchange welcomed the relationship, only that they regarded it as preferable to more intrusive controls. In 1962, 300 members of the London Stock Exchange had signed a petition that noted that 'we can look for hindrance, not help from the present government',[18]

---

[18]   London Stock Exchange, Council Minutes 24 December 1962.

and that was under a pro-business Conservative administration. The level of disillusionment with government policy was even more marked by the mid-1970s when a socialist government headed by Harold Wilson was in power. In 1975, the Council of the London Stock Exchange concluded that:

> No industrial nation has been subjected to the same unending sequence of nationalisation, denationalisation, renationalisation, variation of tax rates, alteration of tax structures, introduction and repeal of investment allowances, initial allowances, capital allowances investment grants, development grants, free depreciation, the Industrial Reorganisation Corporation, Industry Act grants with and without strings attached, the National Enterprise Board, dividend control, price controls, wages controls and similar transitory phenomena all in the space of a few years.[19]

Nevertheless, it continued to cooperate with the government in policing the domestic securities market. Conversely, the government was happy to accept this arrangement as it delivered a reasonably effective mechanism for controlling and supervising the domestic securities market. It did mean, however, that the emerging international market in securities, in the shape of Eurobonds, was located outside the London Stock Exchange, being carried out largely by banks. In addition, the London Stock Exchange became a poor market for both newer and smaller British companies, like those involved in oil exploration or new technologies. Such companies involved a high risk for investors, leading to a public outcry and encouraging government intervention if losses were made. It was thus simpler to ignore them and focus on providing a market for the government's own debt and the stocks of established British companies, as that generated safe business for the London Stock Exchange and its members.

Basically, before the 1980s, the London Stock Exchange was able to exploit its semi-official position and virtual monopoly of the domestic securities market for the advantages for its members through a regime of fixed charges for customers and an array of anti-competitive practices, such as the exclusion of banks and foreign brokers from membership and denying institutional investors direct access to the market. The government's own Monopolies Commission and the Office of Fair Trading were well aware of the situation but found it difficult to take action. That was all to change in the 1980s.

No event in the history of the London Stock Exchange has attracted more media attention than Big Bang. On 27 October 1986, membership of the London Stock Exchange was opened up to both banks and foreign brokers, fixed commissions were abandoned, dealers were allowed to trade directly with investors and the buying and selling of securities became a telephone market. Though the government was directly involved in the negotiations leading to this profound change, it was the abolition of exchange controls in October 1979 that created the conditions

---

[19]   London Stock Exchange, Council Minutes 1 July 1975.

that made them inevitable, and the London Stock Exchange had been informed but not consulted about that decision. The ending of exchange controls destroyed the London Stock Exchange's ability to monopolize its own domestic market and impose its own rules and regulations upon those who traded there. In the early 1980s, those running the London Stock Exchange, though not all the members, recognized that it was now pointless to try to exclude competitors and impose fixed charges as the monopoly that had made this possible no longer existed. In the absence of exchange controls, the large institutional investors could channel their buying and selling through foreign stock exchanges, especially New York where fixed commissions had been abandoned in 1975. The presence in London of so many foreign bankers and brokers, along with advances in telecommunications, made such connections simple and cheap, while the international nature of Britain's largest companies had already created an external market for their securities.

Under these circumstances the Council of the London Stock Exchange reached an agreement with the government in 1983 whereby, in return for an exemption from possible anti-competitive measures, it would abandon its fixed charges by 1986. As in the past, the view on the London Stock Exchange was that virtually anything was preferable to direct intervention by the government in the operation of the market it provided. As the Council of the London Stock Exchange noted in July 1983, 'There was a risk in letting HMG (Her Majesty's Government) become the ultimate controller of our destinies. Politicians tended to be uncertain people'.[20] At that stage, neither the London Stock Exchange nor the British government fully recognized the profound implications of what had been agreed.

Once the regime of fixed charges went there was no way that the London Stock Exchange could prevent direct trading between dealers and large outside investors, as this could always take place through the intermediation of an accommodating broker. This would then undermine brokers, especially in their dealings with large institutional investors. In turn, these brokers would be reluctant to remain members of the London Stock Exchange if that only imposed costs and restrictions compared to non-members and did not deliver benefits, such as exclusive access to the dealers. Once it became evident that this would be the outcome, the London Stock Exchange had no alternative but to embrace wholesale change to its rules and regulations. This involved extending membership to all involved in buying and selling securities, including banks and foreign brokers, and the creation of an electronic marketplace that linked members' own dealing rooms rather than requiring them to use the trading floor. Unless the London Stock Exchange could persuade those trading securities in London to join, its future existence was in doubt. To achieve that involved a radical change in direction. The London Stock Exchange had to cease imposing rules and regulations that disadvantaged its members in comparison to non-members, and to offer trading and related facilities at a price and level of service that made them attractive. However, this radical change meant that the London Stock Exchange's ability to police the

---

[20]   London Stock Exchange, Council Minutes 21–22 July 1983.

whole securities market was undermined. Its own survival now depended not on responding to the wishes of the British government but on meeting the needs of those who used it, who were, increasingly, large banks and brokerage firms with an international profile. These firms could trade elsewhere if they so wished, and so there was no guarantee that the London Stock Exchange would acquiesce to demands from the British government, as they had in the past, if these clashed with the interests of its major users.

It took longer for the British government to recognize that the ending of exchange controls and the abandonment of fixed commissions had destroyed the basis upon which the domestic securities market had been controlled and supervised since the end of the Second World War. No longer did the London Stock Exchange possess the power to impose rules and regulations on the domestic securities market. Instead, the government in 1986 created an independent body to monitor and police the whole securities market, namely the Securities and Investment Board. Though the London Stock Exchange did retain residual powers, the semi-official position it had occupied was now fast disappearing. Even its responsibility for providing the market in the National Debt was lost as this came under the control of the Bank of England and the Treasury. This left the London Stock Exchange as a specialist market for corporate stocks, drawing trading in these not only from British investors but also from abroad.

The liberalization and improvement of the securities market provided by the London Stock Exchange proved attractive to those trading securities in countries where restrictions and controls remained in place, and so such business gravitated to London. In turn, this directed those running the London Stock Exchange away from the domestic securities market, and especially that for the UK government's own debt, and towards the global one. Consequently, during the 1980s, a fundamental change took place in the relationship between the British government and the London Stock Exchange. The British government had created a formal authority to regulate the securities market rather than operate through the London Stock Exchange. This was merged into the newly-created Financial Services Authority in 1997, reflecting the integrated nature of banks and brokers by then. In the process, the London Stock Exchange gradually lost many of the residual regulatory functions that it had once performed. In 1988, it relinquished its role in the policing of broker/client relationships, while in 2000 it stopped vetting all new corporate issues in the UK and the public disclosure of price-sensitive information. Instead, the London Stock Exchange increasingly focused on providing a market for securities that was equally attractive to domestic and foreign issuers, users and investors.

This was especially the case after the conversion of the London Stock Exchange into a public company in 2000. A consequence of that was to make the London Stock Exchange answerable to its shareholders and its users. As both these were, increasingly, international in nature, what mattered were the returns it offered and the service it provided. Under these circumstances, the London Stock Exchange had both less reason and less freedom to act as the unpaid agent of the British government or even respond to its wishes. Indeed, as more and more of the legislation affecting the London Stock Exchange, and those who used it, emanated from the European Union, the significance of the British government's own requirements steadily diminished. Instead, what increasingly existed was a relationship based on the regulation of the London Stock Exchange through the statutory but independent body, the Financial Services Authority.

What an examination of the interaction between the London Stock Exchange and the British government reveals is the complex and changing relationship between financial markets and states over the course of the twentieth century. In the years after the First World War, governments across the world progressively exercised greater and greater influence over stock exchanges. Many stock exchanges were abolished, while the survivors were subjected to varying degrees and types of state control. Even in Britain where, superficially, nothing appeared to have changed, the London Stock Exchange was converted into a semi-official branch of government with responsibility for supervising the securities market. Especially in the years after the Second World War, when the London Stock Exchange was nominally independent, such was the close working relationship between it and the central bank that there was no need for direct government intervention in the securities market. It was not until the ending of exchange controls in 1979, followed by the collapse of its domestic monopoly within the securities market, that this arrangement came to an end.

However, the result was not a return to the pre-1914 relationship between the London Stock Exchange and the British government. Instead, what was adopted was a US-style regulatory agency that had overall responsibility for the British securities market, and this was the almost universal response around the world. Too much had happened in the years since the outbreak of the First World War for governments, including the British government, to abandon responsibility for the stability and successful operation of securities markets. Not only had governments acquired enormously expanded economic and financial responsibilities, but such events as the Wall Street Crash had created a belief that intervention was essential if it was not to happen again.[21] At the same time the environment within which stock exchanges now operated was radically different. No longer was the physical trading floor of a stock exchange central to the securities market, so removing much of the power they had previously possessed over their members. The transformation of communications and computing technology had made possible the creation of electronic marketplaces linking participants directly around the world. As a result, there had emerged large banks with global networks capable of internalizing many of the functions that had once passed through stock exchanges. In response, stock exchanges had internationalized their use and even ownership so that they no longer operated on a purely national basis. Instead, they existed to serve their owners and users who were, increasingly, global banks, international

---

[21]   See R.G. Rajan and L. Zingales, *The Great Reversals. The Politics of Financial Development in the Twentieth Century* (Paris, 2000); E. Dimson, P. Marsh and M. Staunton, *Triumph of the Optimists. 101 years of Global Investment Returns* (Princeton, 2002).

fund managers and multinational companies. Under these circumstances new relationships were forged between stock exchanges and national governments that reflected the much higher degree of global integration possible.

Before 1914, the relationship between national governments and stock exchanges was largely non-existent, with only a few exceptions. That was then replaced with a position where governments largely controlled national securities markets through the power of stock exchanges. Finally, towards the end of the twentieth century there was an acceptance that governments could do little more than regulate national securities markets in full knowledge that excessive interference or charges would encourage the migration of trading activity to an alternative location. In this new world, both stock exchanges and governments had lost the power they once possessed and so the relationship between them mattered much less. In their place had grown up a group of financial businesses of such size and reach that they had become more important than the stock exchanges they used and the governments they dealt with. As with stock exchanges before 1914, all that those who ran these businesses wanted was to be allowed to operate free from the government controls and restrictions that hampered their day-to-day activities. They were not interested in influencing government policy, only in making sure it did not affect them, whatever the political persuasion of the party in power. In that respect nothing had changed and there had been a return to the situation prevailing at the beginning of the twentieth century. However, in all other respects the events and changes of the intervening years had left an indelible mark.

CHAPTER 5

The State in the French Financial System during the Twentieth Century: A Specific Case?*

Laure Quennouëlle-Corre and André Straus

Introduction

The new approaches employed by economists to study financial systems are well established even though certain empirical estimations are open to criticism. Approaches such as 'market-based versus bank-based', 'law and finance', or 'politics and finance' remain useful tools for in-depth historical analysis today. Considered over a long period, the French case is a good illustration of the pertinence of this type of approach. This analysis lets in certain nuances and enables a number of generalizations, though these may sometimes be too hasty, such as the major role played during the interwar period for the increase of the role of States within the financial system (the 'great reversal'[1]). In the case of France, the Great Depression, as elsewhere, led to increasing State intervention in the economy and the financial system. But this intervention was not new and underwent several periods of acceleration during the two world wars and the postwar periods.

There are several ways to study the role of the State in the financial system. First, by studying the evolution of its action as a legislator and regulator of financial markets and the banking system; second, by taking into account its 'financial weight' in the system as a whole. Third, one can study whether financial institutions' ownership by the State could have been a way of influencing the allocation of credit, or not. Finally, direct State financing as an important intervention tool must not be set aside. The links between these phenomena exist, yet they are not systematic. It is true that in France, as elsewhere, the twentieth century saw big changes in the financial sector, but it is also true that in France there exist heavy and ancient trends concerning relationships between the State and the financial system: an important public debt with a dominant position on the bonds market; both support and competition of long standing between the State and banks; various types of State intervention in the financial sphere, sometimes

* We wish to thank S. Battilossi and J. Reis for carefully reading our chapter, and the anonymous reviewer for his helpful comments.

[1] To use the words of R.G. Rajan and L. Zingales, The Great Reversals. The Politics of Financial Development in the 20th Century, Working Paper, University of Chicago, 2000.

indirect and discreet like the so-called 'débudgétisation'; unfair competition on the market (removing tax from certain public financial products, bonuses on financial interest etc.); an informal network of former top civil servants currently working in the banks and able to promote government views within the financial sector.

It is specifically this evolution, viz. the changes in State intervention over the twentieth century, that we propose to study here, by trying to define the features of the 'ebb and flow' of this intervention from a historical viewpoint.

In the second half of the nineteenth century, France's economic behaviour, like Britain's, was typical of a country of 'ancient' capitalism adapting with difficulty to all the range of opportunities offered by the new technologies of the second industrialization.[2] The French economy, after the 'long stagnation' from the 1860s to the mid 1890s, went through a recovery phase until the First World War. But while annual growth rates were comparable to Britain's, France's performances in international trade were marked in various areas by traces inherited from the stagnation period and were less dynamic than those of some newer economic powers like Germany. From a financial viewpoint, as far as this phraseology is still pertinent the French economy at the end of the nineteenth century was a market-based one.[3] Even though the importance of household savings was not as great as historians have said in the past,[4] they allowed both State and firms to be financed in the first place by accumulated savings. Indeed, French firms were largely financed by their own profits, and their needs for external finance were generally low. On the other hand, due to an archaic tax system, public expenses often overtook tax revenue and the State was obliged to call on financial markets. Insofar as big firms, at least the biggest ones, needed external finance in order to develop their investments, they also relied on financial markets.[5]

---

[2]   A. Gerschenkron, *Economic Backwardness in Historical Perspective* (Cambridge MA, 1966).

[3]   For twenty years now there has been a voluminous academic literature, essentially in economics, politics and sociology, focused on the relationship between finance and growth and on the functioning of the financial sphere, but less in history. This is not the place to make a survey of it. Some important overviews are: R. Levine, 'Financial Development and Economic Growth. Views and Agenda', *Journal of Economic Literature*, 35, 2 (1977), pp. 688–726; F. Allen and D. Gale, *Comparing Financial Systems* (Cambridge, MA, 2000); R. Levine, 'Finance and Growth. Theory, Mechanisms and Evidence', in P. Aghion and S.N. Durlauf (eds), *Handbook of Economic Growth* (Amsterdam, 2005). We must also mention the numerous papers from the team of R. Laporta, Lopez-de-Silanes, A. Shleifer, R.W. Vishny on the topic of 'Law and Finance' and many works of political economists like M. Loriaux which attempt to characterize the French case as the well-known 'debt economy' model, like those of J. Zysman, S.S. Cohen or D. Verdier.

[4]   J. Bouvier, 'L'extension des réseaux de circulation de la monnaie et de l'épargne', in F. Braudel and E. Labrousse (eds), *Histoire économique et sociale de la France*, vol. 4, 1 (Paris, 1979), pp. 197f.

[5]   On the French capital market in the nineteenth century, see P.-C. Hautcoeur and G. Gallais-Hamonno (eds), *Le marché financier français au XIXe siècle*, 2 vols (Paris, 2007).

The Financial Market from the 1880s to the First World War and State Control

Between 1880 and 1913, stock-market capitalization on the Paris Bourse[6] doubled from 60 to 116 billion gold francs, representing mean annual growth of 2 per cent. With current and deposit accounts, the ratio in 1913 was at least 1 to 6. In 1913, stock-market capitalization was 2.8 times higher than national income (in 1966 only 0.4). In terms of gross issues related to gross internal production, the ratio went from 4 per cent in 1896 to 9.2 per cent in 1913 (after the Second World War, the ratio remained between 2 and 3.7). In Parisian estates the proportion of stocks and shares rose from 16.6 per cent in 1847 to 51.4 per cent in 1911. One other question is the volume of investment in foreign securities. At the end of the nineteenth century, France was the world's second banker, after Great Britain, though far behind it.[7] While the French economy was obliged to call on British capital at the beginning of the building of railways, the first phase of massive export of capital was the Second Empire: direct investments in the economies of neighbouring countries, Mediterranean ones in particular.[8] From 1866 to 1895, the phenomenon slowed down, and capital exports fell below 2 per cent of GDP on an annual average. With the recovery of economic growth at the end of the century, capital exports underwent a new expansion, rising to 3.5 per cent of GDP, i.e. 28 per cent of gross investment, and grew even more between 1905 and 1913. This was about a third of all issues on the French financial market. That level was never remotely approached at any time until today. The vigour of capital exports resulted from both the big banks' profit-maximization policies and savers' preferences. The deposit banks, which had been disengaged from industrial promotion since the seventies, took a large part of their profits from commissions deducted from investment of foreign securities. They precociously oriented their activity in that direction, prospecting foreign markets and opening agencies; for instance the Crédit Lyonnais, which was interested in the Russian market as early as the 1870s.[9] Savers were inclined to buy these securities because their yield was higher than ones on French bonds. Moreover, most French savers preferred fixed-revenue

---

[6]   We use in English the common term adopted by economic historians. See for instance E. Vidal, *The History and Methods of the Paris Bourse* (Washington, 1910); W. Parker, *The Paris Bourse and French Finance* (New York, 1920); W. Parker, *The Paris Bourse* (Washington, 1930); R. Michie, 'Different in Name only? The London Stock Exchange and Foreign Bourses 1850–1914', *Business History*, 30, 1 (1988), pp. 46–68.

[7]   As emphasized recently once more in Y. Cassis, *Capitals of Capital* (Geneva, 2005).

[8]   M. Lévy-Leboyer (ed.), *La position internationale de la France. Aspects économiques et financiers XIXe–XXe siècles* (Paris, 1977).

[9]   J. Bouvier, *Le Crédit Lyonnais de 1863 à 1882. Les années de formation d'une banque de dépôts* (Paris, 1961); M. Lévy-Leboyer, 'La spécialisation des établissements bancaires', in F. Braudel and E. Labrousse (eds), *Histoire économique et sociale de la France*, vol. 3, 1 (Paris, 1976), pp. 431–71; B. Desjardins, M. Lescure, R. Nougaret, A. Plessis, A. Straus (eds), *Le Crédit Lyonnais* (Geneva, 2003).

stock. But after the 1890s, the French State and local communities borrowed less than before, and on the contrary supplied liquidity to the market through interest paid and amortization.[10] Thus, the Parisian financial market was much more bond-oriented than the London or Berlin ones.

A famous controversy in the 1900s was between a journalist ('Lysis') and a banker ('Testis') concerning French capital exports and their economic consequences, beneficial or otherwise, for growth and trade. But the true question was the capacity of the State to influence these flows. The State had some power on the financial market from the beginning of the nineteenth century. On the one hand, French stockbrokers (the so-called 'agents de change') were nominated by the Ministry of Finance. The law fixed their number and they had a monopoly of the trade on the stock market. Moreover, they could not be bankers or merchants (it was forbidden for stockbrokers to take positions on the market) and so they never occupied the position taken by jobbers in London. The government closely supervised the Paris Bourse, controlling the activities of the Agents de Change and vetting the securities quoted. It had the power to authorize or prohibit the issue of foreign securities and their quotation on the Stock Exchange. There were severe limitations to the liberty of trade on the financial markets. Nonetheless, the market flourished at the end of the nineteenth century and during the years before the war. In fact, right from the beginning, the strengths of the market and the financial needs of the State combined their efforts to liberalize the market. Indeed, the number of official intermediaries was soon too low for the size of the operations. Between 1870 and 1905, while the membership of the London Stock Exchange rose from 1,406 to 5,567, in Paris the membership was set by the government, which kept it at a low level, only increasing it from 60 to 70 in 1898. This led as early as the beginning of the nineteenth century to the emergence and then the development of another market, free and unofficial, called the 'coulisse'. On the other hand, the government, in order to place its loans, required the presence of a counter-party capable of keeping the loans until the savers were finally in condition to buy the 'rentes'. Thus, the relationships between the two markets and the State were a long story of trials, bans and reappearances of the 'coulisse'. At the end of the century, the problem was settled by the decision to tax 'all people usually trading securities,' meaning official stockbrokers plus the 'coulisse'. On the other hand, while theoretically the French State could allow or forbid foreign issues if its recommendations were heeded by the banking groups, the 'Chambre syndicale' of the stockbrokers and the biggest firms of the 'coulisse', in fact it was difficult for it to stop the great deposit banks selling non-authorized bonds, loans known as loans 'émis sous le manteau de la cheminée' (issued under the mantelpiece).[11] Here, the

---

[10]   See A. Straus, 'Trésor public et marché financier', *Revue Historique*, 106 (1982), pp. 65–112; and P. Verley, *Nouvelle histoire économique de la France contemporaine*, vol. 2, *L'industrialisation, 1830–1914* (Paris, 1989).

[11]   R. Girault, *Emprunts russes et investissements français en Russie, 1887–1914* (reprinted, Paris, 1999)

collusion between State and banking groups was much less strong than in Germany. From 1900 to 1910, the proportion of estates including stock-market securities rose from 7 per cent to 10 per cent.[12] This represents a shift in the direction of long-term savings. The proportion of real-estate inheritances can be estimated at about two-thirds in 1851–55 and less than 44 per cent just before the war. The weight of the State in this growing importance of stock-market investments can be evaluated by comparing variable-interest stock non-guaranteed by the State (shares) with fixed-revenue stock or stock promoted by the State (debentures, rentes, foreign securities). Between 1880 and 1895, the proportion of 'guaranteed savings' in stock-market capitalization rose from 53.3 per cent to 63 per cent. But after 1895 – and even more after 1905 – there was a setback: the proportion fell to less than 49 per cent in 1913. From the First World War, and after the stock exchange was closed for some time, the government in 1916 prohibited every foreign issue, and the Paris financial market declined as an international centre, due to the weakening of the French economy (destruction of a large part of its productive potential, selling off of a fair proportion of its foreign assets, high inflation and weakening of the franc) until the stabilization of the franc, de facto in 1926 and de jure in 1928.[13]

Commercial Banks, Public or quasi-State Banks and the State

The favourite kind of savings before 1914 was financial investment, but it did nothing to swell the banks' resources, since they acted purely as intermediaries. It was their capital, reserves and especially deposits (in the case of the deposit banks), which *sustained* the banks' finances. One of the great problems of the banking system during the interwar period was linked to the competition between the private banks and the public or quasi-State banks.[14]

To compare the public area's ability to collect savings with the private area's is not easy, particularly because in banks' balance-sheets current accounts are often lumped together with deposit accounts. Nevertheless, it is clear that in 1891, public channels (this means Banque de France and savings-banks deposits, 'other deposits' and Caisse des Dépôts) were well ahead in the collection of liquidities.

---

[12]   I am largely indebted to André Gueslin for the following passages. A. Gueslin, 'Banks and State in France from the 1880s to the 1930s. The Impossible Advance of the Banks', in Y. Cassis (ed.), *Finance and Financiers in European History, 1880–1960* (Paris and Cambridge, 1992).

[13]   See A. Plessis, 'When Paris Dreamed of Competing with the City…', in Y. Cassis and E. Bussière (eds), *London and Paris as International Financial Centres in the Twentieth Century* (Oxford, 2005).

[14]   D. Verdier's explanation of the development of 'state banking' is mainly political: it came 'in three waves, the first targeting farmers, the second small firms, and the third traditional sectors', see D. Verdier, 'The Rise and Fall of State Banking in OECD Countries', *Comparative Political Studies*, 33, 3 (2000), pp. 283–318.

The imbalance sprang from the run which followed the financial and banking crisis of the early 1880s: between 1880 and 1885, the value of demand deposits dropped from 1.9 to 1.7 billion francs, while the total amount of deposits in savings banks rose from 1.2 to 2.3 billion francs. This early prominence of public channels is especially due to the importance of funds held by the saving banks, particularly since the creation by the State, alongside the private network, of a network of postal savings banks. This had two consequences. First, the post offices succeeded better than the banks in covering the potential market of individuals and small businesses at low costs. Second, since the money deposited was used by the Caisse des Dépôts for investment in *rentes*, the interest that savings banks gave was considerably higher than the banks gave (2.75 and 1.5 per cent respectively in 1913). At a time when people in France had little understanding of how banks worked, it was the State guarantee which fuelled this dynamism. The main drawback was the ceiling on the amount that could be invested in savings banks. In 1881, the ceiling was doubled from 1000 to 2000 francs, but the lowering to 1500 in 1895 explains a (very) relative decline. However, it is clear that the State was managing banking and financial markets at a level which depended more and more on its financial needs. Nevertheless, savings-bank passbooks began to penetrate throughout French society. In 1913, there were 15.1 million passbook holders for 12 million households existing at that time.

The changes in the total collection of deposits in the interwar years are still very hard to determine. The statistics[15] for deposits clearly show the monetary or quasi-monetary character of banks' deposits, unlike those of the savings banks, which were normally less liquid.

They echo the effects of inflation. The change during the 1920s was in favour of bank deposits, and went on until 1930, whereas savings banks may have suffered from the political uncertainties of wartime: the volume of bank deposits rose from 9550 in 1913 to 30480 in 1920 and 89530 in 1930, but fell to 67443 in 1937. After 1926 (date of the stabilization of the franc under Poincaré), the banks' superiority was further reinforced by the influx of external floating capital.

For the birth of banking institutions, the First World War was a determinant. From 1917 to 1938, 'public banking capitalism' (J. Bouvier) grew step by step, with no overall plans, each new body being added to the others for short-term reasons dependent only on circumstances: Crédit agricole, Banques populaires and chèques postaux (1917–18), Crédit national (1919), Crédit hôtelier (1923), Crédit maritime (1928), Caisse de crédit aux départements et aux communes (1931), Caisse des marchés de l'Etat and strict control of the State over the Banque de France (1936), Caisse centrale de crédit coopératif (1938). Those creations added to the older public or semi-public bodies: the enormous Caisse des dépôts et consignations,

---

[15] Of all leading countries, none probably presents the same difficulties to the constructor of economic series. This reflects the absence until recently of official or other estimates of the stock of financial assets. Before the First World War, there is almost an oversupply of estimates that often differ widely and rarely are adequately explained.

which, besides its own resources, centralized the funds of the Caisses d'épargne (savings banks) and of the Assurances sociales, and the Crédit foncier.

The Economic Crisis – A Turning Point for Banking Regulation?

The economic crisis was in fact a turning point for banking regulation. It was the crisis of the 1930s that established State domination of the channels for collection of deposits. The Caisse des Dépôts enjoyed the highest relative growth, due to the rapid rise in deposits representing social insurance funds. But the dynamics came above all from the savings banks, where the volume of deposits rose from 5829m francs in 1913 to 8100m in 1920, 38763m in 1930 and 61638m in 1937.

According to Laufenburger,[16] the total amounts of deposits and creditor current accounts were as follows:

	1913	1938
Private banking sector (banks publishing balance-sheets)	47780m francs (1928)	60298m francs (1928)
Public banking sector	48140m francs (1928)	109229m francs (1928)

With the crisis between 1929 and 1931, the savings banks once again caught up with the banks in terms of relative growth. This was because of State policy: the interest rates on passbooks became more and more favourable. Between 1927 and January 1931, while the banks' rates dropped from 3–4 per cent to 1 per cent, the savings banks' rates remained at 3.5 per cent. The savings banks benefited from other privileges, such as exemption from new direct taxes, conversion of State bonds without commission, and an increase in the ceiling on deposits (from 1500 francs in 1913 to 7500 in April 1925 and 20000 in March 1931). In consequence, savings banks tended more and more to receive the trading capital of small and medium-sized firms, to the great disadvantage of the banks, and it was the political situation rather than the economic crisis which put a brake on the rise of savings banks as of 1936.

The economic crisis, with its bankruptcies and general panic, caused the destruction and transfer of deposits, especially between 1932 and 1935. Some withdrawals went to swell inactive cash hoards of gold and banknotes. The banking crisis first affected small and medium-sized institutions (about 600 banks publishing balance-sheets disappeared, half of them in Paris, the others in the regions[17]), allowing the big banks to increase concentration in the sector.[18]

---

[16]   H. Laufenburger, *Les banques françaises depuis 1914* (Paris, 1940).

[17]   H. Laufenburger, *Les banques françaises*.

[18]   A. Straus, 'La politique des banques régionales dans l'entre-deux-guerres. Entre croissance et rationalisation', in M. Lescure and A. Plessis (eds), *Les banques locales et régionales en Europe au XXe siècle* (Paris, 2004).

With the agreement of the State, indeed under its pressure, large banks like the CIC, which took over the Société Nancéienne, took on the clientele of banks like Banque Renauld that had ceased operations. Some withdrawals swelled the issues of public bodies or went into personal accounts with the Banque de France. By upsetting the equilibrium of banking activities, the crisis of the 1930s assured the domination of State channels. But in contrast with the situation in the United States (1933–34) or in Belgium (1935) – not to mention Italy or Germany – the banking crisis did not lead to a widespread reform of the financial system. The monetary authorities were incapable of seizing the opportunity of the crisis to adapt the policies of the Banque de France to the new needs. Neither Vincent Auriol, Léon Blum nor the new governor, Labeyrie, was capable of taking advantage of the institutional reform the Banque de France was going through at that time to adopt the monetary policies and the banking control the situation was calling for. This would have meant removing the Banque's 'régents' and total State control of the Banque, whose capital still remained in private hands.[19] In spite of the Anglo-Saxon inspiration of the Popular Front's economic policy, the problem of direct discount was not settled; nor was the essential one of new ways for the Banque to intervene on the money market, i.e. an open-market policy.

The open-market policy was established only in spring 1938, with a target aimed at consolidating the situation of the Treasury. In the same years the question of the control of the banks by the Banque de France was discussed, but in vain, and the first banking act dates only from the Vichy government. During the interwar period the influence of the State on the financial system through laws and regulations was weaker than elsewhere. In addition to the importance of public channels, its influence was less formal.

One must for instance emphasize the role of the corps of Inspecteurs des finances. As early as the beginning of the nineteenth century, it began to play an extremely important part contributing to State interventionism in the financial sphere. For instance, Octave Homberg, a finance inspector, was general manager of the Société Générale, auditor of the Banque de France, director of several companies like the Compagnie Générale Transatlantique (1928–31), and even, so it is said, the 'guru' of the Paris Bourse. François Piétri, another finance inspector, progressed through the ranks, ending up with the position of Directeur général des finances du Maroc – Director of Finances for Morocco – a role he played from 1917 to 1924. He became a member of parliament in 1924 and a minister in the government. He viewed 'commercial finance' as the totality of 'everything that lives, stirs and moves in the bank and the bourse'.[20] Two other examples: Emile Moreau, who was the governor of the Banque de France, then became general manager of the Banque de Paris et des Pays-Bas; and in 1930, when the Society

---

[19]   J. Bouvier, *Un siècle de banque française. Les contraintes de l'Etat et les incertitudes des marchés* (Paris, 1973).

[20]   A. Plessis, 'Bankers in French Society, 1860s–1960s', in Y. Cassis (ed.), *Finance and Financiers in European History, 1880–1960* (Paris and Cambridge, 1992).

of alumni of the Ecole libre des Sciences politiques organized its annual lecture series, that year on 'the problems of credit', it called on Olivier Moreau-Néret, director of the Crédit Lyonnais, and Maurice Lorain from the Société Générale, both former finance inspectors.[21]

The Weakness of Commercial Banks in Corporate Finance

In terms of the role of banks in business finance, the interwar period was characterized by both the economic context of the financial markets and the impact of specialized State channels. Between 1880 and 1913, the total credit granted by banks to non-banking agents as a proportion of GDP soared from 7 per cent to over 40 per cent. The financial orthodoxy, a consequence of the troubles borne by the deposit banks in the 1870s and the early 1880s, encouraged short-term credit (mainly discounts – which appeared as 'le pain des banques' – 'the bread of banks'), i.e. the financing of circulating capital even if some repeated renewals of overdrafts or advances were masking a financing of fixed capital.

The regulations of the Banque de France, based on a single rate and the need for three signatures, created a kind of captive market for the deposit banks, something not the case in Britain or Germany. Despite the weakening of those rules at the end of the century, the creation of fiduciary money and bank deposits drew strength from this expansion in the private bills held by the deposit banks.

The main problem was the financing of investments. As we have already seen, the tensions beginning in the 1880s led the deposit banks into 'industrial disengagement'. Before 1913, investment still mainly came from self-financing, from undistributed profits.

But sources of external finance were changing. The proportion of assorted debts fell and the capital from dormant partners remained extremely low, certainly lower than elsewhere. A new stage in the development was reached when the market in transferable securities became capable of allowing an extension of investment. Thus, it might be the direction of that market which explains the importance of self-financing. Numerous analysts were highly critical of the flight of savings from productive channels to the benefit of investment in foreign securities or in *rentes* or investment in current accounts with the Treasury. Big banks were also criticized for their insufficient attempts to help new industries, or small or medium-sized firms.

Three observations may be made. First, savings collected through public channels were not unproductive as a whole. They partly contributed to spending on infrastructure and equipment. The deposit banks not only financed the State's deficits, but also advanced funds to municipalities and public or quasi-public enterprises such as railway companies. Second, too much attention has perhaps been paid to the big banks, to the detriment of local and regional banks. Of course,

---

[21] J. Bouvier, 'Les banques', in A. Sauvy, *Histoire économique de la France entre les deux guerres, divers sujets* (Paris, 1972).

big banks accounted for between half and two-thirds of total banking activity and were strongly inclined towards investment in the public domain, but beneath them were hundreds and hundreds of other banks. In some industrial regions, a local banking system that relied on Banque de France branches existed and was well adapted to their needs. This was the case in the north (textiles and coal) and the east (heavy industry) of the country, and also in the Alps (hydroelectricity).[22] Third, between 1900 and 1913 there was a change of outlook on the financial market: the net contribution of financial savings to the financing of business in France rose from 325m francs to 1500m. Nonetheless, bank intervention remained on a small scale.

Between the wars, the growing needs of the State had a direct effect on the financing of business. The attempts of the banks to adapt to the needs of business (birth of private banks specialized in medium-term loans to firms like UBR, UCINA or CALIF, through the perfecting of rediscounting procedures for medium assets on the part of the Caisse des Dépôts) remained embryonic, and between discounts and advances the banks' strategy scarcely changed from what it had been before the war. All round, the commercial banks' contribution to the economy was less than it had been. The contribution of the public banking sector was still weak, particularly that of 'State banking' (to use Daniel Verdier's terminology), which suffered from a weakness of resources (from 1919 until 1936 the Crédit national and Crédit foncier's issues represented less than 2 per cent of total issues on the market) and the search for security (for instance, in 1924 guarantees of Crédit national loans in public bonds amounted to 83 per cent).[23]

The ever-increasing demand made on the banks by the State was a consequence of the war and was connected to the birth of the Welfare State. State debts, which represented 10 per cent of GDP in 1913, rose to 20 per cent at the end of the war, fell to 14 per cent in 1929 but reached 20 per cent again during the crisis. The banks formed the habit of including in their portfolio a large proportion of 'bons de la défense nationale [national defence bonds]'. Consequently, the level of self-financing rose during the large public issues of the early 1920s and in 1937–38, and the actual volume of bank intervention declined.

By contrast with the former period, in the crisis period the crowding-out effect came into play, in particular between discounts and public assets. In 1934, for instance, the commercial portfolio of the five big deposit banks contracted, to the benefit of the Banque de France, while the portfolio of Treasury bills remained constant.

But the drop in credit to the economy cannot be explained only by this shift in banks' portfolios. It reflected both the drop in their own resources and a search for financial security: at the same time, the importance of the banks was diminishing due

---

[22]   M. Lescure and A. Plessis (eds), *Banques locales et banques régionales en France au XIXe siècle* (Paris, 1999).

[23]   A. Gueslin and M. Lescure, 'Les banques publiques parapubliques et coopératives françaises (vers 1920–vers 1960)' in M. Lévy-Leboyer (ed.), *Les banques en Europe de l'Ouest de 1920 à nos jours* (Paris, 1995).

to the encouragement of public channels (Crédit National, Banques populaires, Crédit Agricole). Nor should one forget that in the thirties demand for funds by firms was low, due to the weakness of investment as a consequence of low market expectations. In conclusion, then, the interwar period shows a consolidation of the rise of the State and, taking into account the probable fall in value of the industrial securities owned by the banks, a certain retreat of the banking system in its contribution to the economic life of the country, especially by comparison with other countries.

As for bank penetration, we can make a comparison with the Anglo-Saxon countries and with the Continent. It was Germany, not France as might be expected, which had the smallest banking network. This can be explained by the prevalence there of savings banks, and above all by the wide-ranging cooperative organizations (Raiffeisenbank, Volksbank). The French banking network, with 9000 banking outlets, was of average size; this can be explained by the large competition from public or quasi-State institutions (ordinary savings banks, Crédit Agricole, Banques populaires, Banque de France, with 10,200 outlets) and 16,800 post offices (dispensing products like Chèques Postaux and the services of the Caisse Nationale d'Epargne).

There was a contrast between Anglo-Saxon countries and Switzerland on the one hand, and the other countries of the Continent on the other, in particular with regard to deposits: 10,100 francs worth of deposits per inhabitant in England, 1700 in France. This 'backwardness' of France before the Second World War can be explained by the existence of channels for financial savings, the competition of the savings banks and the still essentially rural nature of the country. Another brake on the banks' involvement in economic life was the absence of a reliable inter-bank organization: as we have already seen, there was no real money market before 1938. The statutes of the Banque de France prevented it from operating on the open market. As it was in competition with the big commercial banks, the latter avoided any rediscounting with it, and the existence of bilateral relations between banks could not compensate for the absence of an inter-bank market. This lack of organization in the banking sector consolidated the State intervention that had begun in the nineteenth century.

The Second World War – A Decisive Period for State Regulation

For three main reasons, during the war period 1939–45 the financial area underwent a profound change. First of all, scarcity and damages caused by the war obliged the State to intervene more and more in the economy and in financing. Since prices and interest rates were then under the government's control, trading, capital flows, external accounts and so on were severely controlled. Of course, the same war-economy organization also came about in other Western countries, but the French case appears special because of the Germans' four-year occupation, which led to settled experience of regulation. Second, as regulation of the banking system and of the capital market had been postponed after the Great Depression, the Vichy government, in this area as in others, made important laws which were to rule the banking system for nearly 25 years. The 1941 Bank Act obliged the commercial banks to ask in order to open new branches; the banks were split between deposit and investment banks. The law created a supervisor, the Commission de contrôle des banques, which controlled the deposit and investment banks and decided whether a new bank could be registered in France. Yet the semi-public or cooperative banks like Crédit agricole and the savings banks were not concerned by this rule and were directly supervised by the Ministry of Finance. The 1941 banking Act was confirmed after the war and even reinforced by the creation of the Conseil national du crédit, linked with the Banque de France.

Third, while France was occupied by the Germans, the country had to pay 400 million francs per day to them, for four years. Inflation was under control thanks to price policy, but government debt increased considerably, a burden which had to be borne by the financial market. Interest rates were imposed by the government and authorizations had to be secured from the Treasury for new issues on the stock market. Comparatively, in Britain relationships between the State and the City were not so constrained during the war: with both the Stock Exchange and the banks, the Treasury relied on cooperation from the institutions concerned rather than imposing detailed control.[24]

Accordingly, in order to finance public deficit spending, the French Treasury collected most of the specialized financial institutions' funds by setting up the 'circuit du Trésor', a parallel money circuit beside the central bank's. Otherwise, these institutions were devoted to providing firms with funds through government-subsidized loans.[25] Finally, when it needed liquid funds, the Treasury issued new short-term securities, the treasury bills ('bons du Trésor'), that were much appreciated by French savers and banks for their high degree of liquidity. In Britain and the US, government debt also increased dramatically during the war. By 1943, government securities (treasury bills, War Loan, US War Bonds) amounted to 71% of American banks' assets.[26] In France in 1945, two out three investments made by banks were still in treasury bills, whereas English and American banks did not keep government securities in their portfolio and came back after 1946 to supplying private firms' investments. Conversely, after January 1948 French banks were required by a constraining rule to retain a certain fraction of their reserves in treasury bills (by contrast with the prewar period). Thus, after the Second World War the French State established several procedures and institutions that were to be maintained for some forty years.

---

[24]   G.C. Peden, 'The Treasury and the City', in R.C. Michie and P.A. Williamson (eds), *The British Government and the City in the Twentieth Century* (Cambridge, 2005).

[25]   These institutions, usually called 'state credit banks' by D. Verdier in *Moving Money. Banking and Finance in the Industrialized World* (Cambridge, 2002), were already under State control before the war; but State direction was reinforced during and after it.

[26]   H. Laufenburger, *Traité d'économie et de législation financière. Dette publique et richesse privée* (Paris, 1948).

The Postwar Economy – Priority for Direct Financing by the State

After 1945, by contrast with Germany and Britain, which preferred to give priority to monetary policy,[27] France chose growth and sacrificed money. The French political choices went with a 5 per cent growth rate between 1949 and 1973 (the so-called 'trente glorieuses' period) and a gradual internationalization of the French economy.[28] This continuous and intense opening process since 1945 was mainly connected with the manufacturing sector, whereas international and domestic capital flows remained controlled until the 1980s. In this regard, the various aspects of State financial regulation shaped a complex but significant model. A number of steps allowed the State to gain such influence.

First of all, a consensus was reached after the Second World War to give the State the tools for strong intervention, in order to reconstruct and modernize the economy in 1945–46: creation of the Commissariat general au Plan; nationalization of two-thirds of the capitalization of the Paris Bourse, of the four main deposit banks and of insurance companies; and last but not least, the birth of the National Health Service, which impeded the development of pension funds.

In 1948, the Marshall Plan or European Recovery Plan (ERP) was a turning point especially in France, for it allowed the Ministry of Finance to become a banking institution, making loans and receiving funds. Even after the Marshall Plan was over (1952), the Ministry of Finance continued to supply credits for firms, not only through direct subsidies, but also by using the channel of the specialized financial institutions (the semi-public and cooperative banks). Thus, the tools set up before the Second World War were developed over several decades: this is the main difference between France and most of the other Western countries. In terms of volume, State financing for investments in 1949 amounted to 30 per cent of total investment in Britain, 40 per cent in Italy, 50 per cent in Belgium, but 80 per cent in France (Graph 1). Germany and Britain both tried out new guidance tools to regulate financing after 1945: in Britain, in 1946, institutions like the wartime Capital Issues Committee were made permanent, and the National Investment Council (NIC) was created; in Germany, the Kreditanstalt für Wiederaufbau (a State-owned institution) was created by 1948, and four years later a private

---

[27] But their reasons were quite different. The former was haunted by the two inflation periods and was preoccupied with keeping monetary stability. In Britain, sterling policy to maintain both sterling's international position and the City's interests concerned both Treasury and Bank of England officials, even though the link between them started loosening after the 1960s. See C. Schenk, 'The New City and the State in the 1960s', in R.C. Michie and P.A. Williamson (eds), *The British Government and the City of London in the Twentieth Century* (Cambridge, 2004).

[28] See J.C. Asselain and B. Blancheton's recent work, 'L'ouverture internationale en perspective historique. Statut analytique du coefficient d'ouverture et application au cas de la France', *Cahiers du GRES*, no. 2006–09 (mars 2006).

institution for investment, the Industriekreditbank, was set up.[29] However, these financial institutions were only advisory, whereas the French ones remained powerful and strongly linked to the State.

Second, more than in other Western countries, credit and monetary policy was strictly handled, as interest rates were fixed by the government and remained under control until the 1970s. The banking commissions were also under severe control, and this rule was far more constraining than the State ownership established in 1945.[30] By this means, the government aimed at providing funds at the lowest cost for firms and decided which sector had to be subsidized as a priority (agriculture, mortgages, export-development loans). The French Treasury was then really acting as a banking institution: on the one hand, it collected money, and on the other, it granted and warranted credits, for much the same amounts as the whole banking system during the fifties (funds collected: 695bn versus 617bn; loans: 783bn versus 715bn).[31] It appears to have been the main financial institution able to transform short-time money into long-term investment during these decades. Yet, the 'rediscounted' mid-term credit developed since the 1940s allowed commercial banks to supply longer credits to firms. Mid-term credits could be 'rediscounted' at the central bank, so that the lending bank could be paid in advance for its loan. This system was set up thanks to the central bank's support as lender of last resort.

The financial system set up by the French government was based on segmentation between short-term, mid-term and long-term financial institutions. Outside the banking system, but also in competition with it – as it was also working as a banking institution – the Ministry of Finance organized capital flows and transformation within the domestic economy. From a financing perspective, this classification seems more relevant than one based on the private-public distinction, or on the typology of for-profit and non-profit banks.[32]

Capital Markets Under Heavy Supervision

Besides these strong regulations regarding credit and money, the government chose to control all the capital markets, requiring authorization for every issue on the financial market (bonds and stocks) above 250,000 francs (a threshold raised when the financial market improved). Moreover, the issuing commissions were under State control. Consequently, public issues had priority over private issues and were given advantages in terms of amounts and also of rates. The priorities

---

[29]   Furthermore, in Germany tax policy was a government tool earlier than in France. Fiscal incentives in favour of securities, especially bonds, were launched in 1952 and 1955.

[30]   The question of the influence of the State linked with State ownership in the banking area is actually ambiguous. See below.

[31]   About the role of the Treasury, see L. Quennouëlle-Corre, *La direction du Trésor 1947–1967. L'Etat-banquier et la croissance* (Paris, 2000).

[32]   According to Verdier, 'The rise and fall'.

on the bond market were, in order: government issues, State-owned firms' loans, local-authority issues, and, last, private firms' bonds. Only a few firms could access the French market, and foreign issues were quite forbidden until the 1970s.

To convince savers to subscribe for government loans, policy-makers created new tax incentives for public bonds. The French State did not hesitate to play against the competition in various ways in order to preserve its own sources of funds: fiscal advantages, higher interest rates, etc. Such a situation would have seemed impossible in Britain, where the City was considered as a national institution able to influence the government's policy. In Germany, a Central Committee for financial trading was instituted by 1949 to direct capital flows during the European Recovery Programme and fix industrial and mortgage bonds; because it advantaged government issues, industrial companies were averse to the rule and it had disappeared by 1954.

As investment increased, the State continued until the end of the 1960s to control, directly or indirectly, more or less 50 per cent of investments. In this respect, we can say that State ownership was not the main tool for the government's financial direction, whereas monetary, financial and credit policy gave it effective power over the whole financial and banking system.

Comparatively, German and British experiences seem to have had much more freedom. Nonetheless, after the Radcliffe Report in 1959, Britain began considering economic growth as important as strong currency and understood that the decline of sterling did not inhibit the development of the City. The country went through planning in the 1960s, but without any success. Summarizing, we might say that Germany and Britain preferred moral suasion, agreement and cooperation to repressive laws. There was thus a difference in kind between the French State's policy and its neighbours'.

The Fifth Republic Changes: The Beginning of Deregulation?

After General de Gaulle came back to power in 1958, greater financial orthodoxy seemed to set in. International changes played an important role in that liberalization: the European common market, beginning in 1958, and the growth of international trade both obliged France to slowly open its boundaries. In order to make French firms more competitive, it became urgent to broaden the capital markets, modernize credit techniques and improve the collection of savings by the banks.

Policy-makers began then to liberalize the banking and credit system through a number of measures in 1965–67. Banks were given permission to open branches without government authorization. They were encouraged to increase their deposits and reserves, and the reforms sought to eliminate banking specialization. Banking mergers and insurance mergers were decided (by the government). Financial and fiscal incentives were developed in order to increase long-term savings accounts. The Minister of Finance decided to help stock-market revival, to create an independent financial authority (COB) and to open the Paris Bourse, very slowly, to foreign firms. After 1958, the government decided to stop issuing its own large loans on the bond market (Graph 2). But the Ministry of Finance was still arranging the calendar of issues on the bond market and fixing rates of interest, and the COB could not impose the 1967 insider trading law before the end of the 1970s.

But the technocracy did not really want to give up its influence on capital markets, because it feared the consequences for the currency, inflation rates and the Treasury deficit. So the State had a very ambiguous attitude: on the one hand it tried through some reforms to liberalize the market, while on the other it did not want to deprive itself of a monetary and financial tool.

Finally, the financial system was not quite reformed at the end of the Sixties. When direct public financing diminished in the Sixties, that did not mean a State decline: Treasury officials continued to put pressure on the public institutions and to apply the same credit policy, to maintain its influence on industrial investment. In this respect, private as well as State-owned banks were compelled to follow the government orientation.

For instance, monetary policy did not really change. All the interest rates still depended upon the government bills' rate until 1971 (changes were then brought by money-market reform: henceforth interest rates were fixed by the central bank). It is quite interesting to see here that the central bank was unable to decide as regards the credit system, which continued to be in the State's hands. The market was opened only after 1971, central-bank reform was then brought in by 1973, and the official independence of the Banque de France was decided only by 1993.

Second example: the role of specialized financial institutions increased as long as the State seemed to disengage from direct management of the economy.[33] Each special credit institution was devoted to a sector: agriculture, shipping, tourism, and so on. Special credit institutions and long-term credit institutions continue to be a central feature of the French system. They control nearly a third of the capital.[34] Despite reforms, the central features of the French system – established since the beginning of the twentieth century and reinforced after 1945 – remain even after the petroleum crisis in 1973, which brought back strong State intervention to help ailing firms and to fight inflation with heavy credit regulation.

---

[33]   We do not agree here with Verdier, *Moving Money*, p. 131, when he says that 'state credit banking' has been declining in France since the 1960s. Instead, these institutions increased their weight as the State officially withdrew from direct financing (debudgétisation).

[34]   We must specially mention here the increasing role of the Caisse des dépôts as one of the main stakeholders on the bond market and as a State agency on the money market.

State Regulation and the Reinforcement of the Big Banks

About the postwar period, one ranking Paribas figure said: 'The State is everywhere; nothing is possible without the State'. This State domination is partly due to the direct ties between the Ministry of Finance and the banks in two respects: institutional links and personal networks.

1. Banks have been helped by the government to be the foremost financial intermediates

During this period, the French capital market has been the narrowest in the Western world. This weakness can be explained by inflation, which discouraged savers, by nationalizations that withdrew two thirds of stock-exchange capitalization, and also by the high degree of liquidity of French savings. For instance, in 1965, sight deposits and notes amounted to 45 per cent of French savers' investments (only 2 per cent in the USA and 15 per cent in Germany). The fiscal policy also weakened yields, at least until 1965.

In spite of this situation, firms tried to find financing on the market. The negotiations between banks and the State about issuing were rather tough and required the banking industry's intermediation, as banks were the only ones allowed to negotiate with the State. So while the State needs banks' financial help, banks need the State's protection and agreement for their loans or financial activity.

What happened after the 1960s reforms? The banks became stronger and their power grew, as the firms had no other choice for loans than to ask them. Their domestic branches were multiplied by 3 between 1967 and 1973 (20390 bank tellers in 1980) and their international branches grew faster, despite the fact that the State was reluctant to export the franc.[35]

In 1975, firms' financing was still up to 75 per cent supplied by banks (only 51 per cent in the USA, for instance). Thus, firms were more dependent on the banking system than before, for loans but also for issues. Because institutional investors were not very active on the capital market, issuers needed bank intermediation to reach the numerous savers through their local branches. Thus, in the mid 1970s financial intermediation remained rather more important in France than in other Western countries (Tables 5.4 and 5.5).

And issuing expenses were kept high, because of the bank cartel with the State's agreement. The State also helped the 'big four' deposit banks[36] to become the main financial intermediates. They became a central point in the financial apparatus: they drew savings, distributed funds and were the stock market's main go-betweens. Furthermore, the concentration of financing led to a cartel among

---

[35]   E. Bussière, 'French Banks and the Euro-bonds Issue Market during the 1960s', in Y. Cassis and E. Bussière (eds), *London and Paris as International Financial Centres in the Twentieth Century* (Oxford, 2005).

[36]   After the 1966 merger between CNEP and BNCI, there were only three left.

the biggest banks (the three or four deposit banks and the private investment bank Banque de Paris et des Pays-Bas), which were in the best position to negotiate with the State.[37]

2. Finance, State and the corporate-governance issue: the ministry of finance civil servants in management of the financial and industrial sectors

In France, external recruitment in the banking industry is quite specific compared to other countries. As we have seen, since the end of the 19th century top managers were recruited mainly from amongst former high-ranking civil servants. Among them, what we call in French the Inspecteurs des Finances are considered as the government elite.

Since the Second World War, the extension of branch networks in the Western countries entailed the need for banking expertise and allowed the creation of positions reserved for young postgraduates. In France, managers stem from several kinds of external recruitment: civil servants from the Ministry of Finance, engineers from the Polytechnique, and business-school graduates from for example HEC as well as the graduates from the Institut d'Etudes Politiques (Science Po) and the Faculty of Law. From 1960 to 1990, about 650 firms in the banking and industrial sectors customarily recruited high civil servants. Among sectors in which the Inspecteurs des Finances hold a position, the banking industry comes first with 50 per cent of non-governmental jobs. This main trend of the French financial system since the 19th century has been growing since the Second World War, while State-owned banking or semi-public banking was increasing and State intervention occurring, with the nationalization of two thirds of stock-market capitalization. Nonetheless, except for small private merchant banks, every bank has its former civil servant. The totals for Inspecteurs des Finances in the six main banks' top management are 8 in 1950, 13 in 1960, 16 in 1970 and 14 in 1980. Within the banking system, big banks are the great beneficiaries of civil-servant recruitment. As the relations between government and the banking industry were from time to time in conflict, it appears that the Inspecteurs des Finances loosened up the links between them, thus maintaining a stable financial system in France during the twentieth century. Conversely, the government plays its game well through its power of nomination and through empowerment in the financial area. The government's best tool in this area lies in the Ministry of Finance and especially in the Treasury.

On the other hand, this civil-servant recruitment has maintained the status quo of a bank-based financial system, making change more difficult. Moreover, retaining a top management trained for domestic issues and State intervention delayed the internationalization of the French financial system.[38]

---

[37]   See L. Quennouëlle-Corre, 'The State, Banks and Financing for Investments in France from World War II to the 1970s', *Financial History Review*, 12, 1 (2005), pp. 63–86.

[38]   For instance, the first international recruitment in banking industry management occurred only in the eighties, except in the Banque de Paris (Harvard Business School).

The 1980s – Financial Deregulation and State Withdrawal?

From a certain point of view, the economic crisis which broke out in 1973 brought about the beginning of financial deregulation, in France as in other countries, but also the reinforcement of direct State subsidies to industry. Going back to its former habits, the State increased its intervention to help ailing firms. According to J. Zysman,[39] France in the 1970s remained a 'state-based-system', like Japan but contrary to Germany, Britain or the US.

As deficit spending increased, the Government at least became aware of the importance of liberalizing capital markets for financing both corporate and State needs. A powerful incentive to invest (a tax rebate to encourage savings towards financing industry, created by the Monory Act in 1978) and the increase in long-term interest rates both succeeded in boosting the bond market. Between 1979 and 1984, public issues of shares or participating securities increased fourfold. It was chiefly the bond market, to which the State and the banks mainly turned, that developed spectacularly. Share prices also increased fourfold between 1981 and 1984.

With the socialist government's preference for the European Union and a free-market economy over autarky after 1983, the 1980s brought dramatic financial change, bringing in a French-style 'big bang'. The public authorities kept or strengthened encouragements to buy bonds or shares, originating several financial innovations. On the securities markets, the reform movement began in 1982 with the setting up of the Second Market; new markets like MATIF (1986) and MONEP (1987) were then instituted, whereas the primary market was reorganized. All commission and interest rates were free. Deregulation and openness of capital flows allowed the French economy to become a market-based system, which benefited all sorts of firms, especially small and medium-sized ones. Nonetheless, the Paris Bourse's international role remained limited in the 1980s: less than 2 per cent of total transactions were in foreign shares.[40] The total capitalization of equities approached the Western norm by the end of the nineties, with a contraction of the bond market. Nowadays, the degree of financial openness can be measured by the level of foreign capital in the CAC 40:[41] about 40 per cent, one of the highest in the world. In the banking area, the 1984 law began to put an end to specialization among banks and make competition between them a real feature; in this regard, it was followed in 1986 by the privatization of the nationalized banks and insurance

---

Even after the French liberalization in the 1980s and 1990s, even after the Crédit Lyonnais scandal which highlighted the failure of Inspecteurs des Finances and the lack of control, the influence of high civil servants in the private sector remains important.

[39]   J. Zysman, 'The Interventionist Temptation. Financial Structure and Political Purpose', in W.J. Andrews and S. Hoffmann (eds), *The Fifth Republic at Twenty* (Albany, 1981).

[40]   By 1990, the ratio of foreign share transactions to total transactions amounted to 48.7 per cent in London, 2.1 in Germany and 3.8 in Paris.

[41]   The CAC 40 is a share index showing the 40 top-ranked firms listed on the Paris Bourse.

companies, as well as of the Crédit Agricole (1988) and the Caisses d'épargne (2000). Finally, the number of foreign banks established in France rose from 200 in 1984 to 473 in 1999, placing Paris second after London in Europe.

Yet the State's influence remains an important player in the financial world, especially within the banking industry. As a matter of fact, the State – and more specifically the Treasury department – did not want to withdraw from the financial system. The Treasury technocrats, the policy-makers – and many bankers – did not approve self-financing because it did not allow them to control firms' investment decisions. Since the Great Depression bankruptcies, they also did not believe in banks' ability to provide funds. Hence, they relied on their own know-how to make the right decision and on the market to provide for firms' financial needs. But the stock market was not strong enough to supply the necessary funds for both government and firms. Finally, as the State could not by-pass banks as financial intermediaries, it tried to shut them in a restrictive system. That is why a constrained selective credit policy and a segmented system have been applied so long and been so hard to erase.

Conclusion

Two main points have been emphasized throughout this presentation. First, from the First World War until Second – even though the financial turn-round was gradual – the two world wars appear as turning points of the century; a fact that can easily be explained by the country's geographical location. Second, after the Second World War, despite a constraining financial policy, France was one of the most dynamic economies for thirty years. As a matter of fact, French specificity has since the beginning of the century relied on the State's overlapping influence through social networks, institutional links based on a selective policy and a segmented financial system. Nevertheless, despite autarky and strong regulation in the financial sphere, France attained one of the best growth rates after 1945, right up to the 1970s: 5 per cent per year. As a matter of fact, the internationalization of the French economy went well during the same time, partly thanks to the continuous monetary weakening. The gap between economic openness and financial autarky appears in the middle of the second half of the twentieth century. The financial sector actually did succeed in supplying French firms' needs (there was not very much foreign investment) and, despite the weakness of the capital markets, French firms did not, thanks to the State's and the banks' financing, lack funds: the low-cost credit policy was able to offset the lack of funds.

Furthermore, the so-called 'financial repression' that prevailed for almost fifty years did not impede fast deregulation in the 1980s and an evolution toward a 'financial market economy' – a bigger and faster shift than in, for instance, Japan and Germany.

In this respect, the 'ebb and flow' of globalization differs along the time dimension, whether the perspective adopted is that of the 'real economy' or of the financial sphere.

As regards the ways the French State ran its intervention, they changed throughout the century, although some long-term trends can be emphasized. From the 1880s, State intervention focused first on the capital market and then on the settlement of public savings channels; after the First World War, its first preoccupation was the settlement of 'state banking'. Third, after the Second World War, without removing supervision from financial markets' supervision, it concentrated on banking regulation and then, until the 1970s, increasingly on its direct financing role. As a regulator of capital markets and the banking sector or as an actor on the capital markets, the State appears more influential than as an owner of a nationalized bank.

To conclude on French specificity: State regulation was quite different in Germany, in Britain and in France during the twentieth century; although each economic and financial policy shaped a special financial pattern, economic results were quite convergent from a long-term perspective. For instance, financial deregulation since the 1980s has been handled in the same way as in other Western countries like Germany and Italy.

Appendix

Discussion on Data

As all serious economic historians are fully aware, the problem of reconstituting historical series in France is a very difficult one. One of the most brilliant economic historians, Maurice Lévy-Leboyer, spent more than thirty years working on this task, at the macroeconomic level, for the nineteenth century alone. According to R.W. Goldsmith, of all leading countries probably none presents the same difficulties to the constructor of an economic series. This reflects the absence until recently of official or other estimates regarding the stock of financial assets. Before the First World War, there is almost an oversupply of estimates, often differing widely and rarely properly explained; however, during the interwar period there was a drying up of supply. See R.W. Goldsmith, *Comparative National Balance Sheets. A Study of Twenty Countries 1688–1978* (Chicago and London, 1985).

One can illustrate this by the problem of measuring deposits. Before 1945, there were no monetary statistics. The data available was (1) periodic publications of the total of deposits and current accounts for all the balance sheets that were published by banks in 1913, 1921, 1926, 1931, 1935, 1936, 1937, 1938, (2) monthly figures of the Crédit Lyonnais, the Comptoir national d'escompte, the Société générale and the Crédit industriel and after 1918 these plus a fifth bank, the Banque Nationale de Crédit (BNCI in 1932). J. Bouvier, *Un siècle de banque française* (Paris, 1973), considered that the top four Parisian banks represented in 1891, 60 per cent; 1901, 66 per cent; 1913, 51 per cent; 1929, 37 per cent; and 1937, 45 per cent. Michèle Saint Marc, *Histoire monétaire de la France 1800–1980* (Paris, 1983), considered that the same four banks accounted for 46 per cent of the total of demand deposits and current accounts between 1880 and 1913; thereafter she used the INSEE estimates.

J.-P. Patat and M. Lutfalla, *Histoire monétaire de la France au XXe siècle* (Paris, 1986), evaluates the share of these banks at more than 60 per cent in 1913, less than 40 per cent in 1929, more than 50 per cent in 1936 and 48 per cent in 1938. The League of Nations data set uses another multiplier and its evaluations are different for the eve of the First World War and the interwar period.

	Bouvier	Saint Marc	Patat/Lutfalla
1875			
1880		2.30	
1890		2.90	
1895		3.6	
1900		5	
1910		10.4	8.5
1913	9.5	12	10
1919		27	26.2
1929	90.5	84	90.6
1936		74	61.6
1937	67.4	85	65.5

A second example can be given using stock-market capitalization. Between 1880 and 1925, some 42 estimates of it can be found. Some of them are presented in the following table.

1880	Théry	55
	Neymarck	56
	Vignes	200
1888	Théry	40
	Neymarck	74
1898	Foville	61
	Colson	74
1913	Colson	101
	Lescure	122

The weakness and lack of accuracy of French chronological series make any precise international comparison rather difficult. The literature on finance and economic growth in the last fifteen years has benefited from the construction of a large World Bank dataset covering the second half of the twentieth century, which has facilitated a large number of cross-country studies, though sometimes without enough precautions as far as the interpretation of the data is concerned. Time-series data must first be consolidated in order for us to speak with confidence on the role of financial institutions in the real economy within a country or a small number of countries over a transition period before attempting to model and test economic theories by comparisons across countries. Some economic historians have recognized this and are working in this direction (see, e.g., P. Rousseau and P. Wachtel, 'Financial Intermediation and Economic Performance. Historical Evidence from Industrialized Economies', *Journal of Money, Credit and Banking*, 30, 4 (1998), pp. 657–78; R.E. Wright, 'Testing the Finance-Led Growth Hypothesis. Early 19th Century America, Britain, and Canada', Terry School of Business Workshop, University of Georgia, 2004; P. Rousseau and R.E. Sylla, 'Emerging Financial Markets and Early US Growth', *Explorations in Economic History*, 42, 1 (2005), pp. 1–26; M. Bordo and P. Rousseau, Legal-Political Factors and the Historical Evolution of the Finance-Growth Link, NBER Working Paper no. 12035, 2006. However, time-series data have till today remained somewhat scarce).

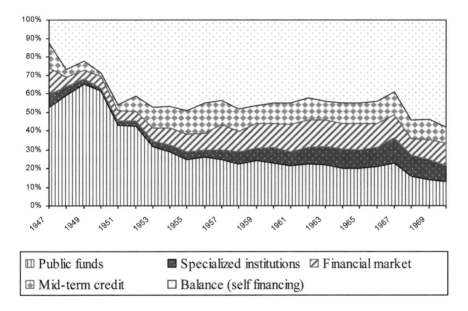

Figure 5.1   Distribution of investment financing funds by percentage

Source: Ministry of Finance

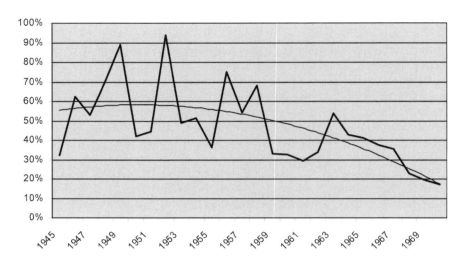

Figure 5.2   Ratio of government bond issues to total bond issues on the Paris Bourse

Source: Annuaire rétrospectif de l'INSEE 1948–88.

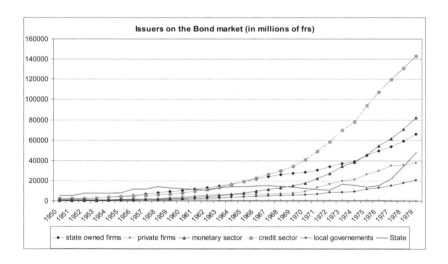

Figure 5.3   Main issuers on the bond market, 1950–80

Source: International Monetary Fund, financial statistics

Table 5.1   Shares of the long-term credit institutions: Liabilities and claims
               with the non-financial sector in 1975

Shares of the long-term credit institutions (per cent)	DEPOSITS	LOANS
France	8.2	32.9
Italy	9.1	29.9
Germany	12.8	23.5
United Kingdom	4.9	21.4

Source: OECD, national accounts

Table 5.2   Ratio Domestic issues/GNP in 1975

Total issues/GNP (per cent)	BONDS	STOCKS
France	16	7
Italy	65	7
Germany	30	13
United Kingdom	43	41

Source: OECD, national accounts

CHAPTER 6

The Emergence of Central Banks
and Banking Supervision
in Comparative Perspective*

Richard S. Grossman

Introduction

Banking is among the most heavily regulated industries in the world.[1] On the national, and increasingly international, level the rules governing all aspects of bank behaviour have proliferated. These include entry restrictions, capital requirements, reserve requirements, auditing and reporting requirements, and restrictions on the types of assets banks are allowed to hold. Although bank regulation is ubiquitous, there is no consensus view on which institution – or combination of institutions – should be responsible for banking supervision. At present, bank supervision is typically undertaken by central banks, government ministries (e.g., finance, economics), sub-national jurisdictions, independent commissions, or by a combination of two or more of these. The goal of this chapter is to determine what factors historically have accounted for the choice of banking supervisor.

Determining the reasons for assignment of supervisory authority is important for both historical and policy viewpoints. First, the forces that lead to the selection of an institution as supervisor may also be responsible for determining other features of national regulatory systems: hence, the exercise will help us better understand the evolution of bank regulation in general. Second, if certain institutions are better suited to be supervisors, the factors that explain that choice may also help to explain a financial system's susceptibility to crisis, and therefore may have implications for national differences in long-run economic growth. Finally, far-reaching changes in financial supervision during the past two decades suggest that the appropriate supervisor is still very much a matter of debate. Hence, the current

* Prepared for the European Association for Banking History conference 'The State and Financial Services. Regulation, Ownership, and Deregulation', Caixa Geral de Depósitos, Lisbon, 26–27 May 2006. I am grateful to conference participants, the editors, and an anonymous referee for helpful comments. The research was supported by the National Science Foundation and the German Marshall Fund of the United States.

[1] W. Möschel, 'Public Law of Banking', in J.S. Ziegel (ed.), *International Encyclopedia of Public Law* (Boston, 1991), chapter 3.

chapter may help us to understand the choices that governments have made, and indicate what sorts of choices they may make in the future.

Briefly, I find that younger central banks were more likely to be called upon to become banking supervisors than their older counterparts. I also find that, among central banks that were entrusted with banking supervision, younger banks were typically given this task earlier than older banks. These results may reflect the fact that younger central banks were less set in their ways, and were perhaps better able to adapt to the dual role of monetary policy-maker and banking supervisor than older central banks.

The remainder of this chapter is outlined as follows. The next section discusses theories of banking regulation. The subsequent section considers the advantages and disadvantages of unified financial supervisory authority and of entrusting the central bank with banking supervision. The following section discusses the emergence of national banks, their development into central banks, and the evolution of banking regulation. The next section presents and analyses data on the choice of supervisor. Conclusions follow.

Banking Regulation

Commercial banks have long been subject to government regulation and supervision. The earliest commercial banks were established by government charters, which frequently specified in detail the conditions under which these institutions could conduct business, including the scope of supervision by State authorities. The earliest comprehensive national banking codes were adopted by Britain (1844) and Sweden (1846); Canada, Finland, Japan, Portugal, and the United States established banking codes in the second half of the nineteenth century; other advanced economies established banking codes in the first half of the twentieth.

Although the form and specifics of banking regulations have long been a popular topic for debate and discussion among journalists, policy-makers, economists, and legal scholars, until recently there has been very little discussion – academic or otherwise – about the identity of the preferred supervisor. Discussion of this issue has been spurred by moves by several countries to establish unified financial supervisory authorities with powers to oversee insurance and securities firms, as well as banks. Norway was the first to adopt a unified supervisor, in 1986; Denmark (1988), Sweden (1991), and the UK (1997) followed. In recent years, a number of countries have adopted – or are considering adopting – a unified supervisor. Table 6.1 illustrates the relatively sharp increase in the number of countries with unified financial-sector supervisors during 1999–2003.

Table 6.1   Single, Semi-Integrated, Multiple Supervisory Agencies

	1999		2003	
	Number	%	Number	%
Separate Supervisors	**35**	**48**	**31**	**40**
Two-sector Regulators, of which:	**25**	**34**	**24**	**31**
Combined Securities and Insurance Regulators	3	4	7	9
Combined Bank and Securities Regulators	9	12	6	8
Combined Bank and Insurance Regulators	13	18	11	14
Single Supervisor	**13**	**18**	**22**	**29**

Sources: R.K. Abrams and M.W. Taylor, Issues in the Unification of Financial Sector Supervision, IMF Working Paper 00/213 (2000); J. De Luna Martinez and T.A. Rose, International Survey of Integrated Financial Sector Supervision, World Bank Policy Research Working Paper 3096 (2003), relying on N. Courtis, *How Countries Supervise Their Banks, Insurance and Securities Markets* (London, 1999).

Two central questions have emerged from the 'who should supervise?' literature. First, should financial-system supervision be consolidated within one agency? Second, to what extent should the central bank take the lead in bank supervision?[2]

As noted above, the trend in recent years has been towards unified supervision. A recent survey of 118 countries finds that approximately two thirds place some or all authority for banking supervision in the hands of the central bank.[3] Among the advanced industrialized countries of the OECD, the proportion of countries in which central banks take the lead in banking supervision is much less – about one third.

What factors should motivate the choice of a supervisor? The remainder of this section will discuss the motivation for regulation in general; the next section will discuss the potential advantages and disadvantages of moving to a unified financial supervisor and of placing the central bank at the head of the supervisory apparatus.

Why should firms, either bank or non-banking firms, be regulated? The impetus to regulate has a variety of sources, which can be separated into: (1) traditional, purely economic motives, and (2) political-economic motives. Purely economic reasoning has long guided economists in their study of regulation and has led to the conclusion that, in the presence of market imperfections such as monopolies or imperfect information, government regulation can result in superior (i.e., more

---

[2]   D.T. Llewellyn, Institutional Structure of Financial Regulation. The Basic Issues, World Bank Seminar, Aligning Supervisory Structures with Country Needs, 2003.

[3]   J. Barth, G. Caprio Jr and R. Levine, 'Banking Systems Around the World. Do Regulations and Ownership Affect Performance and Stability?' in F.S. Mishkin (ed.), *Prudential Supervision. What Works and What Doesn't* (Chicago, 2001).

efficient) outcomes.[4] Thus, regulation is merely a response by the authorities to an imperfect world. In the case of banking, purely economic motives for regulation centre on promoting stability (i.e., avoiding crises) and efficiency. Because of banks' unique role in money creation, in the form of transactions deposits (banknotes, in earlier times), a third economic motive for regulation may also be the government's desire to exert monetary control.

An alternative literature focuses on the political-economic motives for regulation. This literature concentrates on the incentives faced by, and political power of, different actors, and views the evolution of regulation as the outcome of the interplay between different interest groups.[5] Groups with greater numbers, financial resources, and cohesion will successfully support regulations that are favourable to them and had an advantage in competition between different interest groups. This literature also considers politicians and regulators as interest groups that may be motivated by the desire for such non-economic goals as larger budgets, staff, and authority, or to advance a particular ideological agenda.

Although the reasons for regulation described above are distinct, in practice it is difficult to disentangle multiple motivations for a particular reform. For example, the National Banking Acts in the United States (1863–64), which established a new type of bank (national bank), a new regulatory authority (the Comptroller of the Currency), and a bond-backed bank-issued currency (national bank notes), could have been passed on any of the grounds cited above. Since the National Banking Acts established uniform and relatively strict guidelines for granting bank charters, they could be viewed as stability-enhancing. Since the law also required publication of bank balance-sheets, they could be viewed as ameliorating an information asymmetry and therefore be viewed as an efficiency-enhancing reform. Alternatively, since the Acts both established a new national currency and drove notes issued by State banks out of circulation, they could be viewed as enhancing the government's monetary control. Finally, since banks chartered under the Acts were required to secure banknote issues with holdings of government bonds, the laws could be viewed as serving the political-economic goal of increasing demand for federal government bonds during the fiscally demanding Civil War.

The difficulty of disentangling the motives for major legislation is not unique to the US National Banking Acts, but could equally be applied to many banking reforms,

---

[4]   F.M. Scherer, *Industrial Market Structure and Economic Performance* (Chicago, 1980).

[5]   G.J. Stigler, 'The Theory of Economic Regulation', *Bell Journal of Economics and Management Science*, 2, 1 (1971), pp. 3–21; S. Peltzman, 'Towards a More General Theory of Regulation', *Journal of Law and Economics*, 19 (1976), pp. 211–40; G. Becker, 'A Theory of Competition Among Pressure Groups for Political Influence', *Quarterly Journal of Economics*, 98, 3 (1983), pp. 371–400; R.S. Kroszner, Is the Financial System Independent? Perspectives on the Political Economy of Banking and Financial Regulation, Paper prepared for Swedish Government Inquiry on the Competitiveness of the Swedish Financial Sector, 1999, focuses specifically on banking and financial regulation.

including Belgium's Banking Decree of 1935, Japan's National Banking Decree of 1872, Sweden's Banking Code of 1846, and the UK's Joint Stock Bank Act of 1844.

Nonetheless, despite the difficulty of ascribing specific motivations to individual pieces of banking legislation, some patterns do emerge. For example, it is clear that countries in which the central bank had a monopoly on note issue waited much longer to enact banking codes; countries in which the note-issue was in the hands of private banks tended to enact banking codes much sooner, suggesting a monetary-control motive for such banking codes.[6]

Arguments for and against Unified Supervision and a Leading Role for the Central Bank

What are the desirable attributes of a system for bank supervision? According to the Basel Committee on Banking Supervision:

> An effective system of banking supervision will have clear responsibilities and objectives for each agency involved in the supervision of banking organizations. Each such agency should possess adequate resources. A suitable legal framework for banking supervision is also necessary, including provision relating to authorization of banking organizations and their ongoing supervision; powers to address compliance with laws as well as safety and soundness concerns; and legal protections for supervisors. Arrangements for sharing information between supervisors and protecting the confidentiality of such information should be in place.[7]

Given these objectives, what are the advantages of a system of unified financial supervision?

One advantage might be greater efficiency if the skills required to oversee different parts of the financial system are similar,[8] and might command greater resources than separate agencies. Additionally, such a unified agency might be better able to oversee large, complex, financial conglomerates that span more than one area of operation (banking, securities, insurance) than separate supervisors.

---

[6] R.S. Grossman, 'Charters, Corporations, and Codes. Entry Restriction in Modern Banking Law', *Financial History Review*, 8, 2 (2001), pp. 107–21.

[7] Basel Committee on Banking Supervision, *Core Principles for Effective Banking Supervision* (Basel, 1997), p. 7.

[8] See C. Briault, The Rationale for a Single Financial Services Regulator, UK Financial Services Authority Occasional Paper 2, 1999; Abrams et al., Issues; J. De Luna Martinez and T.A. Rose, International Survey of Integrated Financial Sector Supervision, World Bank Policy Research Working Paper 3096, 2003; M. Taylor and A. Fleming, Integrated Financial Supervision. Lessons from Northern European Experience, World Bank Policy Research Working Paper 2223, 1999; and Llewellyn, Institutional Structure, for a summary of arguments in favour of and against a unified financial supervisor.

Given that cross-sector mergers have been common in recent years, this argument has taken on additional weight.[9] Additionally, given regulatory competition, a unified financial supervisor would prevent firms from 'forum shopping', that is, seeking the most lenient of all possible supervisors, and would eliminate the need for coordination and information-sharing among different regulators, since a single agency would have authority for overall supervision. A unified system would also prevent unhealthy competition between supervisors, who might be tempted to be lenient in order to attract more firms into their orbit. Finally, a unified agency would be solely and fully accountable for any and all failures of supervision.

A disadvantage of a unified financial supervisor is that each component of the financial sector may require different expertise; hence, forcing all supervisory personnel to come from the same agency might lead to a reduction in overall efficiency. Opponents of unified supervisors question the existence of scale economies and instead argue that the establishment of a unified authority concentrates too much power in the hands of one agency. Finally, a disadvantage might be that such a supervisor would suffer from a lack of clear objectives. Specifically, the supervisor might pressure stronger firms it oversees to come to the aid of weaker institutions (e.g. banks to insurance companies or vice versa), whether or not such aid was desirable from a public-policy perspective (e.g., Japan in the 1990s).

What are the advantages of having the central bank at the head of the supervisory system?

Goodhart et al. find that central banks tend to hire more economists and fewer lawyers than non-central-bank supervisors.[10] They argue that, to the extent that banking instability (i.e., financial crisis) results from macroeconomic causes, the skill-set of central bankers provide better tools with which to promote stability. Central banks are also typically well funded and relatively prestigious institutions, and hence may well be suited to a powerful role in banking supervision as well as macroeconomic policy. One could also argue that there are synergies between macroeconomic policy-making and banking supervision: Peek et al. argue that the detailed bank-level information gathered by financial supervisors can provide central banks an advantage in making monetary policy; additionally, one could argue that the goals of macroeconomic and financial stability reinforce each other.[11]

Of course, the flip side to the synergies-based argument is that the combination of macroeconomic policy-making and banking supervision may lead to a conflict of interest between a central bank's objectives. For example, banking sector instability might encourage the central bank to conduct a more expansionary

---

[9]   Group of Ten, *Report on Consolidation in the Financial Sector* (Basel, 2001).

[10]   C. Goodhart, D. Schoenmaker and P. Dasgupta, 'The Skill Profile of Central Bankers and Supervisors', *European Finance Review* 6, 3 (2002), pp. 397–427.

[11]   J. Peek, E.S. Rosengren and G.M.B. Tootell, 'Synergies between Bank Supervision and Monetary Policy. Implications for the Design of Bank Regulatory Structure', in F.S. Mishkin (ed.), *Prudential Supervision. What Works and What Doesn't* (Chicago, 2001).

monetary policy – in order to relieve pressure on banks – than it would otherwise undertake. Goodhart and Schoenmaker, for example, find that during the 1980–91 and 1980–87 periods, countries in which banking supervision was undertaken by the central bank had higher rates of inflation than those in which monetary policy and bank supervision were conducted by separate institutions.[12] Yet another potential downside is the fact that an institution that combines monetary policy and banking supervision could become all-powerful; this argument is even more persuasive if all financial regulation is combined into the central bank.

The Emergence of Central Banks

Prior to the last quarter of the nineteenth century, there was no accepted concept of a central bank. Although the modern notion of a central bank can be traced as far back as Baring and Thornton around the turn of the nineteenth century, it was only with the publication of Walter Bagehot's classic *Lombard Street* in 1873 that the concept gained widespread acceptance.[13] In most cases central banks, or the institutions that would evolve into what would later be considered central banks, were merely the first government-chartered banking institutions in the country.[14] For example, the central banks of Sweden (1668), England (1694), Finland (1811), Norway (1816), Austria (1816), and Denmark (1818) were the first chartered banks of any sort in these countries.[15] Because many of these institutions

---

[12]   C. Goodhart and D. Schoenmaker, 'Institutional Separation between Supervisory and Monetary Agencies', in C. Goodhart (ed.), *The Central Bank and the Financial System* (Cambridge, 1995). They also point out that monetary policy should, in theory, be counter-cyclical, while the consequences of banking regulation tend to be pro-cyclical (i.e., capital requirements become more biding when the economy slows), again suggesting a conflict in objectives.

[13]   F. Baring, *Observations on the Establishment of the Bank of England, and on the Paper Circulation of the Country* (1797, reprinted London, 1993), H. Thornton, *An Enquiry into the Nature and Effects of the Paper Credit of Great Britain* (1802, reprinted London, 1939), and W. Bagehot, *Lombard Street* (1873, reprinted London, 1924).

[14]   This was not universal, however. The establishment of a system of commercial banks in Japan predated the establishment of the Bank of Japan by a decade. Australia and Canada did not establish central banks until about a century after the foundation of their first commercial joint-stock banks.

[15]   In some cases, they remained the only bank for a considerable period of time, quite possibly because the demand for banking services was low. Following the charter of the Riksbank (1668) in Sweden, no other bank was chartered for more than 150 years; in Finland and Denmark, additional chartered banks were not established for several decades after the founding of the central banks. Following the establishment of the Bank of England, no other joint-stock bank was chartered for 132 years, although this delay was due to legislation that specifically forbade the establishment of joint-stock banks.

were established well before the concept of a central bank, I refer to these early precursors as 'national banks'.

Frequently, national banks were chartered with a public purpose in mind: clearing up monetary disarray (e.g., Denmark, Norway), raising funds for the government (e.g., England), or facilitating trade by extending banking services (e.g., Sweden, the Netherlands). And the new institutions frequently acted as the government's fiscal agent. Despite these public purposes (sometimes combined with provisions granting the government authority to appoint some of the management), national banks were typically private profit-maximizing institutions, albeit with special privileges and/or public responsibilities.

A key motivation for the establishment of many national banks was to clear up monetary disarray. The Bank of Finland, for example, was founded shortly after the country was annexed to Russia, in order to alleviate the problems caused by the side-by-side circulation of several currencies (including Russian and Swedish). The Austrian National Bank was established following several decades that had been characterized by an over-issue of government currency. And the establishment of national banks in Norway (1816) and Denmark (1818) followed a period of monetary confusion, notably the Statsbankerot (state bankruptcy) in Denmark. Later in the nineteenth century, following unification, the German Reichsbank (1876) and Banca d'Italia (1893) were positioned to consolidate several pre-existing note-issuing institutions.

In addition to any role national banks may have been given in sorting out monetary confusion, they were frequently charged with providing government finance. The classic case is the Bank of England, which was granted a charter in return for a loan of £1.2 million. Napoleon's creation of the Bank of France in 1800 was intended to both provide war finance, and establish monetary order following the collapse of the Revolution's inflationary *assignat* regime. Selling points of both the First (1791–1811) and Second (1816–36) Banks of the United States included enhancing the government's ability to raise funds, as well as promoting credit creation and monetary stability.

Other national banks were established to provide credit to the economy and to stimulate commerce. The Netherlands Bank, for example, was created during a period of slack economic activity. In part, it was established to replace the Wisselbanken of Amsterdam and other cities, which had provided credit to merchants and had begun to decline in the 1790s. The National Bank of Belgium was similarly founded to contribute to domestic commerce following revolutions and monetary disturbances of 1848, as well as to issue notes and handle public moneys.

The functions we associate today with central banks were largely absent during the early years of most national banks. Although, as noted above, a number of national banks were founded in order to clear up monetary disarray, only a minority were, in fact, given a monopoly of domestic note upon establishment.[16]

---

[16]   Examples include the central banks of Austria, Belgium, Denmark, and Norway. By contrast, the central banks of France and the Netherlands (50 years), Finland (75), England

The development of the national bank as a banker's bank and keeper of the reserves of the banking system was also a later development. And national banks did not adopt the role of lender of last resort until well after their founding, typically in the late nineteenth or early twentieth century. Hence, although many modern central banks trace their origins to the early nineteenth century, they did not truly become central banks until some years later.

The role of banking supervisor was assuredly not in the plans of the founders of the various national banks. First of all, these banks were often the first chartered commercial bank of any sort established in a country, and frequently the first for many years. It is therefore extremely unlikely that the founders would have had the foresight to envision a situation in which there would be a banking 'system' to supervise. Any pre-existing private banks, typically partnerships which operated without explicit government sanction or charter, would have been well outside the purview of any supervisory apparatus. Second, as noted above, national banks were private, profit-maximizing institutions. Hence, it is unlikely that governments would have put them in charge of supervising their competitors. It is the evolution of national banks into central banks with supervisory authority to which we now turn.

Central Bankers as Supervisors

How did national banks, ostensibly private, profit-maximizing institutions, evolve into central banks, the public institutions frequently entrusted with supervisory responsibility that we know today? Although the story of this evolution is too long and varied to be adequately described here, three factors need to be mentioned.

Among the first tasks that national banks undertook was the discounting of financial instruments, primarily bills of exchange. As domestic and international commerce grew, banks and other financial houses became more involved in issuing and discounting bills of exchange, and national banks became convenient re-discounters. This had implications for the national bank's relationship with other market participants. For example, the Bank of England maintained a close relationship with discount houses, institutions which financed their holdings of acceptances (bills of exchange) with call loans from the joint stock banks, prior to a falling out after the crisis of 1857. Similarly, because of the growth of new credit institutions in the Netherlands in the 1840s, the Netherlands Bank's re-discounting facilities grew substantially. By the time of the passage of it's charter renewal in 1863, which established a number of new branches throughout the Netherlands, the Bank was already interacting almost exclusively with financial firms.

As banking systems developed, informal, then formal, clearing networks developed to settle accounts between individual banks. Since national banks were large, often well-branched institutions, they were ideally situated to become a key member of these clearing systems. The development of clearing systems further

(150), and Sweden (230) were not granted note-issuing monopolies until some years later.

strengthened the role of national banks in holding the banking reserves of the country and acting as a bankers' bank. The earliest known clearing house was established by London private bankers, probably around 1770.[17] London joint-stock bankers were admitted in 1854, country bankers in 1858, and the Bank of England in 1864.[18] The Swedish Riksbank established a clearing institution in 1899, the Bank of France helped to found one in 1901, and the Bank of Finland established an inter-bank clearing in 1906.

Finally, perhaps most importantly in terms of discouraging competition between national banks and other commercial banks was their development into lenders of last resort. This evolution was pioneered in England, starting with the crisis of 1793 and culminating with the rescue of Baring Brothers in 1890. During that period, the Bank of England gradually evolved into a lender of last resort, providing liquidity to a greater or lesser extent against sound collateral when the banking system was faced with crises in 1825, 1836, 1847, 1857, and 1866.[19]

Capie et al.'s catalogue of central bank histories lists a number of instances during the late nineteenth and early twentieth centuries in which central banks first engaged in lender-of-last-resort activity.[20] For example, the Swedish Riksbank, which was explicitly barred by law from supporting private banking, nonetheless engaged in lender-of-last-resort activities in 1897. Capie et al. chronicle similar lender-of-last-resort actions by central banks in France (1889), Norway (1899), Denmark (1908), and Spain (1913–14).

Table 6.2 presents two pieces of information on each of 18 national/central banks from Europe, Australia, Canada, Japan, and the United States: the year of the bank's establishment and the year in which it was given supervisory responsibility for some part of the banking system. The data presented in this table are problematic for a number of reasons.

First, as noted above, the establishment of a national bank need not signify the establishment of a central bank. Indeed, the Bank of England can be said to have operated for more than a century before taking on the role of a central bank; the Riksbank, for more than two centuries. Nonetheless, Table 6.2 reports the date of the establishment of the national bank, not the year in which it evolved into a central bank, for two reasons: (1) it is impossible to precisely when the transition from national bank to central bank was complete; (2) the date of establishment of

---

[17]   The origin of the London clearing house 'seems to be shrouded in doubt and uncertainty'. The first written evidence of the clearing house dates from 1773. J.G. Cannon, *Clearing-houses. Their History, Methods and Administration* (New York, 1900).

[18]   J.H. Clapham, *The Bank of England. A History* (Cambridge, 1945), vol. 2, pp. 250f.

[19]   It could be argued that a properly functioning lender of last resort constitutes, in some sense, a substitute for a banking supervisor. The latter ensures (among other things) that banks maintain safe levels of reserves; the former ensures that banks that main safe levels of reserves will have adequate liquidity in times of crisis.

[20]   F. Capie, C. Goodhart, S. Fischer and N. Schnadt, *The Future of Central Banking. The Tercentenary Symposium of the Bank of England* (Cambridge, 1994), Appendix B.

the national bank is perhaps more indicative of how firmly established the bank was as a national institution.

Table 6.2   Central/National Banks: Establishment and year given formal responsibility as banking supervisor

| Country | Year | | Bank Name |
	established	supervisor	
Australia	1911	1945	Commonwealth Bank of Australia (1959: Reserve Bank of Australia)
Austria	1816		Oesterreichische Nationalbank
Belgium	1850		Banque Nationale de Belgique
Canada	1934		Bank of Canada
Denmark	1818		Denmarks Nationalbank
Finland	1811		Suomen Pankki
France	1800	1945	Banque de France
Germany	1876	1934	Reichsbank
Italy	1893	1926	Banca d'Italia
Japan	1882	1928	Nippon Ginko
Netherlands	1814	1948	De Nederlandsche Bank
Norway	1816		Norges Bank
Portugal	1846	1925	Banco de Portugal
Spain	1856	1921	Banco de España
Sweden	1668		Sveriges Riksbank
Switzerland	1907		Swiss National Bank
United Kingdom	1694	1946	Bank of England
United States	1914	1914	Federal Reserve System

Average year of establishment
   Central banks that did not become supervisors: 1828
   Central banks that did become supervisors: 1849

Source: F. Capie, C. Goodhart, S. Fischer, and N. Schnadt, *The Future of Central Banking* (Cambridge, 1994).

Second, Table 6.2 indicates the date from which a central bank took formal responsibility for banking supervision. One could argue that the Bank of England, through its supervision of the discount houses, was the banking supervisor in all but name from the later part of the nineteenth century, despite the fact that the Bank was not granted formal supervisory authority until 1946. The Netherlands Bank presents an even more complicated case: the Bank acted as informal supervisor of the Dutch banking system as early as 1900. By 1920, banks had regular consultations with the Bank about lending activities, and by 1931 began voluntarily submitting quarterly returns to the Bank. Formal supervisory authority was not granted to the Bank, however, until 1948. Similarly, the Bank of Portugal had informal supervisory responsibility from 1925, but no formal responsibility until 1975.[21]

Third, Table 6.2 merely notes the date at which supervisory authority was legally granted to the central bank: it provides no data on how extensive supervisory powers were or if those powers changed over time. For example, the Reichsbank was granted extensive supervisory authority over the German banking system under the commercial banking code of 1934. Five years later, however, most supervisory and regulatory authority was transferred to the Ministry of Economics under a revised banking law. In other countries, supervisory powers were both less extensive and more stable.

Despite these shortcomings, the data can help to explain the timing and pattern of countries in which the central bank became the main banking supervisor. In no country did the central bank gain formal responsibility for banking supervision until the twentieth century. In fact, aside from the US Federal Reserve which assumed some supervisory functions upon its establishment in 1914, no central bank was given supervisory authority prior to the end of the First World War. Thus, by the time supervisory authority was entrusted to the national banks, most had already acted as lender of last resort and were no longer in active competition with the institutions that they would oversee.

Considering the countries in which the central bank was never granted responsibility for banking supervision, two patterns stand out. First, none of the Nordic countries (Denmark, Finland, Norway, and Sweden) ever entrusted banking supervision to their central banks. Second, central banks that did become banking supervisors were, on average, founded 20 years later than those that did not become banking supervisors. What can explain these two phenomena?

The Nordic experience can be partially explained by the history of the evolution of the Swedish Riksbank, the world's first national bank. The Riksbank had its origins in a private bank, Stockholms Banco, founded by Johan Palmstruch in 1656. At the time he granted the charter, King Karl X Gustav also established an office of the Chief Inspector of Banks to supervise the new institution.[22] In 1660, the king died and was succeeded by his four-year-old son, Karl XI. During Karl XI's regency, the balance of political power shifted from the monarch to the Diet of the Four Estates (i.e., the Parliament): when Stockholms Banco failed in 1664, the reconstituted bank, Riksens Ständers Bank, or Estates of the Realm Bank, was taken over by the Diet. The eighteenth and much of the nineteenth century witnessed a power struggle between the Diet, which controlled the Riksbank and the national budget, and the king and his bureaucracy, which maintained a monopoly on financial legislation. One result of this struggle was the reluctance of the executive to cede financial power – including the power to supervise banks – to the Riksbank. The next Nordic national bank to be founded, the Suomen

---

[21]   Ibid.

[22]   Finansinspektionen (Swedish Financial Supervisory Authority) web site (http://www.fi.se/Templates/Page____3127.aspx).

Pankki (Bank of Finland), was very much patterned on the Riksbank and it is not surprising that, like the Riksbank, it took no important part in bank regulation.

Another reason that central banks were not involved in bank supervision in the Nordic countries was the presence of well-developed savings banks systems. Savings banks, which were established during the first half of the nineteenth century, were completely distinct from the less well-developed commercial banks and from the national banks. Because of their importance to a large segment of the population, governments had more of an incentive to regulate the activities of savings banks than of commercial banks. Later in the nineteenth century, both Denmark and Norway adopted systems of savings bank regulation (neither adopted commercial bank regulation prior to the twentieth century), including the establishment of a bank inspectorate. In Norway, the savings bank inspectorate was given authority to supervise commercial banks when the first law regulating commercial banks was passed in 1924.

As noted above, national banks that eventually became banking supervisors were founded, on average, 20 years earlier than those that did not become supervisors.[23] What can account for this? One possibility is that younger institutions were more flexible and better able to adapt to include the role of banking supervisor. This might explain why a new institution, the US Federal Reserve, was given some supervisory powers upon its establishment in 1914. Following a severe banking crisis in 1907, Congress created the National Monetary Commission to investigate the working of the banking and monetary system and suggest ways of increasing stability. This led to the establishment of the Federal Reserve System. By contrast, the Bank of Canada, also established in the aftermath of a severe crisis (the Great Depression), did not come into being with any supervisory powers. This was most likely the case because the Canadian banking system – if not the economy as a whole – was quite stable during the Depression.[24]

Of the three next-youngest central banks, Switzerland (1907), Italy (1893), and Japan (1882), those of both Italy and Japan were eventually given responsibility for banking supervision, while the Swiss National Bank was not. Switzerland's experience may be explained by the failure of an earlier attempt to establish a central bank. A proposal for a publicly-owned central bank was defeated in a referendum held on 28 February 1897 (by a vote of 255,984 to 195,764).[25] Among the reasons for the defeat of the referendum were fear of creating a centralized and too-powerful institution.[26] Hence, when the Swiss National Bank was finally

---

[23]   The difference is not, however, statistically significant.

[24]   M.D. Bordo and A. Redish, 'Why Did the Bank of Canada Emerge in 1935?', *Journal of Economic History*, 47, 2 (1987), pp. 405–17, discuss the motivation behind the establishment of the Bank of Canada.

[25]   J. Landmann, 'The Swiss National Bank', *Quarterly Journal of Economics*, 20 (May 1906), pp. 468–82.

[26]   M. Sandoz, 'The Bank-Note System of Switzerland', *Quarterly Journal of Economics*, 1 (April 1898), pp. 280–306, p. 304.

established by less ambitious legislation enacted in 1905, it was created with relatively circumscribed powers.

Does this pattern of younger central banks being more likely to be granted supervisory powers hold when we consider all countries in the sample that eventually did grant supervisory powers to their central banks? The data from Table 6.2 displayed in Figure 6.1 suggest that it does. Younger central banks were typically granted supervisory powers earlier than older central banks.[27] Is it reasonable to suggest that differences of a matter of decades in central-bank age led to much smaller differences in the date of granting the central bank supervisory powers? Without more detailed analyses of the political and economic processes in each country, we cannot conclusively answer this question. Nonetheless, the data presented in Figure 6.1 on those countries that eventually did grant their central banks supervisory powers, combined with information on those countries where the central bank was not given a role in banking supervision, is suggestive.

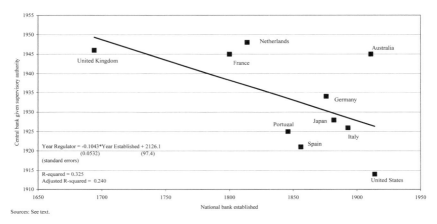

Figure 6.1   Central/National Banks: Establishment and designation as banking supervisor

Conclusion and Extensions

The approach of this chapter has been to take a comparative look at the evolution of central banks and banking supervision in a sample of 18 currently developed countries in order to discern any patterns among countries that entrusted banking supervision to their central banks and those that did not.

The results suggest two conclusions. First, younger central banks were more likely to be called upon to become banking supervisors than their older

---

[27]   The coefficient on the estimated trend line has a p-value of 0.0855. If the UK data point is omitted, the trend remains negative; however, the p-value rises to 0.171.

counterparts. Second, among central banks that were entrusted with banking supervision, younger banks were typically given this task earlier than older banks. These results can be explained by the fact that younger banks were less entrenched in their means of operation, and were perhaps flexible enough to adapt to the dual role of monetary policy-maker and banking supervisor. Older banks were less adaptable and required more time to be brought into this new role – some were not brought in at all.

It is worth returning to two questions that were raised earlier in the chapter and only tangentially addressed in the analysis presented here. First, why are less-developed countries more inclined to have the central bank involved in bank supervision than more developed countries? Second, do the results presented here explain which countries have adopted – and predict which countries will adopt – a unified financial supervisor? Although the answers to these questions await more rigorous analysis, the results presented in this chapter suggest some answers.

One reason for the prominence of central banks in commercial-banking regulation among less-developed countries may be the importance of central banks as institutions. Among newly independent countries, central banks are typically among the first institutions formed, since political independence and monetary independence usually go hand-in-hand. By virtue of their position, they are powerful, prestigious, well funded, and professionally staffed, and hence are well situated to take the lead in financial regulation. They frequently enjoy some degree of autonomy, which may be seen as an advantage in a financial supervisor. Although some of these countries have, and others may yet develop, independent, professional banking regulators, central bankers may well retain an advantage in this field.

A cursory glance at the list of countries that have moved to a unified supervisor suggests a history-based explanation. Among the first countries to move to the unified framework were the Nordic countries – countries in which the central bank has never held supervisory authority over the banking system. Austria, another country in which the central bank never had supervisory authority, has also moved to a unified regulator.[28] Prominent among countries that have taken supervisory authority away from the central bank and given it to a unified agency is Britain – suggestively, among the last of the countries in the sample to grant the central bank supervisory authority.

One conclusion that can be drawn from the above analysis is that central banks, like many institutions, are reluctant to give up powers. The prestige of central bankers – and their ability to resist political power to strip them of the role of banking supervisor – is not limited to the developing world. If this is the case, we would expect to see unified regulators appear where banking supervision is currently outside the purview of the central bank.

---

[28] Categorizations of countries as having unified regulator are not uniform. See De Luna Martinez and Rose, 'International Survey'.

CHAPTER 7

Regulation and Supervision: The Rise of Central Banks' Research Departments*

Pablo Martín-Aceña and Teresa Tortella

Introduction

There have not been many studies on the origins of European central banks' research departments. We know only the work by Ercole Tuccimei (*La ricerca economica a Via Nazionale. Una storia degli 'Studi' da Canovai a Baffi*, 1894–1940), and the book by Pablo Martín-Aceña, *El Servicio de Estudios del Banco de España, 1930–2000*, published some years back. We may add to these the excellent volume published recently by Olivier Feiertag (*Mesurer la monnaie. Banques centrales et construction de l'autorité monétaire, XIXe–XXe siècle*), which includes chapters on the inception of the research departments of Belgium (Ivo Maes and Erik Buyst), Italy (Rosanna Scatamacchia), Spain (Martín-Aceña) and some references to that of the Bank of France (Alain Plessis).

It has not been possible to supplement this lack of references despite having exhaustively trawled the websites of each of the institutions currently comprising the Eurosystem. The information obtained on them refers solely to the current activities of their research departments. We have therefore had to confine our presentation to explaining why research departments were created, and saying something about the people that launched them, for those central banks from which we received information.[1] Moreover, we have compared the salient features of the two Mediterranean countries' departments (Italy and Spain), on which we have the most abundant information.

---

* We would like to thank Ivo Maes from the Bank of Belgium; Sophia Lazaretou and Georgios Mitrofanis from the Bank of Greece; Luis Abreu Nunes and Maria Stella Pereira from the Bank of Portugal; and Joke Mooij from the Nederlandsche Bank, for their help in providing information. We are also grateful to Olivier Feiertag, Alfredo Gigliobianco and Jaime Reis for their suggestions.

[1] It is highly possible there are more articles or monographic studies on this subject, but we have not been able to find them. Nor is there any material on the central banks' websites, except for the activities and publications of recent years. Naturally, our search for information may be assumed to have been limited to date, and our linguistic constraints (material has been sought only in French, English, Italian, Spanish and Portuguese) have prevented us from gaining access to sources written in languages unfamiliar to us.

The oldest research departments were instituted in the three central banks on which much of European financial history in the nineteenth and first third of the twentieth century turned: the Bank of England, the Bank of France and the Bank of Germany. Towards 1900 the three had an office that was responsible for compiling statistics, preparing reports and, where necessary, advising their senior officials. At the remaining European central banks, research offices came into being after the First World War, either in the 1920s (Belgium and Italy, for example), or in the 1930s (Portugal and Spain). A notable exception was the Bank of Greece, belatedly established in 1928, which did not create a research centre until 1956.

That today's central banks did not have research centres or units from the outset is not surprising, since their original functions were confined to issuing banknotes and financing the governments of the day, in addition to operating like any other credit institution. State-regulated as they were, they enjoyed the privilege for the issue of banknotes, but they took some time to assume the functions of genuine central banks with true independence from government, i.e. as monetary policy-makers and as supervisors of their respective financial systems. Indeed, the later they took control of these tasks, the later the creation of research departments and the hiring of economic experts to man them.

In all the cases known to us, the creation of research departments was in response to a common impulse: the need for information on developments in the domestic economy. They were set up to meet the demands for information and advice by the upper echelons of the institutions, who needed to understand financial phenomena and had to act in an increasingly complex economic world. Further, there are particular or national motivations in each of the cases analysed, though the common elements admittedly prevail over the possible differences.

The Beginnings – An Overview

The trigger to establish a research centre at the Bank of France was the publication in 1880 of 'International Statistics of Issuance Banks (*Statistique internationale des banques d'émission*), whose content highlighted the scant contribution of data by the French central bank. Its volume of information was less than that of other issuing institutions featuring in the publication, such as the banks of Germany, Austria-Hungary, Belgium and, above all, the Bank of England. This latter institution already had an effective statistical service whereas its French counterpart did not have a true research office. The Bank of France took due note of its lack of preparedness and of its lag in relation to the Bank of England, and it concluded that the reason for this was that it did not have a true statistical research service. The upshot was the creation in 1894 of its *Bureau des études économiques*.

In Belgium's case, the serious economic difficulties unleashed by the First World War triggered the organization of a research department in its central bank. The inflationary spiral and the heavy depreciation of its currency led the country to a real economic abyss. The search for solutions underscored the pressing need to improve understanding and analysis of monetary phenomena, and hence, amid an economic and monetary storm, the Bank created its *Service d'analyse économique* in 1921.

Having been re-founded in 1894, the Bank of Italy faced a series of problems in its gradual conversion into a central bank. In the 90s, the crisis affecting not only the credit system but the entire economic and financial community and even the structures of the State in Italy was at the root of a small research unit being established to obtain information so as to ascertain what was happening in the country's economy. Thus, the *Ufficio Gabinetto del Direttore Generale* came into being, the seed that would grow over time into a true research office. The latter was created in 1926, when the Bank was legally recognized and was granted the monopoly of currency issuing and entrusted, moreover, with the supervision of credit institutions. The former *Ufficio* was, along with the library, regrouped in an Economic and Statistical Research Department.

The Bank of Portugal's *Divisão de Estatística e Estudos Económicos* was founded in March 1932, though a unit called *Estatística e Arquivo*, which reported to the General Accounting department, had been in place since 1888. In 1930, this unit took the name *Arquivo, Estatística e Estudos Económicos*, and it may be considered as the immediate predecessor of the true research office, which was opened following the reform of the Bank's statutes in 1931. As in other countries, the roots of the research department must be sought in the need for sound quantitative and economic information. The Statistical Division had to take responsibility for analysing world economic policy, compiling bank legislation from other countries and drafting bulletins and reports, along with the Bank's official monthly and annual reports.

The Bank of Greece Economic Research Section was created in May 1928, above all to advise the Bank's management on monetary policy matters and the analysis of the country's general economic situation. From the outset it also conducted studies relating directly to central bank functions, and the departmental staff collaborated in the drafting of the annual report.

As for the Bank of Spain, the direct reason was the severe foreign-exchange crisis of the early 1930s and the Spanish authorities' wish to set the gold standard in place. This drove the Bank's governor to seek help in Paris, specifically at the Bank of France; in London, at the Bank of England; and in Basel, at the Bank for International Settlements. Senior officials at these institutions recommended the creation of a *Servicio de Estudios* (*Research Department*) with an expert staff that could offer advice on the questions of the day. The unit was created in December 1930 and commenced working in January 1931.

A significant common factor to all the cases studied is the link between research departments and the specialized libraries created within central banks. Indeed, if the banks were lacking documentation centres, these were created at the same time as the research offices; and in the banks that already had libraries, these were incorporated into the respective research services. In their capacity as specialized documentation centres, they would receive papers and reports from other central banks, international statistics, economics journals and the financial press.

The Human Factor

From the outset, research departments were staffed with leading and brilliant economists, most drawn from academia. An exceptional figure, in terms of intellect and personality, was usually involved, and one capable of attracting young economists who would form the initial core from which the research unit developed. The other catalyst was the Bank's senior management; very often it was the governor who, concerned to improve the management of the institution, considered it necessary to set in place a small group of monetary and financial experts to advise him.

In France's case the original key personalities were Pierre Des Essars, a mathematician and linguist well connected with French academia, and his assistant Georges Roulleau, a fellow mathematician from the Parisian Higher School of Commerce and the author of numerous articles on economics and statistics in the leading French journals of the time. Jules Décamps joined them in the 20s and later, in the 30s, the outstanding figure of Pierre Quesnay emerged, and he, after having been at the helm of the Bank of France Research Department for several years, moved in 1930 to head the Directorate-General of the Bank for International Settlements in Basel. Throughout this period, the governor, Georges Pallain, played a decisive role in the French central bank. During his term of office he actively promoted the Research Department, providing it with resources that allowed for an improvement in statistical studies, which in turn resulted in an enhancement and modernization of the information available to the Bank's senior management for decision-making purposes. They then began to change the structures of the Bank, commencing the process of converting it into a true central institute.

In Belgium, the key figures were Albert-Édouard Janssen and his eminent pupil Paul Van Zeeland. Janssen joined the Bank in 1908 and rose to the position of Director-General in 1919, where he set about organizing the Research Department. Here he was able to count on the young Van Zeeland, a graduate from the universities of Leuven and Princeton. In the United States, he attended courses imparted by the then famous 'money doctor' Edwin Kemmerer, and worked for some time at the US Federal Reserve. It was Van Zeeland who, at the behest of his mentor Janssen, structured the Department and assumed leadership of it in 1921. It was he, too, who recruited young economists as researchers for the Department. He pursued his career in the Bank and was promoted first to General Secretary in 1924, to Director-General in 1926 and to Deputy Governor in 1934. He was later appointed Minister of Finance and, eventually, Prime Minister in 1935.

In Italy, several personalities shared the honour of promoting the creation of the Bank's Research Department, though it was during the mandate of Bonaldo Stringher, one of the most respected and important governors in the history of the Italian central bank, that a true research and advisory office took root. Its management was entrusted to Tito Canovai and Giovanni Santoponte, two outstanding figures who were capable of attracting to the Bank several notable students whose contributions helped bring about the objectives set. Among these was Paolo Baffi, from the Milan Bocconi University and the London School of Economics; Alberto Campolongo, another Bocconi doctor in economics; the Neapolitan Agostino De Vita, a doctor in economics from the University of Rome and a graduate in statistics, and Giuseppe Di Nardi, a doctor in economics and commerce from the University of Bari and author of an excellent economic history of nineteenth-century Italian banking.

In Portugal, the man credited with establishing and heading the Research Department for several years is Antonio Carlos de Sousa, who joined the Bank in 1918 as an accounts-department employee. A self-taught man, de Sousa devoted his life to the study of economics and finance and became a genuine expert, and the owner moreover of an enormous specialized book collection. In 1932 he was appointed Head of the *Divisão de Estatística e Estudos Económicos* and later, in 1948, Director of the Statistical Services, a position he held until his retirement in 1965.

In Greece, the Economic Research Section, born under the supervision of the General Secretariat, was headed from the outset by Kyriakos Varvaressos, a university professor of economics. He later became a prominent figure in the history of the Bank: deputy governor from 1933 to 1939 and governor from 1939 to 1945. This whole period includes the harsh years of the Second World War, when the country was occupied by German military forces and the Greek Government went into exile. After the liberation of Greece, the Bank's officials returned to Athens and the Economic Research Section resumed its ordinary tasks. Ten years later, in 1955, the Section was renamed and expanded into a fully-fledged Economic Research Department.

At the Bank of Spain we also had two reputable economists from the academic world who had rounded off their academic grounding with stays at European university centres. Both were very familiar with advances in theory and well-trained in mathematics and statistics: on one hand Olegario Fernández Baños, the University of Santiago Professor, and on the other Germán Bernácer, a professor from the Alicante School of Commerce and unquestionably then one of Spain's most prestigious economists.

The Research Departments of the Central Banks of Italy and Spain

The year the *Servizio Studi Economici e Statistica* was created was 1926 but, as Tuccimei indicates, economic research in the Italian central bank should be dated back further to its very origins. Indeed, when the Bank of Italy was created in 1894, the first governor (known then as director-general), Giuseppe Marchiori, wanted to be well informed of the relationship between issuing and credit activity, so as to be able to regulate the financial market when necessary. To do this he established the *Ufficio Gabinetto del Direttore Generale*, which was responsible for collecting economic information published in Italy and abroad and also for translating the most recommended foreign economics papers, particularly those from France and the United Kingdom. He also ordered that a library linked to the recently created *Gabinetto* be set up. To head the *Ufficio*, he chose Tito Canovai, an eminent liberal lawyer and economist well versed in finance and the currency. The reform of the Bank in 1899 extended the powers of the *Ufficio Gabinetto*, entrusting it with the monitoring of the country's economic situation and of developments on international financial markets, and also with compiling statistics on both credit and saving institutions and on industrial and mercantile companies.

When Machiori died he was replaced by Bonaldo Stringher, a forceful personality who shaped the course of the Bank of Italy until his death in 1930. The new governor achieved greater independence for the institution vis-à-vis the Treasury, against which he stood up when necessary. His political power was reinforced thanks to the role he played in the serious 1907 and 1911 crises. As a result, the *Via Nazionale* institution gained in authority and raised its status above that of the rest of the banking system. After the First World War, the Bank was faced with new obligations, such as the search for external financing and the regulation of the foreign exchange market. To face up to the economic complexity of a world in flux, Stringher reinforced and raised the profile of the *Servizio Gabinetto*. He appointed Tito Canovai as deputy director general and created within the *Servizio* an *Ufficio Studi Economici e Finanziari* headed by Giovanni Santoponte, a prolific writer on economic matters and an expert on topical European and North African monetary and financial affairs. Also assigned to the *Servizio Gabinetto* were a press and foreign correspondence office and, of course, an excellent library.

Further to the 1926 monetary reform, the outcome of Stringher's wishes to transform the Italian institution into a true central bank, the Bank assumed the currency-issuing monopoly previously shared with Bank of Naples and Bank of Sicily and took charge of the supervision of the financial system. The reform of its statutes created the post of governor for Stringher, while his number two, Vincenzo Azzolini, was appointed director-general, and Niccola Introna deputy director-general. Now with full powers in the Bank of Italy, Stringher changed the former *Servizio Gabinetto* into the *Servizio Studi Economici e Statistica*, with Santoponte at its head. Divided in turn into an *Ufficio Studi Economici e Finanziari*, headed by C. Rodella, and an *Ufficio Statistica e Biblioteca*, the unit was entrusted with monitoring money markets, compiling corporate documentation, drafting papers and reports, and guiding and advising the Bank's senior management, in particular the governor and the director-general. As Stringher wanted the Bank of Italy to be active on the international stage, he asked the *Servizio* members to remain in permanent contact with the main central banks' research departments.

Between 1926 and 1930, Santoponte and Rodella pursued their activities intensely in the wake of the dynamism deployed by Stringher. They were most competent in responding to the demands and events of the period, for example the stabilization of the lira in 1927, which took up much of the time of those at the head of the *Servizio*. They had to monitor the main international monetary and financial events closely and accurately in order to keep the governor well informed. And yet the number of people working in the unit was small: there were no more than ten people during these years and its position in the Bank's structure was a relatively marginal one, something Rodella complained about on several occasions.

The 1936 banking law, with Azzolini in place as governor, prompted a reform process which converted the Bank of Italy into a public agency. Azzolini took two important measures: to strengthen the internal organization of the *Servizio* and to call on young university graduates to join the department. As a result, four exceptional economists arrived at the Bank of Italy: Baffi, who would become director at the end of the war; Campolongo, De Vita and Di Nardi. Up to nineteen young researchers joined the department with them. With the collaboration of G. Mortara, areas of work were assigned: twelve on the Italian economy and fourteen on the international economy, a specific subject being apportioned to each researcher.

Between 1936 and 1939, the tasks typical for a bank research department were pursued: notes, reports and papers on the agricultural and industrial situation, on international economic developments, on stock-market fluctuations and on foreign-exchange movements, inter alia. The team made up of Baffi, Campolongo, De Vita and Di Nardi also conducted other relevant analyses, including most notably *Statistica Del credito per rami di attività economica* and *L'economia italiana nel sessennio 1931–36*. On one occasion, the fascist authorities asked the *Servizio* to research into the possibilities of setting in place in the short term an autarkic economy so as to give the country the same economic independence that Germany enjoyed. The response from Rodella and Baffi, transmitted to Azzolini, was quite clear: the German model was not applicable in Italy: '[…] L'applicabilità in Italia del modello tedesco, nonostante alcune analogie formali tra i due sistemi, non era proponibile'. One of the reasons given was the scant capacity to generate domestic saving to finance the major investment that such an autarkic strategy would require.

In 1938, Rodella, now director of the *Servizio* (which adopted the name of *Uffici Studi* that year), proposed several reforms to the governor to strengthen the unit, but none prospered. Shortly afterwards, the *Uffici Studi* entered a lengthy period of lethargy: as from 1940, with Italy participating in the Second World War, its activity was drastically cut. Its members, men in the main, were enlisted in the army and their work duly interrupted. Moreover, much of the department's raison d'être was lost, as the war meant that the bank abandoned its monetary policy-setting functions and became, in the words of Luigi Einaudi, the 'longa manus' (long arm) of the Treasury. Only after Rome's liberation by Allied troops in 1944 could the Department, under its former name of *Servizio Studi Economici e Statistica*, resume its work under Paolo Baffi.

The Research Department of the Bank of Spain commenced operating on 2 January 1931. It had the direct support of governor Federico Bas, who in turn was able to count on advice from the Bank of France and, in particular, on personal assistance from Quesnay and his collaborators. The previous year, the Spanish authorities had decided to adopt measures to stabilize the peseta, which was buffeted by strong oscillations owing to the country's political instability and its economic and financial imbalances (the budget and balance-of-payments deficits), inherited from the earlier Dictatorship (1923–29). To do this, they sought the collaboration and advice of European central banks and travelled to Paris, London and also to Basel, the headquarters of the recently created Bank for International Settlements. In Paris, the scene of the most decisive meetings, Bas and a group of experts met Moret, then governor of the Bank of France, and Quesnay, who undertook to design a programme to stabilize the Spanish currency. The report drafted by the French expert contained an essential recommendation: the creation of an economic research unit to analyse developments in the Spanish economy, compile statistics, produce reports and advise the authorities of the Bank and the Ministry of Finance.

To set the Research Department in train, two highly prestigious personalities were engaged: the statistician, mathematician and University of Santiago professor Olegario Fernández Baños, and the high-ranking Treasury official José Larraz. The latter left after a short time, being replaced by Germán Bernácer, an economic theorist of the Keynesian school and director of one of the country's most reputable economics journals. Both co-led the Department until the Civil War, and managed in these few short years to draw together an excellent team. The unit, small in size and on the fringes of the Bank's traditional organization, was divided into three sections: the first covered economic, financial and monetary studies; the second, translation, documentation and library; and the third was entrusted with preparing the stabilization of the peseta, an objective which, given the international economic situation in the early years of that decade, never materialized.

Up until the Civil War, the work of the Research Department, comprising two deputy directors and a small staff, was most intense. There were three key areas of work. The first involved the preparation of reports on Spanish and worldwide economic developments; the best work on the repercussions of the international crisis in Spain, *Ritmo de la crisis económica española en relación con la mundial* (Pace of the Spanish economic crisis in relation to the worldwide crisis), was drafted and completed in 1933. It examined the effects of the Depression and highlighted how this was less acute in Spain owing to the country's agricultural nature and to its lesser degree of external openness. The Department's second mission was to advise the Governing Council of the Bank of Spain and also the Ministry of Finance. As the priority areas in those years were the oscillations of the peseta exchange rate and interest-rate policy, the numerous reports by Fernández-Baños and by Bernácer focused on these two matters. As regards exchange-rate policy, the Research Department economists supported the idea of currency stability, as opposed to the concept of stabilization advocated by the Ministry of Finance. And in opposition to the revaluation intentions of the Bank of Spain Board members, the Research Department economists maintained that adopting the gold standard at that time would be harmful to the Spanish economy; they stated that in order to achieve stabilization, it was necessary beforehand to accommodate monetary and fiscal policy to the needs of exchange-rate policy and that revaluation was not advisable since, according to the results of their studies, the depreciation of the peseta partially isolated the Spanish economy from global deflation since it alleviated the attendant effects on domestic output and industrial employment. For example, in the wake of sterling abandoning the gold standard in September 1931, the Research Department came out in favour of letting the peseta fall and maintaining the stability of domestic prices. They also opposed the policy adopted by the Spanish authorities of keeping the peseta pegged to the French franc.

As regards interest rates, the Research Department's position also ran counter to that of the Ministry of Finance, which was firmly in favour of reducing the cost of money. Since the Bank's economists rejected the monetarist interpretation of the Spanish crisis, they naturally had doubts about the effectiveness of cutting discount rates. Their position throughout the five-year period was that the 'cheap-money policy' would not resolve the serious problems besetting the economy, nor was it a measure that as such could kick-start economic activities that had ground to a halt.

The third area of work involved the search for and reconstruction of economic and financial statistics. In this field the Research Department's work was incessant and truly commendable. In a few short years bank and savings-bank balance sheets were collected and used to estimate 'banking pressure' variables to measure the system's liquidity; the prices of all securities on the three Spanish stock exchanges were brought together, and fixed-income and variable-yield indices were constructed; the Department put together the exchange rates of the peseta and all international currencies; and it compiled highly extensive information on domestic and international prices, drew up consumer and wholesale price indices and also calculated purchasing-power parities, an indicator much in vogue in those years. The Research Department's statistical office also set about gathering together all the information (until then widely dispersed) on agricultural and industrial output, electricity and raw-materials consumption, foreign trade and gold movements, among others. Thanks to its Research Department, the Bank of Spain had by 1935 the biggest and best database on the country's economy and had become the chief producer of statistics.

Yet undoubtedly the most important statistical research was the reconstruction of the Spanish balance of payments for the 1931–34 period. Responsible for this was Francisco Jainaga, an exceptional statistician who was murdered in Madrid in the first weeks of the Civil War. With patience, accuracy and skill, Jainaga compiled data on each of the items of the balances on trade and on services, and also on capital movements. He picked his way through documentation in archives and public and private centres, in libraries, in national and foreign companies, and he also sent a questionnaire to thousands of exporters and importers, companies, consulates and any other agency that might provide him with data. The end result was a magnificent and to date still unsurpassed piece of work. It was thanks to the statistical toils of Jainaga and other Research Department statisticians that Fernández-Baños and Bernácer were able to perform their functions.

The Civil War interrupted the promising future of the Research Department, just as the World War would later curtail the activities of the Italian Research Department. But unlike the latter, which managed to recover as from 1944 thanks to Baffi, the Spanish department fell into a state of protracted lethargy for almost two decades until 1957 when Juan Sardá, a cosmopolitan, influential and Keynesian-school economist, arrived at the Bank at the very time a shift was being prepared in the Franco regime's autarkic policy.

Conclusions

Currently, all central banks operating on the global stage have long-standing and soundly structured in-house research departments amply staffed by experts in all branches of economics. Their economists are influential and their opinions respected and – on many occasions – followed by the monetary authorities. It is not rare for research-department staff to have risen through the ranks to the very top positions of their institutions.

At the outset, however, research departments were small offices with few staff and on the fringes of the organic structure of central banks. They were created to meet the demand for advice in an increasingly complex economic world, and were developed when issuing-bank chiefs, owner-bankers with a traditional background and grounding, voluntarily or obligatorily became central bankers. The vertigo they experienced in having to assume the functions of a monetary authority led them to seek the help of economists.

Among known cases, the history of research departments is indeed a success story. Over time, they consolidated their influence and power within and beyond the central banks in which they were born. And from that starting point they have contributed to increasing the country's statistical pool and have participated decisively in the build-up of human capital, attracting and training young economists and professionals from various fields of science and the humanities.

CHAPTER 8

The Regulation of International Financial Markets from the 1950s to the 1990s

Catherine R. Schenk

After 1945, the regulation of international financial markets became more intense and widespread as part of the system designed to avoid the chaos that had characterized international economic relations in the 1930s. This chapter examines how the postwar consensus about the usefulness of regulating capital flows evolved after the advent of current-account convertibility in 1959. First, an examination of the debate over regulating the Eurodollar market will be used to highlight the contrast between European attitudes to capital markets compared to the views of the USA and the UK, where the differences are not as firm or as reliable as has been portrayed. The archival evidence shows that there were lively concerns about the dangers of the market and vigorous internal discussion about intervention as well as regulation in both London and Washington, and also among banks themselves. Nevertheless, both American and British regulators resisted introducing controls because the benefits of the market for their balance-of-payments policies outweighed the threats. This is not to say that the British and Americans were opposed to capital controls per se. Indeed, this was a time of deliberate intensification of capital controls in the USA on US$ outflows, and in the UK on sterling transactions. This analysis shows that the traditional story, that market innovation undermined the effectiveness of capital controls and therefore led to the collapse of the Bretton Woods system, needs to be adjusted to take account of regulators' roles in allowing that innovation to spread, and how the US and UK deliberately used the market as part of their response to the imbalances in the international economy in the 1960s.

The next part of the chapter develops the history of prudential regulation and supervision of international banking that began after the end of the Bretton Woods system. This area has remained a challenge for regulators for much the same reasons that were present in the 1970s: problems of enforcement, the privacy of banking business, and the primacy of national over international interests. A second theme of the chapter, therefore, is the enduring conflict between the desire to have national sovereignty over financial markets on the one hand, and the need for supranational oversight to ensure consistency and enforcement of prudential supervision and regulation in an increasingly global market.

I

The regulation of international financial markets in the 1950s and 1960s was closely linked to the Bretton Woods solution to the 'trilemma' or 'impossible trinity', which explains that maintaining policy sovereignty in the context of fixed exchange rates requires imposing limits on international capital flows.[1] The over-riding goals of national economic growth and full employment as well as the development of welfare states after 1945 required that national sovereignty was prioritized over freer capital flows.[2] Countries with balance-of-payments deficits used direct controls on outflows to avoid relying solely on higher domestic interest rates. Conversely, countries with pressures for surplus and inflation used regulations to protect their domestic monetary systems from inflows of capital.

The terms of the Bretton Woods agreement reflected a broad international consensus that freer markets in goods were beneficial for growth, employment and incomes overall, but that international financial markets should be closely regulated.[3] While the link between freer trade and growth is fairly well established, there is still no such consensus for the link between liberalization of financial markets and growth. It makes sense to assume that freer capital markets will generate a more efficient global allocation of investment resources and so provide the best prospects for growth. However, empirical research has revealed an ambiguous relationship between capital-account liberalization and economic growth.[4] Crafts has observed that there is 'no evidence that abolishing capital controls per se leads to higher growth …. But there is quite good reason to believe that financial liberalization significantly increases the risk of a subsequent financial/currency crisis'.[5] In 1997, the IMF began to consider including capital-account liberalization in its Articles of Agreement, but this process was stalled in the wake of the financial crises of the late 1990s. In December 2003, Anne Kreuger, Director of the IMF, advised

---

[1]   M. Obstfeld and M. Taylor, *Global Capital Markets. Integration, Crisis, and Growth* (Cambridge, 2004).

[2]   R.G. Rajan and L. Zingales, 'The Great Reversals. The Politics of Financial Development in the Twentieth Century', *Journal of Financial Economics*, 69 (2003), pp. 5–50, here pp. 5–10, pp. 38f.

[3]   R.G. Rajan and L. Zingales, *Saving Capitalism from the Capitalists* (New York, 2003), pp. 242f.

[4]   B. Eichengreen and M. Mussa, *Capital Account Liberalization. Theoretical and Practical Aspects* (Washington, 1998); J. P. Agenor, 'Benefits and Costs of International Financial Integration. Theory and Facts', *World Economy*, 26, 8 (2003), pp. 1089–1119, for a recent review of the literature.

[5]   N. Crafts, Globalization and Growth in the Twentieth Century, IMF Working Papers WP/00/44, 2000, p. 51. See also N. Crafts, 'Globalisation and Economic Growth. A Historical Perspective', *World Economy*, 27, 1 (2004), pp. 45–58. For a similar conclusion, see E.S. Prasad et al., Effects of Financial Globalization on Developing Countries. Some Empirical Evidence, IMF Occasional Paper 220, 2003.

that 'Capital flows are, in some respects, like antibiotics. Anything capable of doing good is also powerful enough to inflict harm when wrongly used. That is not a reason to restrain capital flows, though, but to harness them so that they can do most good'.[6] The history of international financial regulation is the history of the struggle to identify when capital flows were 'wrongly used' and the various 'harnesses' and their outcomes.

II

The persistence of global imbalances after current-account convertibility led to greater reliance on capital controls as a tool to combat short-term balance-of-payments problems. In the UK, controls on a variety of financial and commercial transactions were intensified for balance-of-payments purposes during the 1960s.[7] On the other hand, the Bank of England allowed relatively free transactions denominated solely in foreign currency as part of the City of London's traditional business. This inconsistency eventually led to financial innovation that pierced the barrier between sterling and US$ transactions within the existing rules. In 1955, the Midland Bank began to offer higher interest for US$-denominated deposits that it then used to ease local liquidity constraints.[8] This innovation quickly spread and led to a resurgence in British merchant banking and also a rush of foreign banks opening offices in London to take part in the market.[9] Moorgate, where many US banks found premises, became known as 'America Avenue' and the Eurodollar market quickly moved from being dominated by British banks to being dominated by American banks in London.

The initial regulatory response to the innovation of the Eurodollar market in London was to allow the market to grow, although there were misgivings within the Bank of England and the Treasury over the potential liquidity and volatility of the market. The Bank of England imposed informal prudential supervision by requesting banks to report their monthly Eurodollar balances. Bankers were also warned personally to be cautious about the term structure and liquidity of their Eurodollar business.[10] The effectiveness of this traditional approach to supervision

---

[6]   Anne Kreuger, Director of IMF, 9 December 2003. Speech in Malaysia.

[7]   As late as October 1968, the Labour government re-introduced the control on sterling financing of third party trade that they had imposed in 1957 and removed in 1959.

[8]   C.R. Schenk, 'The Origins of the Eurodollar Market in London, 1955–1963', *Explorations in Economic History*, 35, 2 (1998), pp. 221–38.

[9]   From 1965–71, 69 foreign banks opened branches in London, of which almost 40 per cent were US banks. The assets of accepting houses increased from £955m in 1962 to £3587m in 1970, C.R. Schenk, 'International Financial Centres 1958–71. Competitiveness and Complementarity', in S. Battilossi and Y. Cassis (eds), *European Banks and the American Challenge* (Oxford, 2002).

[10]   G. Burn, *The Re-emergence of Global Finance* (London, 2006), ch. 5.

in the City of London relied on a close relationship between the Bank of England and individual bankers, and therefore became less sustainable as the market became dominated by American bankers less amenable to such 'moral suasion'.[11]

Rajan and Zingales explain the failure to regulate the Eurodollar market as follows: 'It was on British soil, but eventually, many of its players were American. So neither country could unilaterally close it down'.[12] It is clear from archival and contemporary accounts that it was not a lack of cooperation between Washington and London that made it impossible to close the market. Rather, the benefits that the market generated for both parties stymied efforts by *European* regulators to close it down. If they had wanted to, the Bank of England could have eliminated the market in London unilaterally (in the way that European governments did) by prohibiting the payment of interest on non-resident deposits. A major obstacle to imposing new more formal controls in London was the desire to sustain the status of London as an international financial centre. As a report by the Bank of England stated in 1961, 'however much we dislike hot money we cannot be international bankers and refuse to accept money'.[13] Another obstacle to London unilaterally closing the market was that it would merely be driven to other offshore centres with even poorer supervisory systems than London.

Looking more closely, it is clear that the British regulators' motives for supporting the Eurodollar market are rather more complicated than they are portrayed by Helleiner and Rajan and Zingales, whose explanations begin and end with the desire to support London as an international financial centre, or Burn, who sees Britain's toleration of the market as the result of the incestuous relationship between the City and the Bank of England.[14] Certainly, at the time it was believed that the international activities of the City generated prestige and current-account earnings. On the other hand, the Treasury's intensification of controls on many financial transactions in the late 1950s and through the 1960s shows that hurting the interests of the City was not an obstacle to imposing controls if they were deemed necessary for balance-of-payments purposes.[15] As Burn also notes, of more immediate importance was that the growth of the Eurodollar market generated a net inflow of US$ that helped reduce Britain's

---

[11]   C.R. Schenk, 'The New City and the State, 1959–1971', in R.C. Michie and P.A. Williamson (eds), *The British Government and the City of London in the Twentieth Century* (Cambridge, 2004).

[12]   Rajan and Zingales, *Saving Capitalism*, p. 262.

[13]   Report by JML for Hamilton, 19 Oct. 1961. Bank of England Archive, London [hereafter BE] EID10/19.

[14]   Rajan and Zingales, *Saving Capitalism*, p. 261; E. Helleiner, *States and the Re-emergence of Global Finance. From Bretton Woods to the 1990s* (Ithaca NY, 1994), p. 84; Burn, *Re-emergence*.

[15]   For an account of the protests from the City over these controls, see Schenk, 'New City'.

persistent balance-of-payments deficits.[16] The fact that the dollars attracted by Midland Bank reduced the recorded fall in the UK's central reserves in June 1955 from $US56m to US$6m carried considerable weight in the Bank of England and the Treasury. In a time of balance of payments deficits, the UK did not want to introduce new controls on capital *inflows*.

In the US, capital controls on outflows were a major weapon in the battle to rectify the persistent balance-of-payments deficits of the 1960s. The government imposed a series of controls; the IET in 1963, Voluntary Foreign Credit Programme of 1965 and reserve requirements on banks in the US accepting funds from their branches abroad in 1969. These policies encouraged the operation of US banks in London and enhanced the demand for Eurodollar loans there to finance US MNCs and other international borrowers seeking dollar loans. The outcome of the different regulatory environments in the USA and the UK was a reallocation of international banking activity. Britain's share of world banks' foreign assets peaked in 1969 at 26 per cent of the global total, while the share of the USA fell from 21 per cent to less than 10 per cent from 1966–69.

The US Treasury agreed with the Bank of England that there was no immediate need for external supervision or new regulation of the Eurodollar market in London.[17] Burn details the slow realization in the USA of the importance of the market and confusion over its impact the early 1960s.[18] The Under-Secretary of State for monetary affairs, Robert Roosa, told Parsons of the Bank of England early in 1963 that he 'was certain that the Eurodollar market would continue to be a feature of the international financial situation. It was potentially a vehicle for instability but also an important part of liquidity' at a time when the perceived shortage of international liquidity was an important pre-occupation.[19] In talks with US banks, Roosa reminded them that although there was no question of imposing exchange control, they should, in his words, ask themselves whether they are serving the national interest by participating in this sort of activity, which adds to the volume of short-term capital outflow from the US. Mr Roosa was not too optimistic about the outcome.[20]

Roosa was evidently not as confident about the prospects of moral suasion being exercised effectively in the New York market as the Bank of England was in London. However, in 1963 some major US and European banks did agree among

---

[16]   Schenk, 'The Origins'; Burn, *Re-emergence*, p. 127.

[17]   At the beginning of 1963 the US Treasury reassured banks that they did not object to their participation in the market. Memo of conversation with W.B. Eagleson, VP of the Girard Trust Corn Exchange Bank of Philadelphia, with Daane, Trued, Schott, 30 Jan. 1963. US National Archives and Records Administration, Maryland [hereafter NARA]. Papers of Under Secretary of State for monetary affairs [hereafter USSMA], Box 105, RG69-A-407.

[18]   Burn, *Re-emergence*, pp. 151–62.

[19]   Memo of meeting of Roosa with Rickett (HMT) and Parsons (BE), 9 April 1963. NARA, USSMA, Box 106, RG69-A-407.

[20]   Note by S. Goldman of a conversation with Roosa, 1 May 1963. BE EID10/20.

themselves to restrict the inter-bank market and avoid 'pyramiding' of deposits because of fears over the market's stability.[21]

At the end of November 1963, a fraudulent food-oil scam in the USA (dubbed the 'Great Salad Oil Flap' by the *Economist*) brought down the broker Ira Haupte and generated a series of defaults on Eurodollar loans. This sent a shock through the market and brought monetary authorities back to the question of regulation and supervision.[22] The increasing volume of short-term inter-bank flows raised the spectre of the financial crisis of the 1930s but, unlike the 1930s, this did not lead to a reversal of policy.[23] In London, the system of informal supervision continued. As Cromer told Holtrop of the BIS, 'if in an individual case it appeared to us that an unsound situation was developing, we would then discuss the matter with the bank in question'.[24] Governor Daane of the Fed worried about the possibility that 'unsound lending' might lead to a chain of defaults that would cause a banking crisis similar to that of 1933.[25] He was reassured, however, by arguments that the Eurodollar market represented a small proportion of banks' total liquidity and that the market was sensitive to geographical concentration.[26] Like the Bank of England, the Fed used its contacts to obtain more information about the market by asking a small number of leading US corporations why and how they used the Eurodollar market, but they did not put any obstacles in the way of such transactions.[27]

Burn is critical of the late interest the Fed took in the Eurodollar market, noting that it was only in 1960 that they sought to gather intelligence about how the market worked in Europe.[28] The result of this study led them to become more hostile to the market and they considered ways to insulate the US from the Eurodollar market 'by prohibition or patriotic persuasion' or by altering incentives or reserve requirements. The main goal was to curtail the evasion of tight domestic monetary policy through the Eurodollar market. By 1967, they concluded that

a. 'Prohibition might stimulate innovation in methods of avoidance.

---

[21]   Andrew L. Gomory, Executive Vice President of Manufacturers Hanover Trust NY, to Roosa, USSMA, 1 Nov. 1963. NARA, USSMA, Box 105, RG69-A-407. Hermann Abs of Deutsche Bank to Gomory, 5 Sept. 1963. The Director of the Bayerische Vereinsbank told Gomory the same, 1 Sept. 1963. NARA, USSMA, Box 105, RG69-A-407.

[22]   Note by Preston to Bridge, circulated to Selwyn, O'Brien and Parsons, 4 December 1963. BE EID10/22. Losses totalled US$100m. *Economist*, 25 Jan. 1964.

[23]   Bridge to Parsons and O'Brien, 5 Dec. 1963. BE EID10/22.

[24]   Cromer to Holtrop (BIS), 31 Mar. 1964. Bank for International Settlements Historical Archive, Basle [hereafter BIS] FER8 7.18(10).

[25]   Note by Henry N. Goldstein for Mr Young, 17 Feb. 1964. NARA, RG82 Box 76.

[26]   An example was the inability of Italian banks to borrow in the market in November 1962. Note by Henry N. Goldstein for Mr Young, 17 Feb. 1964. NARA, RG82 Box 76.

[27]   Note for the files by Alfred Hayes re: Conversation with W. Braddock Hickman, President of the Federal Reserve Bank of Cleveland, 13 April 1964. NARA RG82 Box 76.

[28]   Burn, *Re-emergence*, pp. 140–44.

b. Efforts at persuasion might bring counter-productive psychological reactions.

c. It would not be sound policy to make what might have to be a permanent change in the framework of reserve requirements for transitory reasons.'[29]

If the Fed wanted to support an integrated world money market, they could not introduce new reserve requirements on foreign deposits of US banks abroad. On the other hand, reserve requirements would 'help us to manage domestic monetary policy effectively – and, incidentally, help simplify other people's management of their domestic and external monetary policies'. Two years later, the Fed opted for domestic priorities and in September 1969 imposed a 10 per cent reserve requirement on net liabilities to foreign branches of US banks in excess of the average amounts outstanding in May 1969. This discouraged foreign branches of US banks from repatriating US$ to their head offices and thus undermining US tight-money policy. The Fed estimated that 30 per cent of foreign-branch resources were used to supply parent offices in 1969 but that in 1970 this had reduced to 2.7 per cent.[30]

At the beginning of 1968, the Fed Board considered injecting additional funds into the market through the Fed-BIS swap mechanism to hold down Eurodollar interest rates.[31] As part of this study, it was revealed that the Fed had intervened in the market in the recent past, but by 1968 most in the Fed were against any further action. In April, the Fed publicly acknowledged that the Eurobond market was an integral part of their balance-of-payments policy: 'It has always been clear that part of the required adjustment in international payments would have to come through increased European financing of capital investment in Europe and elsewhere'.[32] In 1968 new issues of securities in foreign markets by US corporations soared to $2.1b from $US450m in 1967.[33] The US money supply was insulated from the market by reserve requirements in 1969 but offshore borrowing of US$ by foreign companies was encouraged, to ease the pressure on domestic capital markets.

Although taking steps to insulate the US economy, the USA did not push the Bank of England or UK Treasury to impose controls in London. Burn interprets the evidence that the US authorities were concerned by the market in the early 1960s to suggest that they were frustrated by British reluctance to curtail it, but it is not clear from his account what the US wanted Britain to do.[34] The official view was that the US economy was vulnerable to short-term capital movements of many kinds, including the Eurodollar market, and that this problem could not

---

[29]   A.B. Hersey to Robert Solomon, 19 Oct. 1967. NARA RG82 Box 76.

[30]   J. Kelly, *Bankers and Borders. The Case of American Banks in Britain* (Cambridge MA, 1977), p. 101.

[31]   John E. Reynolds to Katz, 8 Jan. 1968. NARA RG82 Box 76.

[32]   Federal Reserve Bulletin, April 1968, p. 353.

[33]   Federal Reserve Bulletin, October 1969, pp. 774–5.

[34]   Burn, *Re-emergence*, pp. 163–7. Burn does not draw on the evidence of discussions at the BIS detailed below.

be contained effectively through further restrictions. On the plus side, the market had increased overseas borrowing of US$, thus relaxing pressure on the New York market directly. By 1970, the view of the President's National Advisory Committee on International Monetary Affairs was that the market was a symptom rather than a cause of instability between national markets and that:

> it would not be possible to achieve tight controls on the access of US banks, companies, or investors to foreign short-term financial markets (including the Eurodollar market).[35]

This section has examined the regulatory response of the supplier and the host of the Eurodollar market. The financial innovation had not been anticipated and reaction was slow in London. The cosy informal networks that had developed in London from the 19th century encouraged the Bank of England to continue to rely on personal contacts and 'moral suasion' despite the fact that the market was changing dramatically with the arrival of US banks. The US Fed was uncertain about the impact of the market on their balance of payments, but found London's facilities eased domestic pressure to relax capital controls and tight money. Both sets of regulators at this point also recognized that this innovation marked a new era of complexity in international finance that was no longer as amenable to national controls. Moreover, the Bank of England was clearly sensitive to the dangers of regulatory competition between international financial centres. The over-riding priority for both governments was minimizing balance-of-payments deficits, and the market had a role to play in this campaign on both sides of the Atlantic.

In continental Europe, the commitment to stable exchange rates strengthened during the 1960s because the process of European integration increased the opportunity costs of fluctuating rates. Germany, with its balance-of-payments surplus, was traditionally the most liberal regime, having abolished controls on outflows as early as 1957, but they reintroduced controls on inflows during the 1960s. Switzerland became among the most restrictive regimes, to prevent the internationalization of the Swiss franc. France began and ended the period more restrictive than many other European countries, but had a brief period of liberalization in 1968. The goal of monetary integration should have led to intra-European liberalization, but in practice domestic monetary sovereignty reigned supreme and controls were maintained. Most countries operated a combination of reserve requirements on Eurodollar deposits and prohibition of interest on short-term foreign deposits. Obstfeld and Taylor note briefly that France and Italy tightened some controls after 1973 to retain exchange-rate stability, but this does not fully capture the widespread affinity for capital controls in Europe.[36] The conflict between capital controls and the European integration project was not finally

---

[35]   Frederick L. Springborn, report for IMF questionnaire, 4 Nov. 1970. NARA RG56 Entry 360D NAC Actions.
[36]   Obstfeld and Taylor, *Global Capital Markets*, p. 160.

resolved until 1990 with the abandonment of remaining controls in favour of the creation of a single market. This finally signalled a new solution to the trilemma for Europe with the abandonment of policy sovereignty and the creation of a single European central bank. Despite monetary union, however, the abandonment of national policy sovereignty and institutional barriers to cross-border capital account transactions remains controversial. [37]

The relatively lax regulation of off-shore international finance in London prompted central bankers in Europe to urge London to impose controls on the Eurodollar market. These efforts foundered over the conflict between national sovereignty and international cooperation, the interests of London and Washington in the continuation of the market, the danger of pushing it to a less well-supervised offshore financial centre, and a lack of consensus over its impact on national and international economic systems. Efforts to improve transparency and supervision were stymied by the priority central banks gave to the privacy of their clients' business. It would take the 1982 LDC Debt Crisis for central banks and the banking community to begin to overcome this inhibition and start to embrace transparency, although obstacles to communication between national financial regulators continued to plague efforts at prudential supervision through the 1980s and 1990s.

The BIS was the ideal forum for this discussion. It used the market in its banking relations with member central banks, and it was a regular meeting place for central bankers away from their governments.[38] In June 1962 Guindey of the BIS sent a letter to member central banks suggesting a meeting of officials to discuss the market. The BIS observed that 'looked at strictly as a competitive phenomenon and as a service to both the lenders and borrowers who use it, the Eurodollar market would appear a useful development. Are there disadvantages or dangers which should be set on the other side of the ledger?', such as counteracting monetary policy, dangers of a liquidity crisis in the market, impact on forward exchange markets. They concluded with the question; 'is it right for the central banks to leave the Eurocurrency markets without supervision or management?'[39] The meeting of experts merely skated over these fundamental questions and concentrated instead on the exchange of statistics.[40]

---

[37]   In 2001, cross-border share trading in Europe cost about ten times that of the USA. *Economist*, Jan. 18, 2001. For the European Commission's study group's response, see Giovannini Group, Second Report on EU cross-border clearing and settlement arrangements, April 2003.

[38]   The involvement of the BIS in the discussions over the Eurocurrency markets is described in G. Toniolo, *Central Bank Cooperation at the BIS 1930–1973* (Cambridge, 2005), pp. 465–71.

[39]   Short paper by BIS as basis for discussion of E$ market at meeting of experts on 6–8 October 1962, 31 Aug. 1962. BIS, 1/3A(3) Meeting of Experts, Volumes 1–2.

[40]   The Americans were particularly keen to see the BIS collect data on the market to help them trace its movements and potential impact on the USA. Fred H. Klopstock,

Central-bank governors met in December 1963, just after the Ira Haupte crisis, and their views show a lack of detailed understanding combined with general suspicion of the market. Hayes of the USA worried about over-extension of credit to a few borrowers and 'inadequate checking between countries of the credit-worthiness of borrowers'.[41] He was still uncertain of the impact on the US balance of payments. Blessing noted that 'the Bundesbank was not concerned about the participation of the German commercial banks in the Eurodollar market'. He felt that the market had similar problems as for all short-term international credit 'but he felt that the Eurodollar market had encouraged foreign bankers to be less cautious than they would normally be in granting foreign credits'. Brunet of the Banque de France remarked that 'he could not say whether the market was good or bad but that the central banks were justified in regarding it with a certain amount of suspicion .... On the other hand, he thought there was no necessity for rigid controls.'[42] Cromer of the Bank of England was unworried by the market. Summing up the discussion, Holtrop concluded that 'the general view seemed to be that there might be problems in connection with the Eurodollar market but that they were not essentially different from the problems that existed in relation to international short-term capital movements in general'. The BIS initiative then focused on the collection of statistics for the next couple of years.

After the Haupte affair, the Bank of England recommended that the BIS should collect and publish statistics of the geographical destination of Eurodollar loans for the 'general health of the Eurodollar market'.[43] This idea was not taken up since data were not easily available from banks. In February 1965 most central-bank officials viewed publishing eurocurrency statistics as an inroad on the confidentiality of bank business, but the central-bank governors nonetheless called for the experts to examine 'concrete possibilities of centralizing on an international level information on bank credits to non-residents' to include eurodollar loans as well as other credits.[44] Such information was a necessary prerequisite to prudential supervision.

The experts duly met in April 1965 to discuss two possibilities, a genuine international risk centre, or merely the collection of national data without the formation of a new institution. France, Italy and Germany each had their own

---

Manager Research Dept of FRBNY to M. Gilbert, 28 May 1962. BIS, 1/3A(3) Meeting of Experts, Volumes 1–2.

[41]   The following account comes from a letter from Ferras to the Governor of Bank of Japan Yamagiwa, who was not present at the meeting, 23 Jan. 1964. BIS, FER8 7.18(10).

[42]   G. Lefort, of the Banque de France, later corrected the French position by emphasizing the need to encourage banks to be more prudent in their lending. G. Lefort comments on Report of Experts draft, 19 Dec. 1963. BIS, 1/3A(3) Meeting of Experts, Volumes 1–2.

[43]   Jasper Rootham (BE) to Martin Gilbert (BIS), 9 March 1964. The suggestion was repeated by Governor Cromer in a letter to Holtrop, 31 March 1964. BIS, FER8 7.18(10).

[44]   Letter from Ferras to central banks, 24 May 1965. BIS, FER8 7.18(10).

risk centres and believed that most legal and administrative differences in their approaches could be overcome to allow data to be communicated to a new international institution. But the other countries were opposed.[45] The British representative was adamant that British law did not permit the creation of such a centre. The Dutch also saw no scope for a new institution. Their central bank received information on use of credits by clients but this information was for exclusive use of the central bank. Sweden received no information officially and did not believe Swedish banks would cooperate. The Fed claimed to receive a lot of information from private banks but nothing on individual borrowers. US companies were so big they often went to more than one bank and it was natural to expect that the banks would exchange information, making any official institution redundant. Swiss banks refused even to exchange information amongst themselves, so there was no possibility of contributing to a risk centre. Given the general antipathy to the idea of a new institution, the experts agreed to recommend the less ambitious plan to report all external credits in foreign and domestic currency to the BIS along the lines of existing Eurodollar reporting.[46]

Multilateral regulation of the market resurfaced at the BIS at the beginning of 1971 after a reduction in US interest rates prompted a massive capital flow into Europe. A group of experts met in February to discuss the prospects for a more interventionist approach, due to fears that the market was inflationary and interfered with domestic monetary policy. However, there was still no consensus that restrictions in the market were advisable.[47] The US and the UK were still the most opposed to intervention. Daane, of the Fed, argued along the lines of the NAC position quoted above that existing problems of the short-term capital market did not arise from the Eurodollar market alone. The US wanted the BIS to pursue a technical approach rather than developing policy. The US authorities, nevertheless, were not wary of exerting national controls on the market to contain its inflationary impact at home. From January 1971 the marginal reserve requirement on Eurodollar borrowings by US banks (Regulation D) was increased from 10 per cent to 20 per cent.

The British remained resistant to regulation, either collective or national. Hollom of the Bank of England stated he 'would be reluctant to say that the market would be much helped by placing restrictions on its activities. If they [the Bank of England] were to do that, they might drive the market into other channels' which would be even more difficult to monitor. On the other hand, Emminger of Bundesbank and Baffi of the Banca d'Italia both remarked on how the market interfered with the effectiveness of monetary policy and wanted to examine how

---

[45]   Antonio D'Aroma, Secretary General BIS, note of experts' meeting on Friday 9 April 1965, drafted 15 April 1965. BIS, FER8 7.18(10).

[46]   On the failure of this proposal, see also Toniolo, *Central Bank Cooperation*, p. 469.

[47]   Informal record of a meeting on the Eurocurrency market held at Netherlands Bank on 18 Feb. 1971. Chaired by Ziljstra. BIS, GILB1.

central banks could influence it collectively. Theron of the Banque de France and Hayami of the Bank of Japan both advised that they protected their markets from capital inflows through national exchange controls. Hay of Banque Nationale Suisse was the most certain of the inflationary impact, estimating the multiplier at 2.5 and complaining about the interference with domestic policy. However, he did not support regulation. Instead 'what was needed was an attempt to get at the root of the problem, i.e. the [deficit] position of the US'.

A consensus eventually emerged that the market was inflationary, but since there was no agreement on controlling private banks' access to the market, the logical progression was to restrict central-bank deposits.[48] At a meeting of experts in April 1971, the mood was irritable, with some resisting the constraints on central-bank freedom that this would involve and others wondering if it was worthwhile, since only the G10 banks would be bound by any such agreement. Morse, of the Bank of England, conceded that there were strong arguments against a permanent ban on central banks using the eurodollar market; however, he noted three rather despairing benefits from the G10 making a public statement pledging not to use the market for the time being: 'one was that they might influence some [other] European central banks and the other was that there was a lot of agitation going on for something to be done about the Eurodollar market and it might be a good idea, therefore to feed those who were calling for action with something. In addition, they would have at least something to say that they had been doing in their meetings'.[49] The G10's self-denying ordinance did not include the OPEC countries that were soon to flood the international capital markets with their surpluses. In 1974 the Committee of Twenty of the IMF also proposed limiting State use of the eurocurrency markets, but the proposal was never formally adopted.[50] The competitive returns in the form of liquidity and high interest rates were too tempting.

Having achieved a standstill on central-bank deposits, the Standing Committee returned to the more thorny issue of regulating or restricting the eurodollar market, but here no consensus was reached.[51] Daane of the Fed argued that in terms of the international financial and monetary crisis, the Eurodollar market was not 'the villain of the piece'.[52] Emminger and Kessler, however, believed that the 1971 crisis made multilateral regulation of the Euromarkets even more pressing, Kessler going so far as to say that failure to deal with the problem would threaten

---

[48]   This was reinforced by a growing academic consensus that the private eurodollar market was probably not itself inflationary but that central banks' participation in the market was inflationary. For a survey of the contemporary debate, see Hawley, 'Protecting'.

[49]   Second meeting of the Standing Committee on the Eurocurrency market. 1 June 1971. BIS, GILB1.

[50]   A. Teck and W.B. Johns, 'Portfolio Decisions of Central Banks', in A.M. George and I.H. Giddy (eds), *International Finance Handbook*, vol. 2 (New York, 1983), p. 10.

[51]   Toniolo relates briefly how the disagreements about both the disease and the cure continued. Toniolo, *Central Bank Cooperation*, pp. 466f.

[52]   Eurocurrency Standing Committee, Informal Meeting, 8 Jan. 1972. BIS, GIL1.

the newly re-established pegged-exchange-rate system. The resulting report of the standing committee to the Governors in March 1972 reflected this disagreement about the depth of the problem and its possible solutions. The Governors deemed it too weak to serve as the basis of policy decisions and referred the question back to the committee.[53]

Acrimonious discussion continued for the next six months. McMahon of the Bank of England supported national approaches to the market, essentially endorsing the status quo of exchange controls on the Continent that benefited the City of London. Emminger argued that EEC members could not accept regulation on a purely national basis since they were concurrently discussing monetary union.[54] The EEC set up a Contact Group of national banking supervisors in 1972 to develop co-operation and to exchange information on banking supervision, but progress was slow. It was not until the end of 1977 that they published their First Directive to co-ordinate laws, regulations and administrative provisions of credit institutions. Meanwhile, at the BIS and at the IMF Germany advocated reserve requirements on Eurodollar deposits but the British reiterated that this would merely push the market to a more hospitable international financial centre.[55] US representatives remained preoccupied with official depositors and went so far as to challenge why so many central banks kept deposits with the BIS at all.[56]

At their meeting on 10 February 1973, amidst disarray in the financial markets, no consensus could be reached among officials.[57] In the end Larre, as Chair, remarked that 'this was not a very propitious day for discussing the question of the regulation of the Eurocurrency market', given large flows of short-term capital that were mostly not Eurodollar flows. It was agreed that Larre should produce a mainly factual report in his own name for the Committee of 20 at the beginning of March 1973.[58]

---

[53]   Informal record of Eurocurrency Standing Committee Meeting, 6 April 1972. BIS, GIL1.

[54]   Larre, in the Chair, noted that not all EEC countries were in favour of monetary union. Informal record of Eurocurrency Standing Committee Meeting, 8 July 1972. BIS, GIL1. The same views are recorded in Informal Record of Eurocurrency Standing Committee Meeting, 6 Jan. 1973. BIS, GIL1.

[55]   A.D. Crockett note for files on Committee of 20 meeting 26 March 1973, Archive of the International Monetary Fund, Washington [hereafter IMF], G142.32 C-20 Ministerial Meetings. Informal record of Eurocurrency Standing Committee Meeting, 9 Dec. 1972. BIS, GIL1.

[56]   Informal record of Standing Committee on Eurocurrency Markets Meeting, 9 Sept. 1972. BIS GIL1. The Fed would have preferred banks to keep their deposits direct with the USA but other countries challenged them to provide better returns on US securities to attract such deposits.

[57]   Informal Record of Standing Committee on Eurocurrency Markets Meeting, 6 Jan. 1973 and 10 Feb. 1973. BIS, GIL1.

[58]   Report on The Eurocurrency Market presented to Committee of 20, 3 March 1973. BIS GIL1.

The deliberations of the Eurocurrency Standing Committee revealed irreconcilable differences over how seriously the market had affected domestic monetary policy and destabilized capital flows, and secondly what controls were necessary or feasible. At their meeting in May 1974, the Governors still could not agree on these issues and multilateral regulation was not achieved.

The case of the Eurodollar market showed that the complexity of international financial flows made it increasingly difficult to formulate effective regulatory responses. This was due to disputes about the economic impact of the new market as well as the challenge of enforcing any regulation given the complexity of the transactions involved. Moreover, the supervision of the market focused attention on the conflict between the benefits of transparency and the costs to business of a loss of privacy. In 1974, floating exchange rates and the oil crisis added to the supervisory challenges of multinational banking and increasingly complex financial markets. Attention soon turned from regulating the Eurodollar market to promoting the stability of multinational banking generally.

III

With the advent of floating exchange rates, doubts about the soundness of many new small and medium-sized banks in the Eurodollar market prompted the emergence of a tiered interest-rate structure in the spring and summer of 1974.[59] Small banks faced a liquidity squeeze as the market contracted, causing the failure of the Herstatt Bank.[60] The market panicked, and the rate on three-month Eurodollar loans soared to an unprecedented 14 per cent in mid-July. At the end of September, the New York Reserve Bank had to take over the foreign-exchange obligations of Franklin National Bank.[61] The contrast between the willingness of the Bundesbank to allow the failure of the Herstatt and the Fed's support of the Franklin highlighted the inconsistency of international practices as lender of last

---

[59]   Johnson and Abrams, *Aspects*, p. 18; I.H. Giddy, 'The Eurocurrency Market', in A.H. George and I.H. Giddy (eds), *International Finance Handbook*, vol. 1 (New York, 1983), p. 18. This section develops material from C.R. Schenk, 'Crisis and Opportunity. The Policy Environment of International Banking in the City of London', in Y. Cassis and E. Bussière (eds), *London and Paris as International Financial Centres in the 20th Century* (Oxford, 2005), pp. 207–28.

[60]   Foreign-exchange trading losses amounting to over US$100m, as against deposits of US$760m. Reid, *Secondary Banking Crisis*, p. 115; Wilson, *The Chase*, p. 213.

[61]   Much larger than the Herstatt, the Franklin was left with 300 contracts outstanding, amounting to forward transactions of US$725m, Federal Reserve Bulletin, March 1975. Franklin National's assets were later sold to European-American Banking Corporation in Aug. 1974; S.J. Weiss, 'Competitive Standards Applied to Foreign and Domestic Acquisitions of US Banks', in *Comptroller of the Currency, Foreign Acquisition of US Banks* (Washington, 1981), pp. 303–27, 324.

resort. The Bank of England took no responsibility for the solvency of subsidiaries of foreign banks in London and so the Israel-British Bank was allowed to fail in July 1974 with outstanding debts of £43m.[62]

Ten years after the American 'invasion' of the city of London, this crisis prompted efforts to co-ordinate lender-of-last-resort facilities to international banks. In September, the Central Bank Governors of the G10 announced that, although detailed rules governing lender of last resort to the eurodollar market were not practical, the market should be reassured that 'means are available for that purpose and will be used if and when necessary'.[63] They also set up the Committee on Banking Regulations and Supervisory Practices in Basle, chaired first by George Blunden and then by Peter Cooke, both of the Bank of England, an institution notorious for its light regulatory hand.

While international regulation stalled, national regulatory changes went ahead. In the City, the Bank of England urged consortium banks to set out formally in letters to the Bank of England that their shareholders would agree to act as lenders of last resort. Foreign banks were asked similarly for commitments that they would support their UK subsidiaries, although these undertakings were not enforceable.[64] At the same time, the Fed announced that it was ready to act as lender of last resort for member banks, to protect them against abrupt withdrawal of petro-dollars or any other deposits. Together, these measures reassured the market and the tiered interest-rate structure contracted early in 1975 as confidence returned.

Ten years earlier, similar crises in Europe related to the Eurodollar market had been contained through informal and ad hoc advice. By 1973–74 the volume of capital flows, greater public sensitivity to the interests of depositors, and UK membership of the EEC required a more formal response. In addition to the traditional personal meetings with individual bank officers, London banks had to make more detailed and continuous statistical reports to enhance prudential supervision. At the end of 1974, the Bank of England sent a letter to all banks in the City advising them to tighten up their internal control systems, particularly the control of foreign-exchange operations by branches and subsidiaries overseas. This was the first time such a formal public instruction had been made. The Bank of England also required London's British Overseas Banks for the first time to report the activities of their overseas offices. Blunden noted that 'the reaction of most banks to our letter has suggested to us that we were right in judging that the banking community as a whole was ready for us to take this new line'. Blunden,

---

[62] Negotiations with the Israeli banking authorities eventually produced a fund to which the Bank of England contributed £3m to pay creditors. Johnson and Abrams, Aspects, pp. 21f; Reid, *Secondary Banking Crisis*, p. 115.

[63] Quoted in Johnson and Abrams, *Aspects*, p. 23.

[64] By the end of February 1975 all consortium banks had given such an undertaking.

nevertheless, promised 'our approach remains flexible, personal, progressive and participative'.[65]

The Basle Committee Concordat in 1975 set out the supervisory responsibility for multinational banks, concluding that solvency of foreign branches was 'essentially a matter for parent supervisory authorities', while foreign subsidiaries and joint ventures lay within the responsibility of the host authorities.[66] The subsequent recommendation of 1978 that solvency should be based on consolidated accounts put greater emphasis on parent authorities to ensure the collection and publication of this information. The Concordat was further amended in 1983 to emphasize the need for cooperation and communication between host and parent supervisory bodies, which was elaborated in recommendations in 1990. The collapse of BCCI led to renewed calls for supervision of multinational banks, and the Concordat recommendations were formalized into minimum standards in 1992, but enforcement was still problematic. The 1992 amendments shifted responsibility back to the host to ensure that parent countries had adequate supervisory structures. Banks were to seek permission for cross-border expansion from both host and parent regulators. These amendments further emphasized international information flows, but by 1996 the BIS recognized that information was not passing easily from some hosts (particularly off-shore financial centres) to the parent supervisory bodies.

The Basle Committee also considered how it could help with risk management, perhaps through central agencies that collected information on total liabilities of particular borrowers that could be accessed by potential lenders. As in the early 1970s, the problem of customer confidentiality and the different standards of disclosure among the various jurisdictions made this impossible.[67] Instead, the BIS reported quarterly data on countries' total external debt and from 1978 included maturity distribution on a half-yearly basis. From December, the Bank of England published the consolidated exposure of banks in the UK. In May 1982 the Basle Committee finally agreed on guidelines on country-risk for banks to consider – just in time for the LDC debt crisis of that year.

The progress of these efforts at international co-ordination was limited by the problems that still confront those seeking to develop global financial standards; different political, legal and institutional structures of financial systems and an antipathy to harmonization. As noted above, the EEC harmonization programme, surely most suited to supranational co-ordination, made little progress in the 1970s. At the International Banking Summer School of 1977 Blunden expressed the Bank of England's dim view of such efforts:

---

[65]   Speech by Blunden to the Institute of European Finance of the University College of North Wales, 17 Mar. 1975 in London, *Bank of England Quarterly Bulletin*, 15, 2 (1975), pp. 188–94, 190.

[66]   Quoted in Johnson and Abrams, *Aspects*, p. 16.

[67]   Speech by Blunden to International Banking Summer School in Stockholm, June 1977, *Bank of England Quarterly Bulletin*, 17, 2 (1977); James, *International Monetary Co-operation*, p. 321.

> The banking system of a country is central to the management and efficiency of its economy; its supervision will inevitably be a jealously guarded national prerogative. Its subordination to an international authority is a highly unlikely development, which would require a degree of political commitment which neither exists nor is conceivable in the foreseeable future.[68]

After relatively smooth sailing from 1975–77, international bank lending surged again in 1978 and coincided with a run on the US$ in the second half of the year. In this volatile environment, the Iranian revolution sparked off the second oil crisis at the end of 1979. Bank lending as a proportion of LDC debt rose from 15 per cent in 1970 to 27 per cent in 1980, contributing to the Latin American Debt Crisis of 1982. The prudential regulation introduced in the 1970s proved inadequate to cope with these pressures, particularly on the assessment of country risk, and the transparency of syndicated lending.

At the end of 1987 the Basle Committee issued a consultative paper on capital adequacy with minimum standards for international banks. The focus of their deliberations reflected the major preoccupation at the time; sovereign default risk.[69] After six months of consultation the proposals were adopted with some minor changes and were implemented by many banking regulators by 1992. The failure of the Capital Adequacy Requirements to forestall the series of financial crises in the 1990s led to a reassessment of risk weightings, in particular since they had been designed mainly with sovereign risk in mind (since this was the problem of the 1980s) rather than risk of private borrowers (which was the case in the Asian Financial Crisis).[70] Basle II also tries to emphasize prudential supervision and better disclosure, partly due to the increased sensitivity to money-laundering in the wake of the US 'War on Terror'. These events renewed efforts by the BIS and the IMF, as well as national regulators, to target financial stability.[71] The focus remains, however, primarily on national application and enforcement, and the future application of Basle II remains uncertain for many nations.

IV

This analysis has highlighted the development of multilateral regulation and supervision of international financial markets by focusing on the Eurodollar market and multinational banking in the 1960s and 1970s as the most important

---

[68] *Bank of England Quarterly Bulletin*, 17, 3 (1977).

[69] At the same time, the European Commission was drawing up common European banking standards.

[70] Basle I also introduced perverse incentives for banks regarding assets with high risk weights, B. Eichengreen, *Capital Flows and Crises* (Cambridge MA, 2003), p. 304.

[71] G.J. Schinasi, *Safeguarding Financial Stability. Theory and Practice* (IMF, 2006). pp. 10f.

financial innovations of this period. These cases reveal the longevity of current obstacles to cooperative international efforts. International finance has remained regulated on a national basis because of practical obstacles to information flows and the dangers of pushing markets to more fragile and poorly supervised offshore centres, as well as an ideological lack of consensus over the costs and benefits of globalization, and the perceived threat to national sovereignty. These obstacles to cooperation derive from the origins of late-20th-century globalization and were as apparent in the 1960s as they have been over the last decade. Efforts at cooperative or collaborative supervision and regulation are most commonly found after a crisis when an international event has threatened national financial systems. This has resulted in the focus of these new guidelines being backward-looking and reactive rather than proactive. Moreover, as each crisis recedes, so does the impetus for regulatory reform.

International finance became extraordinarily more complex and surged in volume relative to 'real' economies in the 1980s and 1990s. However, the seeds of the basic obstacles to cooperative efforts at prudential regulation were already apparent in this earlier era of financial innovation. These debates set the precedent for the priority of national over collective interest and defence of private information over transparency, in the absence of clear evidence that globalization threatened systemic failures. The global financial crisis of 2007–9 dramatically exposed the weaknesses of this approach to international financial regulation, although the responses to the crisis have also demonstrated how difficult these obstacles are to overcome.

CHAPTER 9

The Missing Link: International Banking Supervision in the Archives of the BIS

Piet Clement*

Central banks have always been sensitive to the stability of the financial system in general and of large financial institutions in particular. Indeed, as Padoa-Schioppa has put it: '... the role of central banks in financial stability is part of their genetic code'.[1] However, in many industrialized countries it was only in the wake of the severe banking crises of the 1930s that the regulatory and supervisory powers of central banks were considerably extended or, alternatively, that new and independent supervisory bodies were created. Thus, in the summer of 1931, the collapse of the Danat Bank in Germany, which had a serious knock-on effect on the entire banking sector, was the immediate cause for the establishment of a Reich banking supervisory authority – in which the Reichsbank played an important role – with jurisdiction over all German banks.[2] In other countries, such as the Netherlands, around the same time, regular reporting by commercial banks to the central bank was strengthened considerably, and they voluntarily accepted certain limitations and indirect controls through so-called Gentlemen's Agreements with the central bank.[3]

However, this more or less simultaneous move towards formalized banking supervision did not adequately address the question of how best to regulate or supervise the non-domestic activities of large banks. This question was perhaps not the most burning one in the world of the 1930s to the 1950s, given the drying up of international finance as a result of Depression and war, the pervasive financial regulation in many countries and the generalization of capital controls. It did become acute again from the late 1950s onward, with the achievement of current-account convertibility in western Europe, the gradual relaxation of capital

---

* Views expressed are those of the author and do not necessarily represent the views of the BIS.

[1] T. Padoa-Schioppa, *Regulating Finance, Balancing Freedom and Risk* (Oxford, 2004), p. 97.

[2] 'The Deutsche Bundesbank's Involvement in Banking Supervision', Deutsche Bundesbank Monthly Report (September 2000), pp. 31–43.

[3] J. Mooij and H.M. Prast, A Brief History of the Institutional Design of Banking Supervision in the Netherlands, De Nederlandsche Bank, Research Memorandum WO no. 703, October 2002.

controls and the subsequent rapid growth of international financial flows. It is easy to see that a credible regulation or supervision of the international activities of large financial institutions is essential to reducing risks to international financial stability and to creating a global level playing field. The almost complete absence of such regulation has, for a long time, been the missing link in the international financial architecture. Central bankers from the industrialized world were very much aware of this and from the early 1960s onward they began to discuss this key issue in the context of their monthly meeting weekends at the Bank for International Settlements in Basel. This eventually resulted in the creation of the Group of Ten (G10[4]) Committee on Banking Regulations and Supervisory Practices (later: the Basel Committee on Banking Supervision) in 1974–75, in the wake of the Herstatt crisis, and the adoption of capital-adequacy rules for internationally active banks – the so-called Basel Capital Accord – in 1988, which was substantially revised in 1999–2005 (Basel II).

This chapter very briefly retraces the history of central-bank discussions on banking supervision and regulation in the BIS context. It will then focus on the archival sources for the study of international banking supervision from the 1960s onward. These sources can shed an interesting light on how the thinking of central banks and other relevant players on international financial stability and lender-of-last-resort issues has evolved over the past half century, and how this evolution has been driven by recurrent banking and financial crises. They also highlight the not always easy relationship between the public and private sector in dealing with these issues, as well as, within the public sector, between the central banks and the political authorities. At the same time, many of the main archival sources for the study of international banking supervision remain closed, as they are considered to be either too recent or too sensitive (in particular when referring to domestic crises and the plight of individual commercial banks). Nevertheless, a lot can be gained from the selective opening of relevant records. To this end, it is important to raise awareness among the relevant archive holders of international banking supervision and regulation as a worthy research subject in its own right.

The Basel Process

The inexorable rise of the so-called euro-currency markets in the 1960s was the true catalyst that catapulted the issue of international bank supervision and regulation onto the agenda of policy-makers.[5] The euro-currency market can be defined as a market for short-term deposits and credits, denominated in a currency

---

[4]   G10 = Belgium, Canada, France, Germany, Italy, Japan, the Netherlands, Sweden, the United Kingdom and the United States. Switzerland soon became an associated member.

[5]   On the origins and development of the euro-currency market, see especially: C.R. Schenk, 'The Origins of the Eurodollar Market in London, 1955–1963', *Explorations in Economic History*, 35, 2 (1998), pp. 221–38; and S. Battilossi and Y. Cassis (eds), *European*

different from that of the country in which the deposit-taking and credit-giving bank is located. This market developed strongly from the early 1960s onward, with the City of London as its main hub and the large majority of funds being denominated in US dollars. It proved an attractive outlet for American banks, seeking to 'escape from a stifling banking environment in the United States',[6] and helped fuel the expansion of US corporations in Europe and elsewhere. Within a decade, from 1963 to 1973, the estimated volume of the euro-currency market boomed from some $7 billion to over $130 billion.[7]

Central banks began to concern themselves with the euro-currency market from early on. In May 1961, a group of central bank experts meeting at the BIS in Basel discussed the role of the euro-currency market in cross-border capital movements. An annual meeting of euro-currency market experts soon became a regular fixture on the BIS meeting agenda, and, starting in 1964, the BIS Annual Report contained a special chapter devoted to developments in the euro-currency market. For central bankers, the rapid expansion of the euro-currency market posed three particular challenges: how to define and measure this new phenomenon; the real and supposed effects it had on the effectiveness of domestic monetary policy; and, finally, the prudential risks that seemed to be magnified by the characteristics of this rapidly expanding market.[8] It is this last challenge that interests us here most.

In the 1960s, central bankers became increasingly worried that certain participants in the euro-currency market might be overexposed (especially in view of the large amounts involved), and that there was a considerable – and apparently growing – mismatch between short-term deposits and short- to medium-term credits. These concerns were compounded by the fact that in the euro-currency market quite often the end-users of credits were obscured by the practice of redepositing funds between banks (the share of interbank transactions in total euro-currency banking increased from some 30 per cent in the mid-1960s to an estimated 50 per cent in the early 1980s). These prudential concerns were highlighted as early as 1963, when two reputable international companies, Stinnes and Ira Haupt, suffered heavy losses in their foreign currency business. One result was an abortive discussion among the G10 central banks about the feasibility of creating an international risk office with the task of centralizing information on short-term credits granted by banks operating in any of the G10 countries to 'non-residents'. Nothing came of it, but concerns about the prudential risks associated with the euro-currency markets

---

Banks and the American Challenge. Competition and Cooperation in International Banking under Bretton Woods (Oxford, 2002).

[6]   R. Sylla, 'United States Banks and Europe. Strategy and Attitudes', in S. Battilossi and Y. Cassis (eds), *European Banks and the American Challenge. Competition and Cooperation in International Banking under Bretton Woods* (Oxford, 2002), p. 71.

[7]   Bank for International Settlements, *Annual Report*, Basel, 1964 and 1974.

[8]   On the central banks' position vis-à-vis the euro-currency market, see G. Toniolo, with the assistance of P. Clement, *Central Bank Cooperation at the Bank for International Settlements 1930–1973* (Cambridge, 2005), pp. 452–71.

resurfaced in the Basel context at regular intervals. By the end of the 1960s, more than one central bank Governor believed that the growth of the euro-currency market heightened the potential for financial distress because of the sheer size of the short-term capital flows, but also because of the market's structure, where most operations involved bank consortia or chains of intermediate depositaries, and, last but not least, because of less stringent supervision of the banks' international operations by national authorities. It was feared that a deterioration in confidence might spread rapidly throughout the international markets.

Officially, the central banks and the BIS downplayed these risks, pointing to the market's resilience and to the solidity of the international banks active in it. Nevertheless, they felt it wise to increase the frequency of the meetings of euro-currency market experts held in Basel, creating, in April 1971, a full-fledged G10 Standing Committee on the Euro-Currency Market. Initially, during the twilight years of the Bretton Woods system, the attention of central banks and of the Standing Committee was mainly focused on developments in the euro-currency market that directly affected domestic monetary policy (e.g. interest rate levels, speculative capital flows). This changed in 1974. In the wake of the collapse of Bankhaus Herstatt and of the Franklin National Bank, the G10 Governors gathered in Basel sought to reassure the markets by issuing a declaration underlining the availability of lending of last resort in the euromarkets. Having given this reassurance, the Governors believed it was time to address a fundamental weakness that they felt was at the core of the problems plaguing the international financial system in 1974: the inadequate supervision of international banking activities. For that reason, in December 1974, they created a new G10 standing committee, the Committee on Banking Regulations and Supervisory Practices (later: Basel Committee on Banking Supervision, or 'Basel Committee').

It should be stressed that the Basel Committee on Banking Supervision was set up as a discussion forum and consultative body, bringing together central bank and supervisory authority experts, and not a decision-making body with supranational authority.[9] In the 1970s, as to a lesser degree today, domestic banking supervisory and regulatory practices varied widely among the G10 countries. For instance, in Germany basically the same regulatory restrictions and supervisory obligations applied to the banks' domestic and international activities, whereas in the UK or Luxembourg the international (euro-currency market) activities of large banks were hardly supervised at all. Thus, while the Basel Committee has, from the outset, encouraged international convergence towards common approaches and common standards, it does not attempt harmonization of member countries' supervisory techniques.

The work of the Basel Committee over the three decades since 1975 turned it from an obscure, low-key G10 forum into a much broader-based core body

---

[9]   See: http://www.bis.org/bcbs/history.htm

influencing banking supervisory standards worldwide.[10] This development was punctuated and spurred on by the recurrent financial and banking crises of the 1970s, 1980s and 1990s. In a nutshell, the Basel Committee's work developed along two tracks. In the field of banking supervision, the two main issues were that of the allocation of home-host responsibilities (who supervises what?) and the development of common standards for effective banking supervision (how?). In the field of banking regulation, the overriding aim, as it transpired over the years, was to help create a 'level playing-field' among internationally active banks, mainly through the adoption of common capital-adequacy rules (Basel Capital Accord and Basel II).

The first problem tackled by the newly established Basel Committee was that of the adequate supervision of banks' international activities. The basic principle adopted was that no foreign banking establishment should escape supervision. Soon, a low-key agreement was reached, advocating sharing supervisory responsibility for banks' foreign branches, subsidiaries and joint ventures between host and home-country authorities. This 'Concordat' was endorsed by the G10 governors in 1975, and subsequently revised and tightened in 1983 and 1991, following the failures of Banco Ambrosiano and BCCI respectively. Other key principles that are part of or derive from the Concordat are that international banking groups should be subject to consolidated supervision, and that there should be an efficient flow of prudential information between banking supervisors in different countries. With time, the principles of the Concordat developed into minimum standards that came to be endorsed by supervisory authorities outside the G10 as well. In the 1990s, in close collaboration with non-G10 supervisory authorities, the Basel Committee developed a more formalized set of 'core principles for effective banking supervision'. Since their publication in 1997, these 'core principles', which provide a comprehensive blueprint for an effective supervisory system, have been propagated worldwide, for instance by a specially created liaison group comprising both G10 and non-G10 countries.

The history of the development of regulatory standards through the Basel Committee is no doubt more complex. One of the themes of this volume is the 'great reversal', by which the state-led international financial system of the interwar period and of the Bretton Woods era has gradually made way for a market-led system. In the same vein, in the field of banking regulation, administrative restrictions, which were still prevalent in the 1960s, '… have been increasingly replaced by less intrusive, indirect prudential standards, such as capital requirements'.[11] The Basel Committee has played a key role in the internationalization of such more market-conform standards. It was not, however, the Basel Committee itself that triggered the process that would eventually lead to the Basel Capital Accord of 1988.

---

[10]   'One Hundred and Thirty Years of Central Bank Cooperation. A BIS Perspective', in C. Borio, G. Toniolo and P. Clement (eds), *Past and Future of Central Bank Cooperation* (Cambridge, 2008), p. 61.

[11]   Padoa-Schioppa, *Regulating Finance*, p. 98.

The developing-world debt crisis that erupted in 1982 exposed the inadequate capitalization of many international banks. In an effort to stem the Mexican crisis and avoid contagion from spreading, the US Administration sought additional IMF funding, which Congress was only prepared to grant in exchange for tighter banking regulations, in particular the imposition of minimum capital ratios on large banks in order to shift at least some of the cost of any future bailout from the taxpayers to the banks. In response, the large US banks argued that raising their capital requirements would negatively affect their international competitiveness unless foreign banks too were forced to recapitalize in a similar fashion. This move provided the impetus for the US authorities to push for an international agreement on bank capital adequacy, and the Basel Committee on Banking Supervision quickly emerged as the ideal forum to achieve this.[12]

The Basel Capital Accord was approved by the G10 Governors in July 1988. It provided for a minimum capital standard for internationally active banks of 8 per cent. By September 1993, all the banks in the G10 countries with material international banking business were meeting this minimum capital requirement. This included all the market leaders in international banking, and as a result virtually all other countries with active international banks outside the G10 followed suit.

Once it had become an internationally accepted standard, the Basel Capital Accord generated a dynamic of its own. Further refinements to its rather crude framework were introduced in the course of the 1990s, reflecting both developments in financial technology and products and the impact of the Asian crisis, which turned the spotlight on global financial stability issues. In 1999, the Basel Committee issued a proposal for a new capital-adequacy framework consisting of three pillars: minimum capital requirements; supervisory review of an institution's capital adequacy and internal assessment process; effective use of market discipline as a lever to strengthen disclosure and encourage safe and sound banking practices. The consultation process on the new Accord has been the broadest and most wide-ranging undertaken by the Basel Committee to date, going far beyond the G10 and supervisory authorities alone. Basel II was formally adopted by the G10 Governors in 2004. Nonetheless, some aspects of it remain controversial, raising resistance in some quarters of the banking sector and also at the political level, particularly since the 2008–09 crisis. The Basel process that has

---

[12]   The genesis of the 1988 Basel Capital Accord has been described in detail by E.B. Kapstein, *Supervising International Banks. Origins and Implications of the Basle Accord* (Princeton NJ, 1991). Kapstein conceptualizes cooperation in international financial supervision as the product of power and purpose: '… specifically, the combination of US (and to a lesser extent British) financial market power with the shared or convergent purpose of bank supervisors to provide their home markets with greater financial stability while also addressing the competitive concerns of their domestic firms' (E.B. Kapstein, Architects of Stability? 'International Cooperation among Financial Supervisors', in C. Borio, G. Toniolo and P. Clement (eds), *Past and Future of Central Bank Cooperation* (Cambridge, 2008), p. 119.

yielded the Basel I and II Capital Accords has been subject to criticism because of a perceived lack of transparency and, above all, because it is under the control of a relatively small and closed group of unelected central bankers and banking supervisors and is therefore held to lack democratic legitimacy. It is therefore very likely that the Basel process will have to evolve further, constantly adapting to new circumstances and demands.

Archival Issues

This brief history of international cooperation in the field of cross-border banking supervision already points to the main archival issues it raises. First, there are the many different players involved. Second, there is the highly confidential nature inherent in anything that touches upon the competitive position of the world's main financial intermediaries. Finally, the specific process that has led to the formulation and acceptance of international supervisory and prudential standards poses specific challenges from an archival point of view. Let us now briefly review these three issues.

The most significant players in the history of international banking supervision include national supervisory authorities, the central banks and their cooperative body the Bank for International Settlements, the main commercial banks, national governments, and international political bodies such as the IMF, EU and others. The archival challenge is obvious. To do full justice to the story of how the missing link in the international supervisory architecture was found means putting together the many pieces of a giant jigsaw puzzle. Take for instance the genesis of the first Basel Capital Accord (1988). The historian would at least have to go back to the 1982 Mexico crisis, trace its fallout on the US banking sector, reconstruct the interactions between the IMF and the US Administration, and then between the Federal Reserve System (under the impulse of Paul Volcker) and the Bank of England. Having seen all relevant records and files on one side of the Atlantic, our researcher would have to cross over to Europe to properly gauge the positions of the different national and supranational players there (in particular Germany, France, Italy and the European Commission), then on to Japan to try to get a glimpse at the Ministry of Finance and Bank of Japan files, and back to Europe to witness the story coming to a conclusion as reflected in the records of the Basel Committee on Banking Supervision.

Most of the archives relevant to this story are of course still closed to researchers. In many cases a 30-year access rule applies, which means that only now should the very first records related to the Basel process, which started in 1975, be becoming available. Should be, because many of these records can be expected to be regarded as confidential or sensitive even after the customary 30 years have elapsed. There are two important reasons for this. The first has to do with the type of information-sharing practised by semi-informal bodies such as the G10 central-bank committees. These meetings always work on the presumption of confidentiality: experts can speak their minds in an open and frank manner because they are in a trusted (shielded) environment among colleagues and they know that what they say can be expected to remain within the four walls of the meeting room, or at least within the confines of a closed group of likeminded officials. As a result, the release of, say, the verbatim meeting minutes of the Basel Committee might be held to affect or even jeopardize the confidential nature of present-day discussions and meetings, as the potential release of these minutes – even in a rather remote future – might materially change the discourse of some of the meeting's participants.

The second reason why many of the key records related to the discussions on international banking supervision and regulation over the past 30 years may remain closed for much longer than that can be found in the content itself of many of these discussions. This not only refers to the 'big issues', such as market-stability concerns, moral hazard and lender-of-last-resort issues – on which central banks and supervisory authorities usually prefer to keep their cards close to their chests – but also to more specific instances: for example, if prudential issues regarding a particular commercial bank were being discussed. This sensitivity no doubt also has to do with the fact that not only the Basel process itself, but also its outcomes, remain more or less controversial.[13]

The Basel process is indeed a very specific one, and does not easily lend itself to scrutiny. The experts who engage in it are more often than not appointed officials, and not democratically elected or accountable. The guidelines, standards and 'accords' they produce are usually referred to as soft law. Writing about the 1988 Basel Capital Accord, Steven Solomon has put it as follows: 'Although legally nonbinding – and adopted without any democratic national legislative vote – the central banker club code of honor made it as good as law'.[14] What consequences does this have for archival research? The most important is that the release of much of the key archival material remains very much at the discretion of the institutions involved in the Basel process. While the BIS as an international organization is exempt from any national freedom-of-information legislation, it has voluntarily adopted a 30-year archive access policy. The release of files of the Basel Committee on Banking Supervision is, however, subject to the approval of the individual central banks and supervisory authorities represented on the Committee. Most national central banks and supervisory authorities themselves have to abide by official record-keeping requirements, and usually fall under

---

[13] It has been argued that the 'strengthening of official supervision and regulation', so close to the heart of central banks and supervisory authorities, may not necessarily be conducive to improving the functioning of banks, or that the widespread adoption of common standards may actually increase risks and hamper financial products and services innovation. See: J.R. Barth, G. Caprio Jr and R. Levine, *Rethinking Bank Regulation. Till Angels Govern* (Cambridge MA and New York, 2006), pp. 14 and 67.

[14] S. Solomon, *The Confidence Game. How Unelected Central Bankers Are Governing the Changed Global Economy* (New York and London, 1995), p. 435.

domestic freedom-of-information legislation, although this mostly allows for a broad range of exceptions where it is felt that the release of certain material might negatively affect legitimate third-party interests.[15]

Does this mean that the history of the development of international supervisory standards during the last decades of the twentieth century cannot be written, through a lack of accessible sources? Most certainly not, as testified inter alia by the vast literature that already exists on the subject. A lot of the background material related to the genesis of the Basel I and Basel II Capital Accords has been released by the Basel Committee itself in the course of the extensive consultation rounds that were part and parcel of the process. Moreover, it can reasonably be expected that a lot – though not quite all – of the remaining material will become available at central-bank and public archives and elsewhere after the customary 30 years have passed. This may for instance include the negotiation positions of the different national authorities. It is to be hoped that the archival instances will be able to release as much of this material as possible without jeopardizing legitimate confidentiality concerns. It will no doubt contribute to a better understanding of the Basel process, and how it helped find the missing link in the post-Bretton Woods international financial architecture.

---

[15]   See, for instance, for the USA: *The Freedom of Information Act*, 5 U.S.C. § 552, as amended in 2002 (USA), esp. §552(b); for the UK: *The Freedom of Information Act 2000* (UK), especially articles 21–44; for Germany: *Bundesarchivgesetz*, § 2 (4) and § 5 (3), as well as *Gesetz über das Kreditwesen*, § 9 and *Bundesbankgesetz*, 23 March 2002, § 32 (Germany).

CHAPTER 10

Banking Crises in the North: A Comparative Analysis of Finland and Sweden[1]

Peter Englund and Vesa Vihriälä

Abstract

Finland and Sweden both experienced financial crises in the early 1990s. We give a concise description of the crises, including the background, the evolution of the main events, and the government policies to handle the crises. We discuss the consequences for the real economy, and try to isolate what explained the emergence of the crises and the relatively speedy recoveries. We conclude that the crises were due to a combination of extraordinary shocks and serious mistakes, both in macro policies and in regulatory policies. The crises were preceded by a fundamental financial liberalization in both countries, but this was not sufficient cause for them. The crises exacerbated macro economic problems primarily through their impacts on borrower balance sheets. However, evidence of a so-called credit crunch remains weak. Crisis management was fast and strong-handed. In both countries, the financial sectors were substantially restructured, and recovered from the crisis relatively quickly.

The financial systems in the early 1980s

In the early 1980s, both Sweden and Finland had rather poorly developed financial systems. The Finnish financial sector was much smaller than that of Continental Europe, not to mention the Anglo-Saxon countries, with a ratio of financial assets to GDP of less than 60 per cent of that in Germany. The size of the Swedish financial sector was roughly the same as that of Germany. In terms of structure, the systems were closer to the Continental-European model, with intermediaries dominating the channelling of funds, than the Anglo-Saxon model with the securities markets playing a major role. Stock markets played a limited role, with capitalization remaining under 10 per cent of GDP in Finland and under 30 per

---

[1] This chapter draws on P. Englund and V. Vihriälä, 'Financial Crises in Developed Economies. The Cases of Finland and Sweden', in L. Jonung, J. Kiander and P. Vartia, *Great Financial Crises in Finland and Sweden. The Nordic Experience of Financial Liberalization* (Cheltenham, 2009). Contact authors: peter.englund@hhs.se, Stockholm School of Economics and University of Amsterdam; vesa.vihriala@vnk.fi, Secretariat of the Economic Council, Prime Minister's Office, Helsinki.

cent in Sweden, far below many other countries. Universal banks providing a wide variety of services played a dominant role.

Pervasive regulation confines business opportunities

Financial institutions were tightly regulated. In Finland, lending rates were constrained by ceilings, and deposit rates were required to be linked to the central bank's base rate in order for interest income to be tax exempt for depositors. Lending was not explicitly regulated, but the central bank issued guidelines, requiring priority of business investment over consumption loans. In Sweden, there were outright ceilings on bank lending, and 'liquidity ratios' required banks to hold a minimum fraction of their assets (over 50 per cent around 1980) in bonds issued by the government and by mortgage institutions. This ensured that the desired residential construction could be financed at below-market interest. With more than 50 per cent of their assets in bonds, typically with long maturities and below-market interest rates, Swedish banks and insurance companies had in effect been transformed into repositories for illiquid bonds, crippled in fulfilling their key function of screening and monitoring loans for consumption and investment. The net of regulations imposed on banks benefited other financial institutions. In particular, finance companies, originally focusing on activities like factoring and leasing, expanded aggressively into regular lending.

In both countries, regulated interest rates were kept low relative to inflation, making real rates negative and creating constant excess demand with credit allocated by other means than prices. The absence of alternatives kept depositors willing to deposit in banks. Stock and bond markets were small and illiquid and investments abroad were subject to special permits. Further, the tax systems – with nominal interest payments deductible, as against marginal tax rates from 50 up to 80 per cent in Sweden – contributed to making the after-tax real interest rates even more strongly negative, as illustrated in Figure 10.1. Clearly this was not an equilibrium situation. It could only be sustained through regulations and rationing.

The regulations had a major impact on bank balance sheets, cost structures and risk profiles. Banks held bonds and corporate and household loans, which, even though formally risky, entailed almost no credit risk for several reasons: debt-service burdens never became too severe, real lending rates were low, lending-rate regulation allowed banks to use creditworthiness as the key rationing device, and economic downturns in the economy usually resulted in devaluations.

Deregulation

Many strains developed in the regulated financial systems over time. Circumvention of the regulatory constraints became more widely spread, and technological developments and internationalization made many actors less dependent on domestic markets. As a result, the rationale of regulations was increasingly questioned, and a gradual liberalization process started in the early 1980s in both

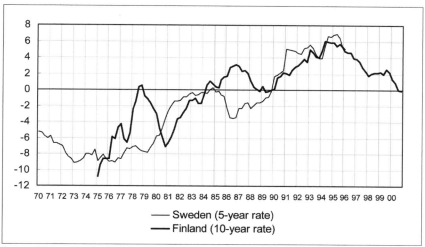

Figure 10.1 Real after-tax interest rates

countries (see Figures 10.2A and B). Key steps were taken in late 1985, when Sweden removed lending ceilings for banks and placement requirements for insurance companies, and in early 1986, when Finland lifted restrictions on lending rates for banks. In both countries, important elements of currency regulations remained. It was only with the final abolition of currency controls in July 1989 that money and bond markets in the Swedish krona were fully integrated with international markets. In Finland, the last restrictions on short-term capital movements were lifted at the end of 1990.

Liberalization expanded the range of assets and liabilities for domestic investors. Instead of being forced to invest in government and housing bonds, Swedish banks were now free to lend where prospects of returns were favourable, and Finnish banks were no longer affected by lending guidelines. Perhaps even more important was the change in refinancing opportunities. Improved access to foreign sources of funds helped banks and other financial intermediaries to reduce their direct dependence on central-bank funding, and the growth of the domestic money market gave them more freedom of funding. Under regulation, obtaining a bank loan had been a sort of privilege. The abolition of lending controls now forced banks to compete freely for borrowers, as in any retail business.

The lending boom

Many years of credit rationing had constrained borrowing by households and smaller firms. Liberalization coupled with a favourable macroeconomic environment now created new conditions. Large devaluations in the early 1980s had improved competitiveness in both countries; and particularly in Sweden, fiscal policy was still expansive. After-tax real interest rates remained negative (measured ex post) as can be seen from Figure 10.1. In Finland, decelerating inflation increased the

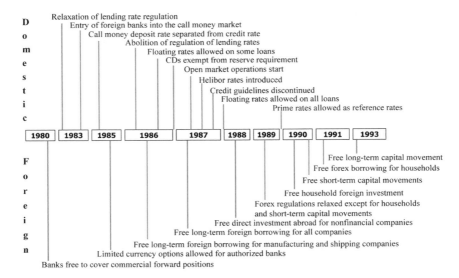

Figure 10.2A Deregulation of financial markets in Finland

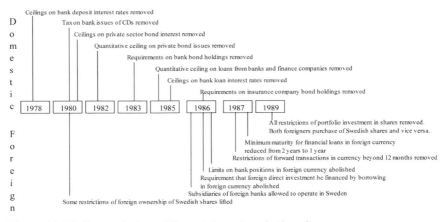

Figure 10.2B Deregulation of financial markets in Sweden

real rate in 1986 and 1987, but faster inflation in 1988 and 1989 brought it back close to zero. The scene was set for a credit boom.

The initial acceleration of credit growth came in 1985 in Finland and in 1986 in Sweden. In Sweden, finance companies and other non-bank intermediaries were particularly active at this initial stage, although bank credit stocks also increased by over 17 per cent in 1986. In Finland, both banks and non-bank intermediaries expanded rapidly in 1985. After a temporary slowdown, credit growth accelerated again in 1988. At this stage banks played the predominant role. In both countries bank lending grew in nominal terms by around 30 per cent. In Finland, tightening of monetary policy and special measures to rein in bank lending slowed down credit expansion in 1989. In Sweden, bank lending continued to expand at a real rate of 15–20 per cent in both 1989 and 1990, and the break came only in the second half of 1990 in response to the combination of tightened monetary policy and a tax reform that cut the marginal tax rate on interest deductions from 50 to 30 per cent. Lending started to fall in real terms from the second quarter of 1991.

Asset prices and bank profits feed back to credit growth

The impact of the lending boom was strongest on those sectors that had been hardest hit by regulation. Consumption of durable goods, housing investment and investment by closed-sector firms were most strongly affected. Readily available finance also spurred merger and acquisition activity. Additional demand inflated real-estate and stock prices, in turn bolstering borrower balance sheets. This supported further lending, which in turn fed back into asset prices. Even though household indebtedness increased substantially in relation to disposable income, it was matched by a parallel increase in asset values. Thus the ratio of debt to total assets remained essentially unchanged at around 22 per cent in Finland and increased by less than 5 percentage points to almost 40 per cent in Sweden by the end of the decade.

Lending was also bolstered by increased bank profitability, which improved solidity. Rapid extension of new loans added to fee income, as did increased stock- and money-market activity. Good earnings growth also made bank cost-effectiveness (revenue/cost-ratios) look better, in many cases masking weak underlying profitability. As subsequent developments were to demonstrate, these profits were largely an illusion, since they did not properly account for credit risks. Fees and interest income were recorded immediately, whereas credit risks manifested themselves only later. With hindsight, it is quite obvious that there was a price bubble in the sense of higher asset prices than could easily be explained by fundamental factors.

Some lenders more aggressive than others

Deregulation triggered competition both within the banking sector and between banks and other financial intermediaries. In Finland, the most aggressive actor was the savings-bank group. Between the end of 1986 and 1990 combined lending by the savings banks grew by over 140 per cent, compared to less than 80 per cent for the commercial banks. The rapid expansion of lending as well as entry into new business areas was a deliberate strategic choice by the Finnish savings banks' central organization (*Skopbank*), with the aim to 'grow out of' profitability problems caused by high costs.

In Sweden, competition had already intensified before the deregulation. Savings banks were gradually losing their traditional dominance in the household

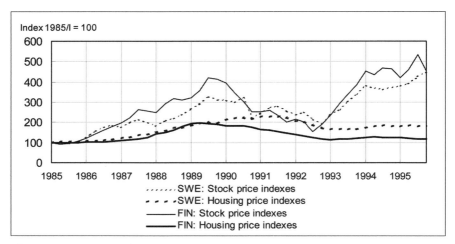

Figure 10.3   Asset prices

deposit market. To compensate, they expanded away into lending to industry. Generally, those banks with a weak position in corporate lending – in particular *Nordbanken* and *Gota Bank* – increased market share. In both countries, the most aggressive actors were the weakest in terms of capital and underlying profitability. This is consistent with a 'gamble for resurrection' response to liberalization: low 'charter value' increases risk appetite.[2] A study by Vihriälä shows that differences in profitability and capital are sufficient to fully explain the difference in lending growth between savings banks and cooperative banks in Finland.[3]

Deregulation also had an impact on competition between banks and other intermediaries. The Swedish finance companies provide a good example. These companies had earlier taken advantage of a loosely regulated position, and expanded from activities such as leasing, factoring and credit cards into direct lending. The effect of the removal of restrictions on banks soon became evident, when these entered into markets previously in the domain of the finance companies, which were now pushed into higher-risk markets. As a result, the finance companies lost market share at a rapid pace starting in 1988. Banks were not only competing against the finance companies, but were also doing business with them in the form of short-term lending and by guaranteeing their commercial paper programmes. In 1990, five per cent of all bank lending went to finance companies, compared to one per cent in 1985. This now turned out to be risky business as the credit losses among finance companies continued to grow.

---

[2]   See M. Keeley, 'Deposit Insurance, Risk, and Market Power in Banking', *American Economic Review*, 80, 5 (1990), pp. 1183–1200.

[3]   V. Vihriälä, *Banks and the Finnish Credit Cycle 1986–1995*, Bank of Finland Studies E:7 (Helsinki, 1990).

Vulnerable financial positions in both the non-financial and financial sectors

Total credit expanded at an unprecedented rate in both countries. By the peak of the boom, household debt as a fraction of disposable income had increased by some 20 percentage points to 80 per cent in Finland and by 30 percentage points to 130 per cent in Sweden. Corporate-sector indebtedness increased in a similar fashion. The ratio of corporate debt to nominal GDP increased from 60 per cent to some 80 per cent in Finland and from about 70 per cent to more than 90 per cent in Sweden. As a whole, the rate of credit growth was rather typical for countries that were to have banking crises, but lower than that in several of the Asian crisis countries of the late 1990s.

A large fraction of borrowing was in foreign currency, even for firms with no foreign revenues that would have needed hedging. Both countries defended fixed exchange rates by high interest rates. As a result, substantial gains could be made by borrowing in foreign currency and investing in kronor or markka – as long as there was no devaluation. In Sweden, the fraction of bank lending to the non-bank public denominated in foreign currency increased from 24 per cent in 1986 to 44 per cent in 1990.[4] In Finland, the share of foreign-denominated debt in total corporate debt rose from 23 per cent in 1986 to 39 per cent in 1990. Since little of this was hedged by forward contracts, the private sectors became vulnerable not only to income and interest-rate shocks but also to exchange-rate shocks.

The Crisis

Tightening monetary conditions stop the expansion

Early signs of over-extension and distress emerged in both countries in 1989. Stock prices and real-estate prices peaked. Interest rates had already started to increase in 1988, primarily as market responses to imbalances in the economies. But apart from occasional episodes to defend the exchange rates, there were few signs so far in the financial markets of either country that signalled a crisis. Attempts by the central banks to rein in credit expansion and over-heating were frustrated by the fixed-exchange-rate regime: interest rates could not be raised very much as long as confidence in the currency peg led to large short-term capital inflows.

Towards the end of 1989 (in Finland) and in early 1990 (in Sweden) there was a significant tightening of monetary conditions, led mainly by market impulses. Foreign interest rates rose substantially and strong depreciation expectations emerged, driving domestic interest rates up even further. Higher interest rates and falling asset prices were soon accompanied by weakened domestic demand. In 1990, private investment started to decline and consumption stagnated in Finland. In

---

[4]   See J. 'Wallander, Bankkrisen – Omfattning. Orsaker. Lärdomar', in *Bankkrisen*, reports from Bankkriskommittén (Stockholm, 1994), tables A1 and A3.

Sweden, consumption was declining but investment still continued to grow in 1990. There was a dramatic reduction in corporate earnings, and some firms started to have problems in servicing their debts. High interest rates and weaker cash flows exerted further downward pressure on asset prices. Lower collateral values in turn increased banks' exposure in the case of default. Recorded credit losses still remained small, but the financial sectors started to feel the pressure in both countries.

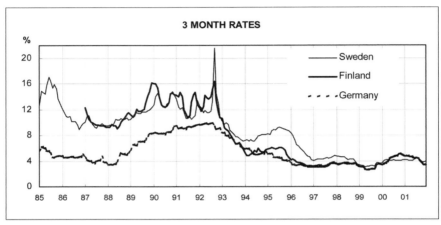

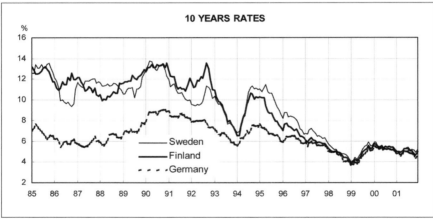

Figure 10.4   Nominal interest rates in Sweden, Finland and Germany

Further shocks increase pressures in the financial markets

Exports started to fall in 1991, driven by the weakness of world market demand – in the case of Finland aggravated by the collapse of the Soviet Union. In Sweden, fiscal policy created a further shock when a long-overdue reform of the income-tax system was finally implemented in 1990–91. A reduction of the marginal tax rate applicable to interest deductions from 50 to 30 per cent finally made after-tax real interest rates positive, but it also created a substantial negative shock to aggregate demand. GDP declined in both countries in 1991, by 6 per cent in Finland and 2 per cent in Sweden.

The shocks impacted on the monetary and financial systems in many ways. The exchange-rate pegs were called into question, putting renewed upward pressure on interest rates. Plummeting corporate profitability weakened borrower capacity to service debt, and the number of bankruptcies doubled between 1990 and 1992. Bank earnings were squeezed by non-performing assets as well as by declining fee income from new lending and trading activity. Falling collateral values increased the costs of bankruptcies to the lending banks.

Swedish finance companies first hit

Reports in early 1990 about sizable credit losses in a couple of minor finance companies went by without much notice.[5] It was only in September 1990 that the mood suddenly changed when one of the finance companies, *Nyckeln* ('the Key'), with heavy exposure to real estate, found itself unable to roll over maturing commercial paper. This was a sort of 'run'; rather than actively running to the bank to withdraw deposits, the commercial-paper holders refused renewed funding in the face of an imminent bankruptcy risk. The crisis spread to the whole market, which dried up in a couple of days. Surviving finance companies had to resort to bank loans. The crisis also affected other segments of the money market, with sharply increasing spreads between t-bills and certificates of deposit. In the next few months a number of other finance companies also went into bankruptcy.[6]

Now the banks, having underwritten the commercial-paper programmes, had two options: either let the finance companies go bankrupt and take the losses right away, or extend new lines of credit with the risk of higher losses further on. As the crisis deepened, the latter option became less attractive, and several finance companies went bankrupt. Now the crisis spread rapidly to the banks. Total credit losses in the bank sector amounted to around one per cent of total lending in 1990, more than twice the level in earlier years.

---

[5]   See L.P. Jennergren, 'The Swedish Finance Company Crisis. Could it have been Anticipated?', *Scandinavian Economic History Review*, 50, 2 (2002), pp. 7–30, for a study documenting the lack of stock-market reaction to the early reports of credit losses among finance companies.

[6]   This crisis bears some resemblance to the crisis of the British 'secondary banks' in 1973. Like the finance companies, they had thriven due to regulation and were put under competitive pressure when the operations of banks were deregulated. See E.P. Davis, *Debt, Financial Fragility and Systemic Risk* (Oxford, 1992), pp. 152f.

Banking problems and exchange rate collapse in Finland

In Finland, problems came out into broad daylight on 19 September 1991, when *Skopbank* could not even obtain overnight funding. As a result, the Bank of Finland took over and invested some FIM 3.5 billion in the bank. The *Skopbank* failure added to the general pessimism, as more bad news was accumulating. Industrial production was declining, while bankruptcies, unemployment and the public deficit were increasing. Devaluation speculations started anew, and short-term interest rates shot up sharply from August and onwards. In defence of the existing parities, the Bank of Finland sold foreign currency, but this did not help in the end. On 14 November 1991, the markka was finally devalued by 13 per cent. This brought short-term interest rates down by some 4 percentage points for a while, but longer-term rates were largely unaffected.

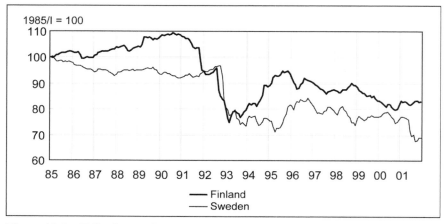

Figure 10.5   Effective exchange rates

The deterioration of the economy with continuing high interest rates progressively weakened all banks. The devaluation was an important element in this process. Although banks' currency positions were closed, they were hurt by bankruptcies among firms with loans denominated in foreign currency. In early 1992, the Finnish government decided to reserve FIM 8 billion to bolster the capital base of the deposit banks across the board through a capital injection. Furthermore, a completely new authority, the Government Guarantee Fund (GGF), was authorized to use up to FIM 20 billion for support operations. At this stage, the Swedish authorities did not yet admit any reason for similar precautionary measures; the banking problems were still seen as isolated to a couple of banks and not to be handled as a systemic crisis.

It did not take long for new problems to emerge, particularly among the savings banks, as a large fraction of their loans turned non-performing. By October 1992, yet another bank, *STS*-bank, was failing and was taken over by one of the two largest commercial banks (*KOP*). Total bank-sector capital fell by almost 40 per cent. By then, three banks had been taken over by the State, and the remainder of the banking system now depended on government support. In the spring of 1992 new pressures started to mount on the Finnish markka. Both short- and long-term interest rates increased, and the Bank of Finland had to sell foreign exchange to support the exchange rate. In the end, the peg was finally abandoned on September 8. The markka immediately depreciated by some 12 per cent.

The Swedish Crisis Spreads to the Banks

In Sweden, bank credit losses reached an annual rate of 3.5 per cent of lending by the end of 1991, and 7.5 per cent of lending at the peak of the crisis in the final quarter of 1992, about twice the operating profits of the banking sector. Over the period 1990–93, accumulated losses came to a total of nearly 17 per cent of lending.[7] The evolving crisis was closely connected with a sharp downturn in the real-estate market, with prices in central Stockholm falling by 35 per cent in 1991 and by another 15 per cent the following year.[8] Lending 'related to real estate'[9] accounted for between 40 and 50 per cent of all losses, but only 10–15 per cent of all lending.

The fraction of lending going into real estate and the pace of lending expansion in previous years are the key factors that explain why some banks had larger credit losses than others. The first signs of solvency problems came in the fall of 1991, when two of the six major banks, *Första Sparbanken* and *Nordbanken*, needed new capital to fulfill their capital requirements. Just as in Finland, problems were at first seen to be limited to a couple of banks. In *Nordbanken* the state had to act in its capacity as the main owner and injected SEK 5 billion of new equity in December 1991. A major restructuring was decided by parliament in June 1992, and private minority owners of the bank were bailed out. A 'bad bank', *Securum*, was founded and a quarter of *Nordbanken*'s credit stock, at an original book value of SEK 67 billion, was transferred to *Securum*.

During the spring of 1992, problems also surfaced in *Gota Bank*, the bank that in the end turned out to have made the largest losses. On September 9 1992 the holding company owning *Gota Bank* went bankrupt. Only at this stage were the banking problems dealt with as a systemic crisis. Sweden had no formal deposit insurance at the time, but now the government immediately announced that it guaranteed *Gota*'s liabilities. A similar guarantee, covering all forms of bank debt, was extended to all banks a few weeks later. Subsequently, the State took over *Gota* at a price of one krona, but with recapitalization costing a total of SEK 25 billion.

---

[7] These numbers include provisions for future losses on loans that were still performing.

[8] These are particularly uncertain estimates as the market dried up, with few transactions, making the empirical ground for the appraised values thinner than usual.

[9] See Wallander, *Bankkrisen*, tables 4 and 5. The concept was defined by the Financial Supervisory Authority and includes loans to the real-estate and construction industries but also other loans against real-estate collateral.

The unrest on the European currency markets during the summer of 1992 spilled over with particular force on Sweden and Finland, not surprisingly given their legacies of high inflation and recurring devaluations. Increased interest rates rescued the krona for the moment, but deepened the problems for many bank customers, with adverse effects on Swedish banks' international funding. With more than 40 per cent of their lending in foreign currency, banks were heavily dependent on access to international financial markets, and with increasing signs of crisis loan maturities shortened.

In early September 1992 the pound and the lira touched the lower limits of their currency bands and on September 8 the Finnish markka started floating. This led to speculations against the krona and on September 9 (the day of the Gota bankruptcy) the overnight rate was raised to 75 per cent. On September 16 and 17, when the UK and Italy left the ERM, the Riksbank had to increase the overnight rate to 500 per cent to defend the krona. Now, the general bank guarantee played an important role in securing continued international funding for Swedish banks. The Riksbank also provided liquidity by depositing a part of the foreign-exchange reserves with the banks, thereby insuring banks against funding problems. During the fall, the government presented some restrictive fiscal measures, but this brought only temporary relief. In November speculation resumed, and on November 19 the krona was left to float, leading to an immediate depreciation the next day by 9 per cent, and by 20 per cent by the turn of the year.

The interaction between the currency crisis and the banking crisis is complex. The fact that the banking crisis started at least a year before the currency crisis, with credit losses culminating in the fall of 1992 – *before* the fixed rate was abandoned – indicates that there was no strong *direct* link from currency losses to the banking crisis. In this regard the Swedish crisis process differs from that in Finland, where the 1991 devaluation had a direct impact on the debt-service burden of the corporate sector, thereby adding to credit losses early in the process. On the other hand, there was an *indirect* link, which was particularly important in Sweden, with the defence of the krona by high interest rates, causing credit losses and deepening the banking crisis.

The Swedish private sector had built up a large stock of foreign currency debt, estimated to be SEK 541 billion in September 1992 (35 per cent of GDP). Most of this was intermediated by the banking sector, whose net position in foreign currency was essentially balanced. The spot position was positive (SEK 20 billion), but the position on the forward market was minus SEK 65 billion.[10] This situation involved two risk elements for the banks. One was the liquidity risk: even if banks did not directly take excessive exchange risk, they faced the risk of foreign lenders refusing to roll over short-term credit lines. This mechanism

---

[10]   These figures are based on unpublished calculations within the Riksbank. We are grateful to Anders Lindström and Kerstin Mitlid for making these figures available to us.

contributed to deepening many other banking and currency crises.[11] In the end, the liquidity support provided by the Riksbank played an important role in avoiding this risk.

The other risk element relates to bank customers. Whereas the banks themselves had a balanced position, many of their customers were heavily exposed in foreign currency. In the aggregate, the private sector held foreign-currency assets to offset the debt. Financial assets in foreign currency amounted to SEK 174 billion, making the net financial position in foreign currency minus SEK 367 billion in September 1992. Adding direct investments abroad and holdings of foreign shares made the total net position a trivial minus SEK 13 billion. But this balanced average concealed an uneven distribution, with many small and medium-sized bank customers heavily exposed to currency movements.

The banking crisis and the currency crisis reinforced each other. As the precarious situation of the Swedish banks became recognized internationally during 1992, it was clear that the banks and many of their customers would not be able to survive an extended period of very high interest rates. This improved the odds from speculating against the Swedish krona, in the end making it unavoidable to abandon the fixed parity.

Further bank support and stabilization

Towards the spring of 1993 pressures in the financial markets started to recede in both countries. In Finland, interest rates had been falling since the currency was left floating. But it was only after the first signs of a more sustained improvement in the current account in the second quarter that the financial markets calmed down. The markka started to appreciate while the Bank of Finland bought foreign currency, and interest rates continued to decline. From mid-1993, the real economy started growing again. Despite these improvements, further bank support was needed. The two major commercial banks were given guarantees for raising new capital, and the restructuring of *Skopbank* and the Savings Bank of Finland continued with full force. The restructuring of failed institutions and the associated disposal of assets required substantial public funding for several years to come. Total payments over the government budget have been estimated at FIM 52 billion.

Also in Sweden, financial indicators started to return to normal levels in 1993, with interest rates falling continuously during the year. By the end of 1993, both short- and long-term rates were down at around 7 per cent. The depreciation of the krona was halted in February 1993, but in contrast to the markka it was not strengthened until 1995. Lower interest rates eased the situation for the banks, and after 1993 no more government support was needed. Out of total government payments of SEK

---

[11] See, e.g., F.S. Mishkin, 'Lessons from the Tequila Crisis', *Journal of Banking & Finance*, 23, 10 (1999), pp. 1521–33 on Mexico, and G. Corsetti, P. Pesenti, and N. Roubini, 'What Caused the Asian Currency and Financial Crisis?', *Japan and the World Economy*, 11, 3 (1999), pp. 305–73 on Asia.

65 billion, only 3 billion went to the old bank owners. By and large, the government followed the principle of saving the banks but not their owners.

Effects on the Real Economy

Aggregate observations consistent with the importance of financial factors

The production decline during the crisis was associated with a significant reduction both of aggregate credit and of the importance of bank loans in relation to other sources of funds. In Finland, the ratio of total liabilities of non-financial enterprises to GDP declined from 65 per cent in 1992 to 40 per cent in 1995, and the share of bank loans in those liabilities fell from 52 per cent to 49 per cent. The pattern was similar in Sweden, where total liabilities fell from 126 per cent of GDP in 1992 to 83 per cent in 1995, and the fraction of bank loans among total liabilities decreased from 28 to 25 per cent.

This is consistent with credit constraints becoming more important, but declining credit volume could also be explained by weak demand owing to high interest rates and weak profitability prospects and income expectations. Survey data indicate a sharp increase in the proportion of Finnish firms reporting funding difficulties, suggesting a role for tighter financial constraints, be they on the side of borrowers or of lenders. Further evidence comes from econometric studies on aggregate time-series data. Analysing quarterly data for all Nordic countries, it has been found that total lending by credit institutions, along with house prices, has a strong predictive power (Granger causes) for bankruptcies.[12] For Finland, VAR models indicate that shocks to bank credit explain a significant proportion of the variation in GDP.[13] A more structural analysis supports the idea that supply is indeed responsible for at least a part of the decline of credit in Finland in the early 1990s.[14]

For Sweden, Hallsten tested the hypothesis of a lending channel for monetary policy within the framework of an IS/LM model extended with a loan market.[15] The model implies that the mix between bank loans and other sources of private-sector funding should vary with the stance of monetary conditions, and further that this mix should have an impact on production, investment and consumption.

[12]   J. Hansen, Financial Cycles and Bankruptcies in the Nordic Countries, Sveriges Riksbank Working Paper No. 149 (Stockholm, 2003).

[13]   A. Anari, J. Kolari, S. Pynnönen and A. Suvanto, 'Further Evidence on the Credit View. The Case of Finland', *Applied Economics*, 34, 3 (2002), pp. 267–78.

[14]   C. Pazarbaşioğlu, A Credit Crunch? Finland in the Aftermath of the Banking Crisis, IMF Staff Papers, 44 (1997).

[15]   K. Hallsten, Bank Loans and the Transmission Mechanism of Monetary Policy, in K. Hallsten, Essays on the Effects of Monetary Policy, Dissertation in Economics 1999, 2, Department of Economics, Stockholm University (Stockholm, 1999).

Her study documents a pronounced decline in the share of bank loans in various broader credit aggregates between 1991 and 1993. In a regression analysis on quarterly data from 1985 to 1995, she finds that an increased proportion of bank loans have a significantly positive impact on GDP.

Unfortunately, aggregate relationships cannot say much about the nature of the link between financing problems and real outcomes. Even if credit shocks are identified as stemming from the supply side it is not obvious whether they reflect reduced credit supply to constant-quality borrowers, or weakened borrower creditworthiness. Using the terminology of Holmström and Tirole, one has to distinguish between a 'credit crunch' and a 'collateral squeeze'.[16] This is not easy in practice because declining asset prices reduce both collateral values and lender net worth. Similarly, bankruptcies and associated credit losses deplete lender capital while also signalling an increased bankruptcy risk among borrowers in general.

Borrower Balance Sheets Played a Role

Let us now look in some more detail at the connection between private-sector balance sheets and consumption and investment. Starting with firms' investment, there is evidence that firms' weak balance sheets had a negative impact on fixed investment in Finland in the early 1990s. Honkapohja and Koskela show,[17] for panel data on the 500 largest Finnish firms for the years 1986 through 1996, that investment spending was much more dependent on cash flow (positively) and on debt (negatively) for firms that on a priori grounds could be considered financially constrained than for other firms. Furthermore, the effect of cash flow was stronger during the depression than in an average year. With somewhat different specifications but using essentially similar though shorter data, Brunila also found that investment depends positively on cash flow and negatively on indebtedness.[18] The effects turned out to be stronger for non-manufacturing than for manufacturing firms, which may reflect differences in the nature of available collateral assets. Similar patterns are found in time-series data.

For Sweden, Hansen and Lindberg estimated the impact of financial constraints using an unbalanced panel of manufacturing firms in existence for at least six years during the period 1979 to 1994.[19] They captured borrowing restrictions by treating

[16]   B. Holmström and J. Tirole, 'Financial Intermediation, Loanable Funds and the Real Sector', *Quarterly Journal of Economics*, 112, 3 (1997), pp. 663–91.

[17]   S. Honkapohja and E. Koskela, 'The Economic Crisis of the 1990s in Finland', *Economic Policy*, 29 (1999), pp. 399–424. Firms were classified as financially constrained if they could not meet the interest payments on their debt from profits in the previous period.

[18]   A. Brunila, Investment and Financing Considerations. Evidence from Finnish Panel Data, Bank of Finland Discussion Paper 4/94 (Helsinki, 1994).

[19]   S. Hansen and S. Lindberg, Agency Costs, Financial Deregulation, and Corporate Investment. An Euler Equation Approach to Panel Data for Swedish Firms, Working Paper 1997:20, Department of Economics, Uppsala University (Uppsala, 1997).

the marginal cost of capital as an increasing function of indebtedness. They found a significant, but quantitatively small, effect of indebtedness on the cost of capital, consistent with the importance of financial constraints.

All in all, the evidence indicates that high debt levels tend to constrain investment. In particular, the Finnish results are in accordance with the idea that borrower balance sheets have a rather non-linear impact on investment. Marginal changes in indebtedness at low debt levels, particularly under favorable macroeconomic conditions, do not matter greatly, but at high debt levels increased indebtedness can be a significant constraining factor, particularly in bad macroeconomic circumstances. This is likely to have played a role at least in the Finnish financial crisis.

The evidence with regard to consumption is less clear-cut. In neither country have there been studies based on panel data for individual households, and we have to rely on aggregate time series. For Finland, Honkapohja and Koskela estimate a consumption function augmented by measures of net wealth and credit growth, and find that private consumption depends, apart from on disposable income, positively on net wealth and credit growth and negatively on the nominal interest rate.[20] This is in line with corresponding studies for Sweden.[21]

A further approach rests on the assumption that financially unconstrained households follow an inter-temporally optimal consumption plan, implying that changes in the marginal utility of consumption are random (white noise), i.e., in a time-series regression the coefficient on (the marginal utility of) lagged consumption should be unity. Adding current income as an independent variable, its regression coefficient should indicate the fraction of total consumption that is limited by credit constraints. Employing such an Euler-equation approach it has been found that private consumption has been sensitive to current disposable income, and that this sensitivity increased after 1991.[22] The fraction of credit-constrained consumers seems to have increased during the crisis.

Weak evidence for 'Credit Crunch' due to insufficient bank capital

Inferring the role of bank balance sheets requires bank-level analysis. To really distinguish between 'collateral squeeze' and 'credit crunch' one should ideally

---

[20]   Honkapohja and Koskela, 'The Economic Crisis', interpret the finding that the nominal rather than real rate of interest affects consumption as evidence of liquidity constraints.

[21]   See L. Berg and R. Bergström, 'Housing and Financial Wealth, Financial Deregulation, and Consumption. The Swedish Case', *Scandinavian Journal of Economics*, 97, 3 (1995), pp. 421–39, and J. Agell, L. Berg, and P.-A. Edin, 'The Swedish Boom-to-Bust Cycle. Tax Reform, Consumption, and Asset Structure', *Swedish Economic Policy Review*, 2, 2 (1995), pp. 271–314.

[22]   See J. Agell and L. Berg, 'Does Financial Deregulation Cause a Consumption Boom?', *Scandinavian Journal of Economics*, 98, 7 (1996), pp. 579–601; and K. Takala, *Studies in Time Series Analysis of Consumption, Asset Prices and Forecasting*, Bank of Finland Studies E:22 (Helsinki, 2001).

combine data on individual firms with those of individual banks. Unfortunately, a lack of data has largely prevented such analyses. Kinnunen and Vihriälä examine how the likelihood that a firm terminated its operations in Finland in the early 1990s depended on the firm's characteristics and on whether it had a lending relationship with the most troubled part of the Finnish banking system, i.e. the Savings Bank of Finland and *Skopbank*.[23] The results, for 474 small and medium-sized firms, suggest that even accounting for the effects of liquidity, current profitability, indebtedness, age and size, firms with a lending relationship with the *SBF* and *Skopbank* in 1992 were more likely to close than other firms. The statistical significance of the finding is not very strong, however.[24]

Another study with Finnish data follows the widely used cross-sectional approach of examining how the rate of credit growth is affected by bank capital.[25] Vihriälä estimates reduced-form equations for the loan growth of 313 individual savings and cooperative banks in the early 1990s.[26] The study controls for demand factors using data on the economic conditions in the banks' regions of operation and for borrower quality by the share of non-performing assets in each bank's loan stock. There is no significant effect of bank capital on credit growth, a finding that is robust to various definitions of capital.

As a whole, the Finnish evidence supports the conclusion that financial factors exacerbated the economic downturn in the early 1990s. This seems to stem mainly from weak borrower balance sheets. The Swedish evidence is generally weaker, perhaps because the crisis was not quite as deep in Sweden as in Finland.

What really mattered

The Swedish and Finnish banking crises share many features of the crises experienced elsewhere. Geographically, the closest case is Norway, but many similarities can also be seen with the crises of several developing countries, particularly in East Asia. These experiences allow one to draw some broad conclusions about the factors that triggered the crises, contributed to their depth, and shaped the pattern of recovery. Distinguishing between triggering factors ('shocks') on the one hand and factors that affected responses to these shocks ('propagation mechanisms') on the other, it seems that the Nordic crises were due to the combination of extraordinary shocks with a propagation mechanism that was fundamentally altered as a result of financial deregulation.

---

[23]   H. Kinnunen and V. Vihriälä, Bank Relationships and Small-business Closures during the Finnish Recession of the 1990s, Bank of Finland Discussion Paper 13/99 (Helsinki, 1999).

[24]   The critical coefficient has a *t*-value of 1.83, implying a marginal significance level of 6 per cent.

[25]   These credit-crunch studies were initiated by B. Bernanke and C. Lown, The Credit Crunch, Brookings Papers on Economic Activity, 1991, pp. 205–47.

[26]   Vihriälä, *Banks and the Finnish Credit Cycle*, chapter 4.

Liberalization and credit boom not the whole story

It is often claimed that the key shock occurred several years before the crises: the deregulation of the financial markets in the mid-80s. Such reforms, undertaken in many countries all over the world, stimulated increased activity in the financial markets. Securities markets flourished and banks and other intermediaries expanded credit supply. Credit was partly reallocated away from previously unregulated lending like trade credits. But to a large extent there was a real credit expansion. Many countries, like Sweden and Finland, saw periods of exceptional credit growth.

Such credit booms often precede financial crises.[27] But while liberalization occurred in most developed and many developing countries, it was followed by a lending boom in only a few, and only a minority of booms ended in banking or currency crises with associated credit busts.[28] In Sweden and Finland, the credit booms were certainly partly triggered by the deregulations, but they had a strong impact on aggregate demand only when combined with other macroeconomic disturbances and expansive macro policies. Furthermore, deregulation was instrumental in leading to a crisis only because of the absence of effective supervision or other institutional arrangements giving banks the right incentives vis-à-vis risk taking.

External macro shocks important, particularly for Finland

Both Sweden and Finland are small open economies heavily exposed to external events. The years around 1990 were unusually turbulent, with a series of negative international macro shocks. First, the increase in European interest rates was particularly important for countries with high government debt, like Sweden. Second, external demand declined in response to the higher interest rates and the crisis in the Persian Gulf. Third, the ERM crisis initiated a general turmoil in exchange markets with a strong impact on small countries like Sweden and Finland, trying to defend fixed exchange parities increasingly removed from their fundamental values. Finally, the collapse of the Soviet export market hit Finland much more strongly than other countries. In fact, Finland was the only OECD country to experience declining overall export-market growth in 1991.[29]

---

[27]   See, for example, A. Demirgüç-Kunt and E. Detragiache, The Determinants of Banking Crises in Developing and Developed Countries, IMF Staff Papers 45 (1998), pp. 81–109.

[28]   P. Gourinhas, R. Valdés, and O. Landerretche, 'Lending Booms. Latin America and the World', *Economía*, 1 (2001), pp. 47–99, find that a credit boom, defined as a deviation of the ratio of private credit to GDP from a stochastic trend, was followed by a banking crisis in only 10 to 21 per cent of all cases depending on the precise definitions of boom and crisis.

[29]   J. Pesola, The Role of Macroeconomic Shocks in Banking Crises, Bank of Finland Discussion Papers 6/2001 (Helsinki, 2006), uses panel data for the four Nordic countries

Fixed but adjustable exchange-rate regime fatal

The great majority of financial crises of the 1990s occurred in countries with a fixed-exchange-rate regime. When liberalization unleashed suppressed demand and stimulated growth, attempts to tighten monetary policy were largely futile. Interest rates could not be raised sufficiently, as capital inflows responded strongly to higher short-term rates. Ironically, the authorities – supported by a large majority of academic economists – strongly emphasized that the era of recurring devaluations was over for good.[30] This historically exceptionally strong commitment to unchanging exchange rates increased public confidence in the exchange rate, irrespective of underlying economic realities.

When the financial positions became vulnerable, a confidence crisis was quick to arise. In the end, the fixed-rate regimes had to be abandoned. The markka was first devalued in late 1991 and then floated in September 1992. Sweden attempted to defend the krona even further, with exceptional interest rates in the fall of 1992.[31] The early Finnish devaluation helped export recovery to start earlier. But the decision to devalue rather than float left the exchange-rate regime still vulnerable to speculation, thereby contributing to high interest rates. This, combined with windfall losses from currency loans, weakened the financial position of the domestic sectors in Finland. It therefore seems that the Finnish approach to floating was more unfortunate from the point of view of the domestic sectors – and banks – than the Swedish one, with just a brief period of high interest rates before floating. Be that as it may, with hindsight it is obvious that both countries would have benefited from earlier floating.

The first downturn in a recently deregulated economy

In retrospect, the processes of deregulation may appear inevitable; the time was ripe. However, at the time the swiftness of the process came as a surprise. As a result, many actors, not least among them regulators and financial institutions, were ill prepared for the new situation. It did not take long, however, for the financial sector to realize that the competitive environment had been fundamentally altered.

---

to quantify the shocks to aggregate demand occurring in the early 1990s. He finds external macro shocks to be of major importance in Finland (on the order of 8 per cent of GDP in 1991) but not in the other countries.

[30]   In Finland the government in power in 1987–1991 described its economic policy strategy as one of 'managed structural change' as opposed to the 'soft' devaluation-prone policies of earlier governments. Prior to the spring 1991 general election, furthermore, the governing coalition made the 'stable markka' a central plank of its election platform.

[31]   The rates were so high that no financial system could sustain such pressures for more than a few days. The exorbitant rates were probably central to making the banking crisis acute in Sweden in the fall of 1992. In fact, the crisis in Gota occurred on 9 September, the very same day that the overnight interest rate was increased to 75 per cent.

Lending restrictions no longer conserved relative positions and competition over market shares was unhampered.

It took longer for banks and regulators to learn to understand the nature of financial risks in the new situation. Credit losses had been minuscule for as long as any active banker could remember. Few had studied the banking history of the 1920s and 30s, and little was learnt from the current crisis experience in nearby Norway. Credit risks were evaluated casually, and banks had little overview of their portfolio of loans, including exposure towards a single borrower or a particular sector.

The recession that started in both countries around 1990 was the first downturn after deregulation. It hit a bank system with low solidity, high-risk loan portfolios and highly leveraged borrowers. This triggered dynamic responses that banks and regulators were quite unaccustomed to. In particular the interaction between asset prices, collateral values and credit losses was a new phenomenon, or rather a rediscovery of a phenomenon well-known decades ago to Irving Fisher and his contemporaries.[32] It was the combination of strong negative shocks and a fundamentally altered propagation mechanism that was at the heart of the crisis.

---

[32]   I. Fisher, 'The Debt-Deflation Theory of Great Depressions', *Econometrica*, 1, 4 (1933), pp. 337–57.

Bibliography

M. Abramovitz and P.A. David, 'Growth in the Era of Knowledge-Based Progress', in S. Engerman and R.E. Gallman, *The Cambridge Economic History of the United States*, vol. 3 (Cambridge, 2000).

R.K. Abrams and M.W. Taylor, *Issues in Financial Sector Supervision*, IMF Working Paper 00/213 (2000).

J. Agell and L. Berg, 'Does Financial Deregulation Cause a Consumption Boom?', *Scandinavian Journal of Economics*, 98, 7 (1996), pp. 579–601.

J. Agell, L. Berg, and P.-A. Edin, 'The Swedish Boom-to-Bust Cycle. Tax Reform, Consumption, and Asset Structure', *Swedish Economic Policy Review*, 2, 2 (1995), pp. 271–314.

J.P. Agenor, 'Benefits and Costs of International Financial Integration. Theory and Facts', *World Economy*, 26, 8 (2003), pp. 1089–1119.

A. Alesina, V. Grilli and G.M. Milesi-Ferretti, 'The Political Economy of Capital Controls', in L. Leiderman and A. Razin (eds), *Capital Mobility. The Impact on Consumption, Investment and Growth* (Cambridge, 1994).

A. Alesina and G. Tabellini, 'External Debt, Capital Flight and Political Risk', *Journal of International Economics*, 27, 3–4 (1989), pp. 199–220.

F. Allen and D. Gale, *Comparing Financial Systems* (Cambridge MA, 2000).

B. Anan'ich, 'State Power and Finance in Russia, 1802–1917', in R. Sylla et al. (eds), *The State, the Financial System and Economic Modernization* (Cambridge, 1999).

A. Anari, J. Kolari, S. Pynnönen and A. Suvanto, 'Further Evidence on the Credit View. The Case of Finland', *Applied Economics*, 34, 3 (2002), pp. 267–78.

J.C. Asselain and B. Blancheton, 'L'ouverture internationale en perspective historique. Statut analytique du coefficient d'ouverture et application au cas de la France', *Cahiers du GRES*, no. 2006–09 (March 2006).

J. Atack, 'Industrial Structure and the Emergence of the Modern Industrial Corporation', *Explorations in Economic History*, 22, 1 (1985), pp. 29–55.

W. Bagehot, *Lombard Street* (1873, reprinted London, 1924).

A.F.P. Bakker, *The Liberalization of Capital Movements in Europe. The Monetary Committee and Financial Integration, 1958–1994* (Dordrecht, Boston and London, 1996).

F. Baring, *Observations on the Establishment of the Bank of England, and on the Paper Circulation of the Country* (1797, reprinted London, 1993).

G.L. Barrow, *The Emergence of the Irish Banking System 1820–1845* (Dublin, 1975).

J. Barth, G. Caprio Jr. and R. Levine, 'Banking Systems Around the World. Do Regulations and Ownership Affect Performance and Stability?', in F.S. Mishkin (ed.), *Prudential Supervision. What Works and What Doesn't* (Chicago, 2001).

J.R. Barth, G. Caprio Jr and R. Levine, *Rethinking Bank Regulation. Till Angels Govern* (Cambridge, Mass., and New York, 2006).

Basel Committee on Banking Supervision, *Core Principles for Effective Banking Supervision* (Basel, 1997).

A.S.J. Baster, *The Imperial Banks* (London, 1929).

——, 'The Origins of British Banking Expansion in the Near East', *Economic History Review*, 5, 1 (1934), pp. 76–86.

S. Battilossi and Y. Cassis (eds), *European Banks and the American Challenge. Competition and Cooperation in International Banking under Bretton Woods* (Oxford, 2002).

G. Becker, 'A Theory of Competition Among Pressure Groups for Political Influence', *Quarterly Journal of Economics*, 98, 3 (1983), pp. 371–400.

E. Benmelech and T. Moskowitz, The Political Economy of Financial Regulation. Evidence from US State Usury Laws in the 18th and 19th centuries, NBER Working Paper no. 12851, 2007.

G. Benston, *The Separation of Commercial and Investment Banking. The Glass-Steagall Act Revisited and Reconsidered* (Oxford, 1990).

L. Berg and R. Bergström, 'Housing and Financial Wealth, Financial Deregulation, and Consumption – the Swedish Case', *Scandinavian Journal of Economics*, 97, 3 (1995), pp. 421–39.

E. Berglof and H. Rosenthal, The Political Economy of American Bankruptcy. The Evidence from Roll Call Voting, 1800–1978, Mimeo, Princeton University (1998).

B. Bernanke and C. Lown, The Credit Crunch, Brookings Papers on Economic Activity, 1991.

S. Bhattacharya and A. Thakor, 'Contemporary Banking Theory', *Journal of Financial Intermediation*, 3, 1 (1993), pp. 2–50.

I.S. Black, 'Money, Information and Space. Banking in Early Nineteenth-century England and Wales', *Journal of Historical Geography*, 21 (1995), pp. 398–412.

H. Bodenhorn, *A History of Banking in Antebellum America. Financial Markets and Economic Development in an Era of Nation-building* (Cambridge, 2000).

——, 'Bank Chartering and Political Corruption in Antebellum New York. Free Banking as Reform', in E. Glaeser, C. Goldin (eds), *Corruption and Reform. Lessons from America's Economic History* (Chicago, 2006).

——, *State Banking in Early America. A New Economic History* (Oxford, 2003).

——, 'The More Perfect Union. Regional Interest Rates in the United States 1880–1960', in M.D. Bordo and R.E. Sylla, *Anglo-American Finance* (New York, 1995).

L. Bolaffio, *Il concordato preventivo secondo le sue tre leggi disciplinatrici* (Turin, 1932).

G. Bonelli, *Del Fallimento. Commentario al codice di commercio* (Milan, 1907–1909).

M. Bordo, 'The Lender of Last Resort. Alternative Views and Historical Experience', in C. Goodhart and G. Illing (eds), *Financial Crises, Contagion, and the Lender of Last Resort. A Reader* (Oxford, 2002).

M. Bordo and B. Eichengreen, 'Is our Current International Economic Environment Unusually Crisis Prone?', in D. Gruen and L. Gower (eds), *Capital Flows and the International Financial System* (Sydney, 1999).

M.D. Bordo and A. Redish, 'Why Did the Bank of Canada Emerge in 1935?', *Journal of Economic History*, 47, 2 (1987), pp. 405–17.

M.D. Bordo, H. Rockoff and A. Redish, 'The US Banking System From a Northern Exposure. Stability versus Efficiency,' *Journal of Economic History*, 54, 2 (1994), pp. 325–57.

M. Bordo and P. Rousseau, Legal-Political Factors and the Historical Evolution of the Finance-Growth Link, NBER Working Paper no. 12035, 2006.

C. Borio and A. Filardo, Back to the Future? Assessing the Deflation Record, BIS Working Paper, no. 152, 2004.

C. Borio and P. Lowe, Asset Prices, Financial and Monetary Stability. Exploring the Nexus, BIS Working Papers, no. 114, 2002.

C. Borio and G. Toniolo, One Hundred and Thirty Years of Central Bank Cooperation. A BIS Perspective, BIS Working Papers, no. 197 (February 2006).

D.G. Boshkoff, 'Limited, Conditional, and Suspended Discharge in Anglo-American Bankruptcy Proceedings', *University of Pennsylvania Law Review*, 131, 1 (1982), pp. 69–125.

J. Bouvier, *Le Crédit lyonnais de 1863 à 1882. Les années de formation d'une banque de dépôts* (Paris, 1961).

J. Bouvier, 'Les banques', in A. Sauvy, *Histoire économique de la France entre les deux guerres, divers sujets* (Paris, 1972).

——, 'L'extension des réseaux de circulation de la monnaie et de l'épargne', in F. Braudel and E. Labrousse (eds.), *Histoire économique et sociale de la France*, vol. 4, 1 (Paris, 1979), pp. 197f.

——, *Un siècle de banque française. Les contraintes de l'Etat et les incertitudes des marchés* (Paris, 1973).

H.V. Bowen and P.L. Cottrell, 'Banking and the Evolution of the British Economy', in A. Teichova et al. (eds), *Banking Trade and Industry. Europe, America and Asia from the Thirteenth to the Twentieth Century* (Cambridge, 1997).

J. Bradford De Long, 'Did J.P. Morgan's Men Add Value. An Economist's Perspective on Financial Capitalism', in P. Temin (ed.), *Inside the Business Enterprise. Historical Perspectives on the Use of Information* (Chicago, 1992).

T.F. Bresnahan and M. Trajtenberg, 'General Purpose Technologies. Engines of Growth?', *Journal of Econometrics*, 65, 1 (1995), pp. 83–108.

C. Briault, The Rationale for a Single Financial Services Regulator, UK Financial Services Authority Occasional Paper 2 (1999).

J.L. Brosz and R.S. Grossman, 'Paying for Privilege. The Political Economy of Bank of England Charters, 1694–1844', *Explorations in Economic History*, 41, 1 (2004), pp. 48–72.

A. Brunila, Investment and Financing Considerations. Evidence from Finnish Panel Data, Bank of Finland Discussion Paper 4/94 (Helsinki, 1994).

R.A. Bryer, 'The Mercantile Laws Commission of 1854 and the Political Economy of Limited Liability', *Economic History Review*, 50, 1 (1997), pp. 37–56.

W.L. Buenger and J.A. Pratt, *But Also Good Business. Tax Commerce Banks and the Financing of Houston and Texas 1886–1986* (College Station, 1986).

G. Burn, *The Re-emergence of Global Finance* (London, 2006).

E. Bussière, 'French Banks and the Euro-bonds Issue Market during the 1960s', in Y. Cassis and E. Bussière (eds), *London and Paris as International Financial Centres in the Twentieth Century* (Oxford, 2005).

S.J. Butlin, *Australia and New Zealand Bank. The Bank of Australia and the Union Bank of Australia Limited 1828–1951* (London, 1961).

A. Cairncross (ed.), *The Robert Hall Diaries* (London, 1989).

C.A. Calomiris and E.N. White, 'The Origins of Federal Deposit Insurance,' in C. Goldin and G.D. Libecap (eds), *The Regulated Economy. A Historical Approach to Political Economy* (Cambridge, 1994), pp. 145–88.

R. Cameron, 'Scotland, 1750–1845', in R. Cameron et al., *Banking in the Early Stages of Industrialization* (New York Oxford, 1967).

J.G. Cannon, *Clearing-houses. Their History, Methods and Administration* (New York, 1900).

F. Capie, C. Goodhart, S. Fischer and N. Schnadt, *The Future of Central Banking. The Tercentenary Symposium of the Bank of England* (Cambridge, 1994).

G. Caprio, J.A. Hanson and R. Litan (eds), *Financial Crises. Lessons from the Past, Preparation for the Future* (Washington DC, 2005).

G. Caprio and P. Honohan, Banking Crises, Institute for International Integration Studies, Trinity College, Dublin, Discussion Paper no. 242, 2008.

V.P. Carosso, *Investment Banking in America. A History* (Cambridge, 1970).

Y. Cassis, *Capitals of Capital* (Geneva, 2005).

G. Chandler, *Four Centuries of Banking, vol. 1, The Grasshopper and the Liver Bird. Liverpool and London* (London, 1964).

S.G. Checkland, *Scottish Banking. A History, 1695–1973* (Glasgow, 1975).

J.H. Clapham, *The Bank of England. A History* (Cambridge, 1945).

C.G.A. Clay, 'Henry Hoare, Banker, his Family and the Stourhead Estate', in F.M.L. Thompson (ed.), *Landowners, Capitalists and Entrepreneurs. Essays for Sir John Habakkuk* (Oxford, 1994).

G. Corsetti, P. Pesenti, and N. Roubini, 'What Caused the Asian Currency and Financial Crisis?', *Japan and the World Economy*, 11, 3 (1999), pp. 305–73.

P.L. Cottrell, 'Credit, Morals and Sunspots. The Financial Boom of the 1860s and Trade Cycle Theory', in P.L. Cottrell and D.E. Moggridge (eds), *Money and Power. Essays in Honour of L.S. Pressnell* (Houndmills, 1988).

——, *Industrial Finance 1830–1914. The Finance and Organization of English Manufacturing Industry* (London, 1980).

——, 'The Coalescence of a Cluster of Corporate International Banks, 1855–1875', *Business History*, 33, 3 (1991), pp. 31–52.

P.L. Cottrell and L. Newton, 'Banking Liberalisation in England and Wales, 1826–1844', in R. Sylla et al. (eds), *The State, the Financial System and Economic Modernization* (Cambridge, 1999).

N. Courtis, *How Countries Supervise Their Banks, Insurance and Securities Markets* (London, 1999).

N. Crafts, 'Globalisation and Economic Growth. A Historical Perspective', *World Economy*, 27, 1 (2004), pp. 45–58.

——, Globalization and Growth in the Twentieth Century, IMF Working Papers WP/00/44, 2000.

A. Crockett, T. Harris, F. Mishkin, and E.N. White, *Conflicts of Interest in the Financial Services Industry. What Should We Do About Them?* (London, 2004).

J.-P. Danthine, F. Giavazzi, X. Vives, E.L. von Thadden, *Monitoring European Integration*, vol. 9 (London, 1999).

P.A. David, 'Clio and the Economics of QWERTY', *American Economic Review*, 7, 2 (1985), pp. 332–6.

P. David, 'Why Are Institutions the "Carriers of History"? Path-dependency and the Evolution of Conventions, Organizations and Institutions', *Structural Change and Economic Dynamics*, 7, 5 (1994), pp. 205–20.

E.P. Davis, *Debt, Financial Fragility and Systemic Risk* (Oxford, 1992).

L.E. Davis, 'The Investment Market, 1870–1914. The Evolution of a National Market', *Journal of Economic History*, 25, 3 (1965), pp. 355–99.

——, 'The New England Textile Mills and Capital Markets. A Study of Industrial Borrowing, 1840–1860', *Journal of Economic History*, 20, 1 (1960), pp. 1–43.

J. De Luna Martinez and T.A. Rose, International Survey of Integrated Financial Sector Supervision, World Bank Policy Research Working Paper 3096 (2003).

C. Del Marmol, *La faillite en Droit Anglo-Saxon. Etude de législation et de jurisprudence faite dans le cadre de la loi anglaise de 1914* (Paris et Bruxelles, 1936).

A. Demirgüç-Kunt and E. Detragiache, The Determinants of Banking Crises in Developing and Developed Countries, IMF Staff Papers 45 (1998).

B. Desjardins, M. Lescure, R. Nougaret, A. Plessis, A. Straus (eds), *Le Crédit lyonnais* (Geneva, 2003).

D.W. Diamond, 'Financial Intermediation and Delegated Monitoring', *Review of Economic Studies*, 51 (1984), pp. 393–414.

D.W. Diamond and P.H. Dybvig, 'Bank Runs, Deposit Insurance and Liquidity', *Journal of Political Economy*, 91, 3 (1983), pp. 401–19.

P. Di Martino, 'Approaching Disaster. A Comparison between Personal Bankruptcy Legislation in Italy and England (c.1880–1939)', *Business History*, 47, 1 (2005), pp. 23–43.

N. Dimsdale and M. Prevezer (eds), *Capital Markets and Corporate Governance* (Oxford, 1994).

E. Dimson, P. Marsh and M. Staunton, *Triumph of the Optimists. 101 Years of Global Investment Returns* (Princeton, 2002).

R. Dodd, The Economic Rationale for Financial Market Regulation, Financial Policy Forum, Special Policy Report no. 12, 2002.

P.J. Drake, *Money, Finance and Development* (Oxford, 1980).

I.P.H. Duffy, *Bankruptcy and Insolvency in London during the Industrial Revolution* (New York and London, 1985).

N. Economides, R.G. Hubbard and D. Palia, 'The Political Economy of Branch Restrictions and Deposit Insurance', *Journal of Law and Economics*, 29 (1996), pp. 667–704.

B. Eichengreen, *Capital Flows and Crises* (Cambridge, Mass., 2003).

——, *Globalizing Capital* (Princeton, 1996).

B. Eichengreen and M. Mussa, *Capital Account Liberalization. Theoretical and Practical Aspects* (Washington, 1998).

Federal Deposit Insurance Corporation (FDIC), *History of the 1980s. Lessons for the Future, vol. 1, An Examination of the Banking Crises of the 1980s and early 1990s* (Washington, 1997).

O. Feiertag (ed.), *Mesurer la monnaie. Banques centrales et construction de l'autorité monétaire, XIXe–XXe siècle* (Paris, 2005).

E.H. Feijen and E. Perotti, The Political Economy of Financial Fragility, CEPR Discussion Papers no. 5317, 2005.

F.W. Fetter, *Development of British Monetary Orthodoxy 1797–1875* (Cambridge, Mass., 1965).

A.J. Field, 'Technical Change and US Economic Growth. The Interwar Period and the 1990s', in P.W. Rhode and G. Toniolo (eds), *The Global Economy in the 1990s. A Long-run Perspective* (Cambridge, 2006).

I. Fisher, 'The Debt-Deflation Theory of Great Depressions', *Econometrica*, 1, 4 (1933), pp. 337–57.

X. Freixas, C. Giannini, G. Hoggarth and F. Soussa, 'Lender of Last Resort. A Review of the Literature', in C. Goodhart and G. Illing (eds), *Financial Crises, Contagion, and the Lender of Last Resort. A Reader* (Oxford, 2002).

M. Friedman and A.J. Schwartz, *A Monetary History of the United States, 1863–1960* (Princeton, 1963).

R.E. Gallman, 'Economic Growth and Structural Change in the Long Nineteenth Century', in S. Engerman and R.E. Gallman, *The Cambridge Economic History of the United States*, vol. 2 (Cambridge, 2000).

E.P.M. Gardener and P. Molyneux, *Changes in Western European Banking* (London, 1994).

E.P.M. Gardener, P. Molyneux and J. Williams, 'Competitive Banking in the EU and Euroland', in A.W. Mullineux and V. Murinde (eds), *Handbook of International Banking* (Cheltenham, 2003).

G. Gary and D. Mullineaux, 'The Joint Production of Confidence. Endogenous Regulation and Nineteenth Century Commercial-bank Clearinghouses,' *Journal of Money Credit and Banking*, 19, 4 (1987), pp. 457–68.

A. Gerschenkron, *Economic Backwardness in Historical Perspective* (Cambridge, Mass., 1966).

I.H. Giddy, 'The Eurocurrency Market', in A.H. George and I.H. Giddy (eds), *International Finance Handbook,* vol. 1 (New York, 1983).

D.C. Giedeman, 'Branch Banking Restrictions and Finance Constraints in Early Twentieth Century America,' *Journal of Economic History*, 65, 1 (2005), pp. 129–51.

J.W. Gilbart, *A Practical Treatise on Banking* (London, 1828).

A. Giovannini and M. De Melo, 'Government Revenues from Financial Repression', *American Economic Review*, 83, 4 (1993), pp. 953–63.

R. Girault, *Emprunts russes et investissements français en Russie, 1887–1914* (reprinted, Paris, 1999).

R.W. Goldsmith, *Comparative National Balance Sheets. A Study of Twenty Countries 1688–1978* (Chicago and London, 1985).

——, *Financial Intermediaries in the American Economy* (Princeton, 1958).

C. Goodhart, 'The Political Economy of Financial Harmonization in Europe', in J.M. Kremers, D. Schoenmaker and P. Wierts (eds), *Financial Supervision in Europe* (Cheltenham, 2003).

C. Goodhart, F. Capie and N. Schnadt, 'The Development of Central Banking', in F. Capie et al., *The Future of Central Banking. The Tercentenary Symposium of the Bank of England* (Cambridge, 1994).

C. Goodhart and D. Schoenmaker, 'Institutional Separation between Supervisory and Monetary Agencies', in C. Goodhart (ed.), *The Central Bank and the Financial System* (Cambridge, 1995).

C. Goodhart, D. Schoenmaker and P. Dasgupta, 'The Skill Profile of Central Bankers and Supervisors', *European Finance Review*, 6, 3 (2002), pp. 397–427.

R.J. Gordon, 'Does the "New Economy" Measure up to the Great Inventions of the Past?', *Journal of Economic Perspectives*, 14, 4 (2000), pp. 49–74.

P. Gourinhas, R. Valdés, and O. Landerretche, 'Lending Booms. Latin America and the World', *Economía*, 1 (2001), pp. 47–99.

T.E. Gregory, *The Westminster Bank through a Century*, vol. 2 (London, 1936).

A. Greif, *Institutions and the Path to the Modern Economy. Lessons from Medieval Trade* (Cambridge, 2006).

W.J. Greenwood, *American and Foreign Stock Exchange Practice, Stock and Bond Trading and the Business Corporation Laws of all Nations* (New York, 1921).

V. Grilli, G.M. Milesi Ferretti, Economic Effects and Structural Determinants of Capital Controls, IMF Staff Papers, 42, 1995.

L.H. Grindon, *Manchester Banks and Bankers* (Manchester, 1877).

R.S. Grossman, 'Charters, Corporations, and Codes. Entry Restriction in Modern Banking Law', *Financial History Review*, 8, 2 (2001), pp. 107–21.

Group of Ten, *Report on Consolidation in the Financial Sector* (Basel, 2001).

A. Gueslin, 'Banks and State in France from the 1880s to the 1930s. The Impossible Advance of the Banks', in Y. Cassis (ed.), *Finance and Financiers in European History, 1880–1960* (Paris and Cambridge, 1992).

A. Gueslin and M. Lescure, 'Les banques publiques parapubliques et coopératives françaises (vers 1920–vers 1960)', in M. Lévy-Leboyer (ed.), *Les banques en Europe de l'Ouest de 1920 à nos jours* (Paris, 1995).

S. Haber, D.C. North and B. Weingast (eds), *Political Institutions and Financial Development* (Stanford, 2007).

S. Haber and R. Perotti, The Political Economy of Financial Systems, Timbergen Institution Discussion Paper, no. 045/2, 2008.

S. Haber, A. Razo and N. Maurer, *The Politics of Property Rights. Political Instability, Credible Commitments, and Economic Growth in Mexico 1876–1929* (Cambridge, 2003).

C.T. Hallinan, *American Investments in Europe* (London, 1927).

K. Hallsten, Bank Loans and the Transmission Mechanism of Monetary Policy, in K. Hallsten, Essays on the Effects of Monetary Policy, Dissertation in Economics 1999, 2, Department of Economics, Stockholm University (Stockholm, 1999).

B. Hansen, 'Commercial Associations and the Creation of a National Economy. The Demand for Federal Bankruptcy Law', *Business History Review*, 72, 1 (1998), pp. 86–113.

B.A. Hansen and M.E. Hansen, The Role of Path-dependency in the Development of US Bankruptcy Law, 1880–1938, American University, Department of Economics Working Paper Series (2005).

J. Hansen, Financial Cycles and Bankruptcies in the Nordic Countries, Sveriges Riksbank Working Paper No. 149 (Stockholm, 2003).

S. Hansen and S. Lindberg, Agency Costs, Financial Deregulation, and Corporate Investment. An Euler Equation Approach to Panel Data for Swedish Firms, Working Paper 1997:20, Department of Economics, Uppsala University (Uppsala, 1997).

P.-C. Hautcoeur and G. Gallais-Hamonno (eds), *Le marché financier français au XIXe siècle*, 2 vols (Paris, 2007).

E. Helleiner, *States and the Re-emergence of Global Finance. From Bretton Woods to the 1990s* (Ithaca NY, 1994).

B. Hilton, *Corn, Cash, Commerce. The Economic Policies of the Tory Governments 1815–1830* (Oxford, 1977).

B. Holmström and J. Tirole, 'Financial Intermediation, Loanable Funds and the Real Sector', *Quarterly Journal of Economics*, 112, 3 (1997), pp. 663–91.

S. Honkapohja and E. Koskela, 'The Economic Crisis of the 1990s in Finland', *Economic Policy*, 29 (1999), pp. 399–424.

A.C.F. Houben, *The Evolution of Monetary Policy Strategies in Europe* (Dordrecht, Boston and London, 2000).

S.S. Huebner, 'The Scope and Functions of the Stock Market', *Annals of the American Academy of Political and Social Science* 35 (1910), pp. 1–23.

R. Ingham, 'Mill on limited liability partnerships', *Journal of Liberal Democrat History*, 23 (1999), pp. 16 and 28 seguitur.

J.A. James, *Money and Capital Markets in Postbellum America* (Princeton, 1978).

L.P. Jennergren, 'The Swedish Finance Company Crisis. Could it have been Anticipated?', *Scandinavian Economic History Review*, 50, 2 (2002), pp. 7–30.

F.S. Jones, 'Instant Banking in the 1830s. The Founding of the Northern & Central Bank of England', *Bankers' Magazine*, 211 (1971), pp. 130–35.

——, 'The Cotton Industry and Joint-stock Banking in Manchester 1825–1850', *Business History Review*, 20, 2 (1978), pp. 65–85.

——, 'The Manchester Cotton Magnates' Move into Banking, 1826–50', *Textile History*, 9 (1978), pp. 90–111.

G. Jones, *British Multinational Banking 1830–1990* (Oxford, 1993).

S. Jones, 'The Professional Background of Company Law Pressure Groups', *Accounting, Business and Financial History*, 7, 2 (1997), pp. 233–42.

L. Jonung, J. Kiander and P. Vartia, *The Great Financial Crisis in Finland and Sweden. The Nordic Experience of Financial Liberalization* (Cheltenham, 2009).

T. Joplin, *An Examination of the Report of the Joint Stock Bank Committee* (London, 2nd edn, 1837).

D.M. Joslin, 'London Bankers in Wartime, 1739–84', in L.S. Pressnell (ed.), *Studies in the Industrial Revolution Presented to T.S. Ashton* (London, 1960).

——, 'London Private Bankers, 1720–1785', *Economic History Review*, 2nd series, 7 (1954), pp. 167–86.

——, 'Private Banking in London's West End, 1750–1830', *London Journal*, 28 (2003).

——, 'The London Agency System in English Banking, 1780–1825', *London Journal*, 21 (1996).

E. Kane, 'Accelerating Inflation, Technological Innovation, and the Decreasing Effectiveness of Banking Regulation', *Journal of Finance*, 36, 2 (1981), pp. 355–67.

——, 'Competitive Financial Reregulation. An International Perspective', in R. Portes and A. Swoboda (eds), *Threats to International Financial Stability* (Cambridge, 1987).

——, 'Technological and Regulatory Forces in the Developing Fusion of Financial-Services Competition', *Journal of Finance*, 39, 3 (1984), pp. 759–72.

——, 'Tension between Competition and Coordination in International Financial Regulation', in C. England (ed.), *Governing Banking's Future. Markets vs. Regulation* (Boston, 1991).

E.B. Kapstein, Architects of Stability? International Cooperation among Financial Supervisors, BIS Working Papers, no. 199, February 2006.

——, *Supervising International Banks. Origins and Implications of the Basle Accord* (Princeton NJ, 1991).

J.H. Kareken, 'Federal Bank Regulatory Policy. A Description and Some Observations', *The Journal of Business*, 59, 1 (1986), pp. 3–48.

J. Kay, *The Truth About Markets* (London, 2004).

M. Keeley, 'Deposit Insurance, Risk, and Market Power in Banking', *American Economic Review*, 80, 5 (1990), pp. 1183–1200.

J. Kelly, *Bankers and Borders. The Case of American Banks in Britain* (Cambridge, Mass., 1977).

F.H.H. King, 'Structural Alternatives and Constraints in the Evolution of Exchange Banking', in G. Jones (ed.), *Banks as Multinationals* (London, 1990).

R. King and R. Levine, 'Finance and Growth. Schumpeter Might Be Right', *Quarterly Journal of Economics*, 108, 3 (1993), pp. 717–37.

H. Kinnunen and V. Vihriälä, Bank Relationships and Small-business Closures during the Finnish Recession of the 1990s, Bank of Finland Discussion Paper 13/99 (Helsinki, 1999).

M. Klausner, 'Bank Regulatory Reform and Bank Structure', in M. Klausner, L.J. White (eds), *Structural Change in Banking* (Homewood, Ill., 1993).

J.M. Kremers, D. Schoenmaker and P. Wierts (eds), *Financial Supervision in Europe* (Cheltenham, 2003).

R.S. Kroszner, Is the Financial System Independent? Perspectives on the Political Economy of Banking and Financial Regulation, Paper Prepared for Swedish Government Inquiry on the Competitiveness of the Swedish Financial Sector, 1999.

R.S. Kroszner and R.G. Rajan, 'Is the Glass-Steagall Act Justified? A Study of the US Experience with Universal Banking before 1933', *American Economic Review*, 84, 4 (1994), pp. 810–32.

R.S. Kroszner and P.E. Strahan, 'What Drives Deregulation? Economics and Politics of the Relaxation of Bank Branching Restrictions', *Quarterly Journal of Economics*, 114, 4 (1999), pp. 1437–67.

N. Lamoreaux, *Insider Lending. Banks, Personal Connections, and Economic Development in Inudstrial New England* (Cambridge, 1994).

N. Lamoreaux and J.-L. Rosenthal, Corporate Governance and the Plight of Minority Shareholders in the US before the Great Depression, NBER Working Paper no. 10900, 2004.

J. Landmann, 'The Swiss National Bank', *Quarterly Journal of Economics*, 20 (May 1906), pp. 468–82.

R. Laporta, F. Lopez-de-Silanes et al., 'Law and Finance', *Journal of Political Economy*, 106, 6 (1998), pp. 1113–55.

H. Laufenburger, *Les banques françaises depuis 1914* (Paris, 1940).

——, *Traité d'économie et de législation financière. Dette publique et richesse privée* (Paris, 1948).

M. Lescure and A. Plessis (eds), *Banques locales et banques régionales en France au XIXe siècle* (Paris, 1999).

V.M. Lester, *Victorian Insolvency. Bankruptcy, Imprisonment for Debt, and Company Winding-up in Nineteenth-Century England* (Oxford, 1994).

R. Levine, 'Finance and Growth. Theory, Mechanisms and Evidence', in P. Aghion and S.N. Durlauf (eds), *Handbook of Economic Growth* (Amsterdam, 2005).

——, 'Financial Development and Economic Growth. Views and Agenda', *Journal of Economic Literature*, 35, 2 (1977), pp. 688–726.

——, 'The Legal Environment, Banks, and Long-Run Economic Growth', *Journal of Money, Credit and Banking*, 30, 3 (1998), pp. 596–620.

R. Levine and S. Zervos, 'Stock Markets, Banks, and Economic Growth', *American Economic Review*, 88, 3 (1998), pp. 537–58.

M. Lévy-Leboyer (ed.), La position internationale de la France. Aspects économiques et financiers XIXe–XXe siècles (Paris, 1977).

M. Lévy-Leboyer, 'La spécialisation des établissements bancaires', in F. Braudel and E. Labrousse (eds), *Histoire économique et sociale de la France*, vol. 3, 1 (Paris, 1976).

D.T. Llewellyn, 'Institutional Structure of Financial Regulation. The Basic Issues', World Bank Seminar, Aligning Supervisory Structures with Country Needs (2003).

D. Loftus, 'Capital and Community. Limited Liability and Attempts to Democratize the Market in Mid-nineteenth Century England', *Victorian Studies*, 45, 4 (2002), pp. 93–120.

I. Maes and E. Buyst, 'La création d´un service d´études à la Banque nationale de Belgique au début des années 1920', in O. Feiertag (ed.), *Mesurer la monnaie. Banques centrales et construction de l'autorité monétaire, XIXe–XXe siècle* (Paris, 2005).

P.G. Mahoney, 'The Origins of the Blue-Sky Laws. A Test of Competing Hypotheses', *Journal of Law and Economics*, 46, 1 (2003), pp. 229–51.

——, 'The Political Economy of the Securities Act of 1933', *Journal of Legal Studies*, 30, 1 (2001), pp. 1–31.

R.C. Marston, *International Financial Integration. A Study of Interest Differentials between the Major Industrial Countries* (Cambridge, 1995).

P. Martín-Aceña, *El Servicio de Estudios del Banco de España, 1930–2000* (Madrid, 2000).

——, 'La Banque de France, la BRI et la création du service d'études de la Banque d´Espagne au début des années 1930', in O. Feiertag (ed.), *Mesurer la monnaie. Banques centrales et construction de l'autorité monétaire, XIXe–XXe siècle* (Paris, 2005).

N. Maurer and A. Gomberg, 'When the State is Untrustworthy. Public Finance and Private Banking in Porfirian Mexico', *Journal of Economic History*, 64, 4 (2004), pp. 1087–1107.

J.E. Meeker, *Short Selling* (New York, 1932).

F.T. Melton, 'Robert and Sir Francis Gosling. 18th Century Bankers and Stationers', in R. Myer and M.R.A. Harris (eds), *Economics of the British Book Trade, 1605–1939* (Cambridge, 1985).

——, 'Deposit Banking in London, 1700–90', *Business History*, 28, 3 (1986), pp. 40–50.

R. Michie, 'Different in Name only? The London Stock Exchange and Foreign Bourses 1850–1914', *Business History*, 30, 1 (1988), pp. 46–68.

——, *The Global Securities Market. A History* (Oxford, 2006).

——, *The London Stock Exchange. A History* (Oxford, 1999).

R. C. Michie and P.A. Williamson (eds), *The British Government and the City of London in the Twentieth Century* (Cambridge, 2004).

J. Miron 'Financial Panics, the Seasonality of the Nominal Interest Rate and the Founding of the Fed', *American Economic Review*, 76, 1 (1986), pp. 125–40.

F.S. Mishkin, 'Lessons from the Tequila Crisis', *Journal of Banking & Finance*, 23, 10 (1999), pp. 1521–33.

J. Mooij and H.M. Prast, A Brief History of the Institutional Design of Banking Supervision in the Netherlands, De Nederlandsche Bank, Research Memorandum WO no. 703, October 2002.

W. Möschel, 'Public Law of Banking', in J.S. Ziegel (ed.), *International Encyclopedia of Public Law* (Boston, 1991).

C.W. Munn, 'Banking on Branches. The Origins and Development of Branch Banking in the United Kingdom', in P.L. Cottrell et al. (eds), *Finance in the Age of the Corporate Economy. The Third Anglo-Japanese Business History Conference* (Aldershot, 1997).

——, 'The Coming of Joint-stock Banking in Scotland and Ireland 1820–25', in T.M. Devine and D. Dickson (eds), *Scotland and Ireland* (Edinburgh, 1983).

——, 'The Emergence of Joint-stock Banking in the British Isles. A Comparative Approach', *Business History*, 30, 1 (1988), pp. 69–83.

——, *The Scottish provincial banking companies 1747–1864* (Edinburgh, 1981).

R.R. Nelson and S.A. Winter, *An Evolutionary Theory of Economic Change* (Cambridge, Mass., 1982).

L. Newton and P.L. Cottrell, 'Joint-stock Banking in the English Provinces 1826–1857. To Branch or not to Branch?', *Business and Economic History*, 27, 1 (1998), pp. 115–28.

K. Ng, 'Free Banking Laws and Barriers to Entry in Banking, 1838–1860', *Journal of Economic History*, 48, 4 (1998), pp. 877–89.

J.P. Nicolini, 'Tax Evasion and the Optimal Inflation Tax', *Journal of Development Economics*, 55, 1 (1998), pp. 215–32.

S. Nishimura, *The Decline of Inland Bills of Exchange in the London Money Market 1855–1913* (Cambridge, 1971).

D.C. North, *Institutions, Institutional Change and Economic Performance* (Cambridge, 1990).

D. North, 'Life Insurance and Investment Banking at the Time of the Armstrong Investigation of 1905–1906', *Journal of Economic History*, 14, 3 (1954), pp. 209–28.

M. Obstfeld and M. Taylor, *Global Capital Markets. Integration, Crisis, and Growth* (Cambridge, 2004).

T. Padoa-Schioppa, *Regulating Finance, Balancing Freedom and Risk* (Oxford, 2004).

M. Pagano, P. Volpin, 'The Political Economy of Finance', *Oxford Review of Economic Policy*, 17, 4 (2001), pp. 502–19.

J.-P. Patat and M. Lutfalla, *Histoire monétaire de la France au XXe siècle* (Paris, 1986).

W. Parker, *The Paris Bourse* (Washington, 1930).

——, *The Paris Bourse and French Finance* (New York, 1920).

C. Pazarbaşioğlu, A Credit Crunch? Finland in the Aftermath of the Banking Crisis, IMF Staff Papers, 44, 1997.

W.N. Peach, *Security Affiliates of National Banks* (Baltimore, 1941).

G.C. Peden, 'The Treasury and the City', in R. Michie and Ph. Williamson (eds), *The British Government and the City in the Twentieth Century* (Cambridge, 2005).

J. Peek, E.S. Rosengren and G.M.B. Tootell, 'Synergies between Bank Supervision and Monetary Policy. Implications for the Design of Bank Regulatory Structure', in F.S. Mishkin (ed.), *Prudential Supervision. What Works and What Doesn't* (Chicago, 2001).

S. Peltzman, The Economic Theory of Regulation after a Decade of Deregulation, Brookings Papers in Economic Activity, Special Issue: Microeconomics, 1989, pp. 1–59.

——, 'Towards a More General Theory of Regulation', *Journal of Law and Economics* 19 (1976), pp. 211–40.

G. Pepper, *Official Order – Real Chaos* (London, 1990).

S.A. Perez, *Banking on Privilege. The Politics of Spanish Financial Reform* (Ithaca, 1997).

E. Perotti and E.-L. von Thadden, 'The Political Economy of Corporate Control and Labor Rents', *Journal of Political Economy*, 114, 1 (2006), pp. 145–75.

J. Pesola, The Role of Macroeconomic Shocks in Banking Crises, Bank of Finland Discussion Papers 6/2001 (Helsinki, 2006).

B. Pimlott, *Harold Wilson* (London, 1992).

U. Pipia, *Del Fallimento* (Turin, 1932).

A. Plessis, 'Bankers in French Society, 1860s–1960s', in Y. Cassis (ed.), *Finance and Financiers in European History, 1880–1960* (Paris and Cambridge, 1992).

——, 'La Banque de France et la production de statistiques au XIXe siècle', in O. Feiertag (ed.), *Mesurer la monnaie. Banques centrales et construction de l'autorité monétaire, XIXe–XXe siècle* (Paris, 2005).

——, 'When Paris Dreamed of Competing with the City...', in Y. Cassis and E. Bussière (eds), *London and Paris as International Financial Centres in the Twentieth Century* (Oxford, 2005).

E.S. Prasad et al., Effects of Financial Globalization on Developing Countries. Some Empirical Evidence, IMF Occasional Paper 220, 2003.

L.S. Pressnell, *Country Banking in the Industrial Revolution* (Oxford, 1956).

——, 'Gold Reserves, Banking Reserves and the Baring Crisis of 1890', in C.R. Whittlesey and J.S.G. Wilson (eds), *Essays in Money and Banking in Honour of R.S. Sayers* (Oxford, 1968).

L. Quennouëlle-Corre, *La direction du Trésor 1947–1967. L'Etat-banquier et la croissance* (Paris, 2000).

——, 'The State, Banks and Financing for Investments in France from World War II to the 1970s', *Financial History Review*, 12, 1 (2005), pp. 63–86.

M. Radin, 'Discharge in Bankruptcy', *New York University Law Quarterly Review*, 9, 1 (1931), pp. 39–48.

J.P. Raines, *Economists and the Stock Market: Speculative theories of stock market fluctuations* (Cheltenham, 2000).

R.G. Rajan and L. Zingales, *Saving Capitalism from the Capitalists* (New York, 2003).

——, 'The Great Reversals. The Politics of Financial Development in the Twentieth Century', *Journal of Financial Economics*, 69, 1 (2003), pp. 5–50.

——, *The Great Reversals. The Politics of Financial Development in the Twentieth Century* (Paris 2000).

——, The Great Reversals. The Politics of Financial Development in the 20th Century, Working Paper, University of Chicago, 2000.

C. Reinhart and K. Rogoff, Banking Crises. An Equal Opportunity Menace, NBER Working Paper no. 14587, 2008.

J. Rezzara, *Il concordato nella storia, nella dottrina, nella giurisprudenza: Studio di diritto commerciale* (Turin, 1901).

R. Robertson, *The Comptroller and Bank Supervision. A Historical Appraisal* (Washington, DC, 1968).

A. Rocco, 'Il disegno di legge sul fallimento e sul concordato preventivo', *Rivista di Diritto Commerciale*, 28 (1930).

N. Roubini, X. Sala-i-Martin, 'A Growth Model of Inflation, Tax Evasion and Financial Repression', *Journal of Monetary Economics*, 35, 2 (1995), pp. 275–301.

P. Rousseau, 'General-purpose Technologies then and now', in P.W. Rhode and G. Toniolo, *The Global Economy in the 1990s. A Long-Run Perspective* (Cambridge, 2006), pp. 118–38.

P. Rousseau and R.E. Sylla, 'Emerging Financial Markets and Early US Growth', *Explorations in Economic History*, 42, 1 (2005), pp. 1–26.

P. Rousseau and P. Wachtel, 'Financial Intermediation and Economic Performance. Historical Evidence from Industrialized Economies', *Journal of Money, Credit and Banking*, 30, 4 (1998), pp. 657–78.

M. Saint Marc, *Histoire monétaire de la France 1800–1980* (Paris, 1983).

M. Sandoz, 'The Bank-Note System of Switzerland', *Quarterly Journal of Economics*, 1 (April 1898), pp. 280–306.

R. Scatamacchia, 'L'émergence du service d'études de la Banque d'Italie et le développement de sa fonction d'expertise, 1894–1947', in O. Feiertag, *Mesurer la monnaie. Banques centrales et construction de l'autorité monétaire, XIXe–XXe siècle* (Paris, 2005).

C.R. Schenk, 'Crisis and Opportunity. The Policy Environment of International Banking in the City of London', in Y. Cassis and E. Bussière (eds), *London and Paris as International Financial Centres in the 20th Century* (Oxford, 2005).

——, 'International Financial Centres 1958–71. Competitiveness and Complementarity', in S. Battilossi and Y. Cassis (eds), *European Banks and the American Challenge* (Oxford, 2002).

——, 'The New City and the State in the 1960s', in R.C. Michie and P.A. Williamson (eds), *The British Government and the City of London in the Twentieth Century* (Cambridge, 2004).

——, 'The Origins of the Eurodollar Market in London, 1955–1963', *Explorations in Economic History*, 35, 2 (1998), pp. 221–38.

F.M. Scherer, *Industrial Market Structure and Economic Performance* (Chicago, 1980).

G.J. Schinasi, *Safeguarding Financial Stability. Theory and Practice* (IMF, 2006).

W. Seifert et al., *European Capital Markets* (Basingstoke, 2000).

J. Sgard, 'Do Legal Origins Matter? The Case of Bankruptcy Laws in Europe 1808–1914', *European Review of Economic History*, 10, 3 (2006), pp. 389–419.

R.J. Shiller, *Irrational Exuberance* (New York, 2001).

D.A.J. Skeel, *Debt's Dominion. A History of Bankruptcy Law in America* (Princeton, 2001).

S. Solomon, *The Confidence Game. How Unelected Central Bankers Are Governing the Changed Global Economy* (New York London, 1995).

E.E. Spicer, *The Money Market in relation to Trade and Commerce* (London, 4th edn, 1924).

K. Spong, *Banking Regulation. Its Purposes, Implementation and Effects* (Kansas City, 2000).

G.J. Stigler, 'The Theory of Economic Regulation', *Bell Journal of Economics and Management Science*, 2, 1 (1971), pp. 3–21.

A. Straus, 'La politique des banques régionales dans l'entre-deux-guerres. Entre croissance et rationalisation', in M. Lescure and A. Plessis (eds), *Les banques locales et régionales en Europe au XXe siècle* (Paris, 2004).

——, 'Trésor public et marché financier', *Revue historique*, 106 (1982), pp. 65–112.

R.E. Sylla, Comparing the UK and US Financial Systems, 1790–1830, mimeo, April 2006.

R. Sylla, 'US Banks and Europe. Strategy and Attitudes', in S. Battilossi and Y. Cassis (eds), *European Banks and the American Challenge. Competition and Cooperation in International Banking under Bretton Woods* (Oxford, 2002).

——, 'U.S. Securities Markets and the Banking System, 1790–1840', *Federal Reserve Bank of St Louis Review* (May/June, 1998), pp. 83–98.

C.J. Tabb, 'The Historical Evolution of the Bankruptcy Discharge', *American Bankruptcy Law Journal*, 65 (1991), pp. 325–71.

——, 'The History of Bankruptcy Laws in the United States', *American Bankruptcy Institute Law Review*, 3, 1 (1995), pp. 5–51.

K. Takala, *Studies in Time Series Analysis of Consumption, Asset Prices and Forecasting*, Bank of Finland Studies E:22 (Helsinki, 2001).

M. Taylor and A. Fleming, 'Integrated Financial Supervision. Lessons from Northern European Experience', World Bank Policy Research Working Paper 2223 (1999).

A. Teck and W.B. Johns, 'Portfolio Decisions of Central Banks', in A.M. George and I.H. Giddy (eds), *International Finance Handbook*, vol. 2 (New York, 1983).

S.E. Thomas, *The Rise and Growth of Joint Stock Banking*, vol. 1, Britain: to 1860 (London, 1934).

H. Thornton, *An Enquiry into the Nature and Effects of the Paper Credit of Great Britain* (1802, reprinted London, 1939).

K.S. Toft, 'A Mid-century Attempt at Banking Control', *Revue Internationale d'Histoire de la Banque*, 3 (1970), pp. 149–67.

G. Toniolo, with the assistance of P. Clement, *Central Bank Cooperation at the Bank for International Settlements 1930–1973* (Cambridge, 2005).

E. Tuccimei, 'La ricerca economica a Via Nazionale. Una storia degli 'Studi' da Canovai a Baffi', *Banca d'Italia. Quaderni dell'Ufficio Ricerche Storiche*, 9 (September 2005).

P. Tufano, 'Business Failure, Judicial Intervention, and Financial Innovation. Restructuring U.S. Railroads in the Nineteenth Century', *Business History Review*, 71, 1 (1997), pp. 1–40.

H.B. van Cleveland and T.F. Huertas, *Citibank. 1812–1970* (Cambridge, 1985).

D. Verdier, *Moving Money. Banking and Finance in the Industrialized World* (Cambridge, 2002).

——, 'The Rise and Fall of State Banking in OECD Countries', *Comparative Political Studies*, 33, 3 (2000), pp. 283–318.

P. Verley, *Nouvelle histoire économique de la France contemporaine, vol. 2, L'industrialisation, 1830–1914* (Paris, 1989).

E. Vidal, *The History and Methods of the Paris Bourse* (Washington, 1910).

V. Vihriälä, *Banks and the Finnish Credit Cycle 1986–1995*, Bank of Finland Studies E:7 (Helsinki, 1990).

C. Vivante, 'Il fallimento civile', in P. Ascoli et al. (eds), *Il codice di commercio commentato* (Turin, 1909).

H.-J. Voth, 'Convertibility, Currency Controls and the Cost of Capital in Western Europe, 1950–1999', *International Journal of Finance and Economics*, 8, 3 (2003), pp. 255–76.

J.E. Wadsworth (ed.), *The Banks and the Monetary System in the UK 1959–1971* (London, 1973).

N.B. Wainwright, *The History of the Philadelphia National Bank* (Philadelphia, 1953).

D. Waldenstrom, *A Century of Securities Transaction Taxes. Origins and Effects* (Stockholm, 2000).

S.J. Weiss, 'Competitive Standards Applied to Foreign and Domestic Acquisitions of US Banks', in Comptroller of the Currency, *Foreign Acquisition of US Banks* (Washington, 1981).

E.N. White, 'Banking and Finance in the Twentieth Century', in S.L. Engerman and R.E. Gallman, *The Cambridge Economic History of the United States*, III (Cambridge, 2000).

——, 'Before the Glass-Steagall Act. An Analysis of the Investment Banking Activities of National Banks', *Explorations in Economic History*, 23, 1 (1986), pp. 33–55.

——, 'The Political Economy of Banking Regulation, 1864–1933', *Journal of Economic History*, 42, 1 (1982), pp. 33–40.

——, *The Regulation and Reform of the American Banking System, 1900–1929* (Princeton, 1983).

——, 'The 1990s in the Mirror of the 1920s', in P. Rhode and G. Toniolo, *The Global Economy in the 1990s. A Long-run Perspective* (Cambridge, 2006).

——, 'Were Banks Special Intermediaries in Late Nineteenth Century America?', *Federal Reserve Bank of St Louis Review* (May/June 1998), pp. 13–32.

J.H. Wood, 'Bagehot's Lender of Last Resort. A Hollow Hallowed Tradition', *The Independent Review*, 7, 3 (2003), pp. 343–51.

R.E. Wright, Testing the Finance-Led Growth Hypothesis. Early 19th Century America, Britain, and Canada, Terry School of Business Workshop, University of Georgia, 2004.

C. Wyplosz, 'Exchange Rate Regimes. Some Lessons from Post-war Europe', in G. Caprio et al. (eds), *Financial Liberalization. How Far, How Fast?* (Cambridge, 2001).

J. Zysman, 'The Interventionist Temptation. Financial Structure and Political Purpose', in W.J. Andrews and S. Hoffmann (eds), *The Fifth Republic at Twenty* (Albany, 1981).

Index